The Music Lover's Library

A PIANOFORTE BY CRISTOFORI.

In the Crosby Brown Collection, Metropolitan Museum of Art, New York.

The Music Lover's Library

The Pianoforte and Its Music

By

Henry Edward Krehbiel H. E.

*Author of "How to Listen to Music," "Music and Manners
in the Classical Period," "Studies in the Wagnerian Drama," "Chapters of Opera," "A
Book of Operas," "The Philharmonic
Society of New York," etc., etc.*

With Portraits and Illustrations

Charles Scribner's Sons

New York : : : : : 1911

ML 265
K87
c. 1

Copyright, 1910, by H. E. Krehbiel

Copyright, 1911, by Charles Scribner's Sons

Published January, 1911

reel 9/99

TO

IGNAZ JAN PADEREWSKI

Blue Hill, Maine,
Summer of 1910.

Contents

PART I

THE INSTRUMENT

PAGE

I.   Principles and Primitive Prototypes .   .   3

II. Mediæval Precursors   17

III. The Pianoforte of To-Day   29

PART II

THE COMPOSERS

IV.   The Earliest Clavier Music   53

V.   The English Virginalists   62

VI.   French and Italian Clavecinists   .   .   .   87

VII. The German School—Bach and Handel .   100

VIII. Classicism and the Sonata   122

IX.   Beethoven—an Intermezzo   146

X.   The Romantic School   180

XI.   National Schools   229

PART III

THE PLAYERS

XII. Virtuosi and Their Development .   .   .   261

vii

Illustrations

A Pianoforte by Cristofori . . . . . . *Frontispiece*
In the Crosby Brown Collection, Metropolitan Museum of
Art, New York.

PAGE

Evolution of the Musical Bow . . . . *Facing* 12

Group of Clavichord Keys 18

A Harpischord Jack 18

Hammer-action of a Grand Pianoforte . . . 45

Jean Philippe Rameau . . . . . . *Facing* 88

Domenico Scarlatti . . . . " 98

Franz Liszt . . . . " 144
After a drawing by S. Mittag.

François Frédéric Chopin . . . . . " 200

Ignaz Jan Paderewski . . . . . . " 242

Carl Tausig . . . . " 262

Part I
The Instrument

I

Principles and Primitive Prototypes

IN this book I have undertaken a study of the origin and development of the pianoforte, the music composed for it, and the performers who have brought that music home to the understanding and enjoyment of the people who have lived since the instrument acquired the predominant influence which it occupies in modern culture. There is that in the title of the series of works to which this little book belongs which justifies a trust in the graciousness, gentleness, and serious-mindedness of those who shall, haply, read it; and therefore I begin with a warning that an earnest purpose lies at the bottom of my undertaking: I am more desirous to instruct than to entertain, though I would not assert that in this instance instruction and entertainment need be divorced. Nevertheless, it was this desire that determined the method which I shall follow in the discussion and which I shall believe to be successful in the degree that it excites the imagination and quickens the perceptions of my readers without burdening the faculty which historical study, as commonly conducted, taxes most severely—that is to say, the faculty of memory. I shall care little for dates and much for principles. Names shall not affright me, and I shall not attempt to

> distinguish and divide
> A hair 'twixt south and south-west side

when it comes to enumerating or describing the instruments which some centuries ago filled the place in musical practice now occupied by that instrument universal—the pianoforte. Yet I shall strive to point out why and how the structural principles of those instruments influenced the music which they were called upon to utter, and pointed the way to the art of to-day. It is one of the cheering and amiable features of historical study pursued in this manner that it refuses to be kept in the dusty road tramped by date-mongers and takes into account the utterances of poets, the testimony of ancient carvings and drawings, as well as the records of prosy chroniclers. Many are the by-paths which lead into the avenue of scientific fact—varied and lovely are the vistas which they open.

We are concerned in this portion of our study with the story which shall tell us how the pianoforte came into existence. As we know it, this instrument is practically a product of the nineteenth century; yet poetical traditions which have come down to us from the earliest civilizations are at one with the conclusions of scientific research in telling us what was the common origin of the instruments to which the pianoforte has borne relationship since music began. Let me, before showing this, classify these instruments. They are known technically as "stringed" instruments, because their tones are generated by the vibrations of tense strings, or chords. Now:

(a) *Instruments of the viol family yield tones when their strings are rubbed;*

(b) *Those of the harp family when they are twanged, plucked, or picked;*

(c) *Those of the dulcimer family when they are struck.*

All these instruments are interrelated, and at one time or another in its long history the instrument which we call the piano for short (but which ought always to be called the pianoforte, for reasons which shall appear presently) has embodied the fundamental principle of each. There are differences, however, which determine further divisions. Thus, some stringed instruments yield many more tones than they have strings through the mediumship of a finger-board which enables a player to shorten the vibrating segment of each string by pressure upon it with the fingers—"stopping," as it is called by the musicians; some have fewer tones than strings, the latter being doubled, or even trebled, in unison for the sake of greater sonority; some are plucked or twanged with the

5

bare fingers, some with a bit of metal, ivory, or wood, anciently called a plectrum. The feature which differentiates the pianoforte from its companions is the keyboard. This is a mechanical contrivance by which the blow against the strings is not only delivered, but by means of which it can also be regulated so as to produce gradations of power and a considerable range of expression. It is to the first of these capacities that the instrument owes its name—the "pianoforte" (*piano e forte* as it was first called) is the "soft and loud." This is very rudimentary talk, but its significance will appear later.

If, now, I were asked to give a brief but comprehensive definition of the pianoforte, whose origin, growth, and present status are to occupy our attention in the first large subdivision of this study, I should say that it is an instrument of music the tones of which are generated by strings set in vibration by blows delivered by hammers controlled by a keyboard, the mechanism of which is so adjusted that the force of the blow and the dynamic intensity of the resultant tone are measurably at the command of the player. Also that it has a sound-board, or resonance-box, to augment the tone after its creation.

The beginning of such an instrument may be sought for in the legends of antiquity, the somewhat confusing records of mediæval scholastics, and

the rude inventions of the savages who live to-day
to tell us something about things which antedate the
civilization of which our time has been so boastful.
Mediæval records are equidistant between the imaginative and scientific periods. Now, imagination
not only

> bodies forth
> The forms of things unknown,

but also preserves a record of things forgotten. I
am, therefore, pleased first to invite its aid.

The god of music of the ancient Greeks was also
their archer-god. Recall the description of Apollo's answer to the supplication of Chryses in the
first book of the "Iliad." The aged priest implores
the god to avenge the wrong done by Agamemnon.

> Hear me, thou bearer of the silver bow,

he prays; and thus the poet describes the god's
answer to the appeal:

> Phœbus Apollo hearkened. Down he came,
> Down from the summit of the Olympian mount,
> Wrathful in heart; his shoulder bore the bow
> And hollow quiver; there the arrows rang
> Upon the shoulders of the angry god
> As on he moved. He came as comes the night,
> And, seated from the ships aloof, sent forth
> An arrow; terrible was heard the clang
> Of that resplendent bow.

7

The Instrument

It was not a mere chance that the poet equipped the god of music with a bow, nor yet a striving after picturesque effect. A Homer would not have juggled so with words and images. Apollo bore the bow on this occasion because it fell to him to mete out retribution; but he was the god of music because he bore the bow. I cannot recall where, but I have seen somewhere another of these beautiful old Greek legends which presents Apollo listening entranced to the musical twang of his bowstring, which gave out sweet sounds even while it sped the arrow on its errand of death. Also there comes to mind the passage in the "Odyssey" which describes Ulysses's trial of his own bow after the suitors of Penelope had put it by in despair—when he drew the arrow to its head and the string rang shrill and sweet as the note of a swallow as he let it go. A version of an old legend given by Censorinus says that the use of the tense string of his bow for musical purposes was suggested to Apollo by the twang made by the bowstring of his huntress sister Diana.

Tales like these preserve a record which antedates history as commonly understood. The bow was the first stringed instrument of music—that is what these tales tell us; and note how the old lesson is illustrated in the life of to-day: There lives no boy brought up where the bow is a plaything who has not made Apollo's discovery for himself. For all such boys it is a common amusement to pluck at the bowstring and catch the faint musical tone which results by putting the bow to the ear or between the teeth. The savage probably did the same thing thousands of years ago; he certainly does it now pretty much all the world over. In the Smithsonian Institution at Washington there is a musical instrument which used to be described in the catalogue as a guitar of the Yaquima Indians of Sonora, Mexico. It is nothing else than a bow provided with a tuning peg. While picking the string with his right hand the savage varied the pitch of the tone by slipping the left along the string. Travellers have found half a dozen tribes in Africa whose principal instrument of music differs but in little from the bow. Some savages, indeed, use the same bow in their music-making that they do in war and the chase. The n-kungu of the Angola negroes is a springy piece of wood bent by a string of twisted fibre. Near one end another bit of fibre is lashed around the bow, drawing the string tighter, and a hollow gourd is fastened to the wood to augment the sound. Here we have the primitive resonator, or sound-box. The performer holds his rude instrument upright in his left arm, the gourd resting on his left hip, or his stomach, and while he twangs the string with a splint of wood he slips the fingers of his left hand along it to raise and lower the tone. In the Crosby Brown collection of musical instruments, housed at the Metropolitan Museum of Art in New York, there is an instrument from Brazil which has its counterpart in two specimens from the Gaboon River, Africa, preserved in the National Museum at Washington. It is made from the midrib of a large palm leaf. In the Washington specimens strips of the outer skin of the midrib are cut loose and raised up on a vertical bridge, the ends being left attached. Around the ends and the midrib are little bands of plaited fibre by which the vibrating length of the strings can be adjusted. As in the Angola instrument, a gourd forms the resonator. The hunting-bow has here grown into an instrument capable of giving out eight tones. The instrument was introduced in America by slaves who came from Africa; this, at least, is the contention of Professor Mason, of the National Museum.

The theory which finds the origin of all musical instruments of the stringed tribe in the bow of the savage has a triple commendation: the Hellenic myths suggest it; reason approves it; the practice of modern savages confirms it. Suppose primitive man to conceive the desire to add to the number of tones possible to his improvised musical instruments so as to enjoy that sequence or combination which, when pleasingly ordered, we call melody or harmony—how would he go about it? Most naturally by adding strings to his bow; and a bow with more than one string is already a rudimentary harp. As Homer came to our support in the first instance, so the ancient sculptor helps us now. The oldest rock pictures which archæologists have found in Egypt show us harps that retain enough of the bow form plainly to suggest their origin. The body of the instrument is still shaped like a bow; the single string has received three fellows; the gourd of the n-kungu has developed into a sound-box of wood. The instrument was carried on the left shoulder and its strings were plucked with the fingers. The mural paintings and sculptures of Egypt discover many varieties of harps, some showing a marvellous degree of perfection, but even the largest and finest lacks the pole which completes the triangular form of the modern harp and is essential to its strength and rigidity.

There is no relic of the bow in the shapes of the harps and lyres of the Greeks and Romans, but, instead, suggestions of the tortoise-shell which, according to the familiar legend told by Apollodorus, gave Mercury the idea exemplified in the classic lyre. According to this story, the god one day accidentally kicked a tortoise-shell stretched in the interior of which there remained some cartilages after the flesh had been dried out by the sun. These chords gave forth a sound, and Mercury at once conceived the idea of the lyre, made the instrument in the shape of a tortoise-shell and strung it with the dried sinews of animals. This legend originates the two principles of a vibrating string and a resonator simultaneously, and is obviously of a later date than the myth which made Apollo

> The lord of the unerring bow,
> The god of life, and poetry, and light.

But we ought now to look away from all the ancient instruments whose strings were twanged or plucked, whether with the unarmed fingers or with plectra of various kinds, and seek for the earliest form of an instrument embodying the principle of a struck string. The oldest illustrations of this manner of producing musical sounds that have been discovered are Assyrian. Among the bas-relief sculptures taken from the tumuli which mark the places where Nineveh, Nimroud, Khorsabad, and Kuijundschik once stood (they are now safely housed in the British Museum, to the great glory of the English people) is one representing a portion of a triumphal procession in honor of Saos-du-Khin, an Assyrian king whose reign began 667 years before Christ. In this group there is what I have ventured to look upon as an Assyrian dulcimer player. The instrument, apparently a sound-box with strings stretched across the top (though they are depicted as bending over each other in the air in agreement with ancient notions of art, which made perspective wait upon delineation of actualities),

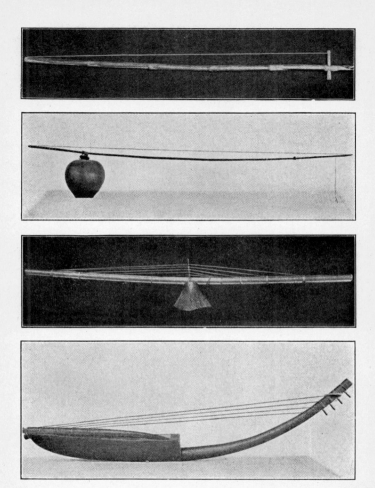

EVOLUTION OF THE MUSICAL BOW.

was suspended in front of the player by a band from the neck, since both hands are occupied in playing upon it—the right hand striking the strings with an instrument apparently about a foot long, the left seemingly checking the vibrations of the strings.

If this instrument was really a dulcimer, it may stand as the true prototype among the civilized ancients of the modern pianoforte. Varied in shape, with many names, it has lived till to-day. It is still popular in the Orient. It is the Persian santir; it was the Greek psalterion, and its use was general throughout Europe as early as the sixth century. The Italians called it the dolcimelo, compounding the word out of the Latin *dulce* and the Greek *melos*. The ruder Germans, taking a suggestion, probably, from the motion of the players' hands, which suggested that of the butchers' in the preparation of their favorite viand, called it Hackbrett— that is, chopping board. By this time the instrument had attained its present form, a box of thin boards pierced on the top with sound holes, having wire strings stretched over bridges, played upon with two hammers with slender handles and cork heads. Once it was played upon with two sticks slightly bent at one end, making an elongated head, one side of which was covered with cloth. By striking the wires with the cloth-covered surface soft effects were obtained—a noteworthy device in this history, for it suggested the pianoforte to the mind

13

of one of its inventors. The capabilities of the dulcimer may be studied to-day in the music of the ubiquitous gypsy band.

We have now seen something of the origin and growth of two of the vital principles of the modern pianoforte—the principle of a vibrating string as a medium of tone generation and of a blow against the string as a means of tone production. For a third distinguishing principle, that by which the two media are brought into mutual service, the journey of discovery must again be into the classic past. The keyboard was borrowed from instruments of the organ kind, and its antiquity cannot clearly be determined. Organs were the possession of both Greeks and Hebrews before the Christian era, and their existence in anything beyond the simplest forms, as exemplified in the syrinx, presupposes some contrivance for admitting and excluding wind from the pipes at the will of the player. At first, and even after the instrument got into literature, this contrivance may have been a series of rods which could be drawn forth and pushed back under the mouths of the pipes, but in the sixth century A.D. Cassiodorus, in a commentary on Psalm cl., wrote a description of a pneumatic organ which leaves no doubt that the commentator was familiar with something like our key-action. He mentions the presence in the interior of the instrument of "movements of wood which are pressed down by the fingers of the player" in order to "express agreeable melodies." We do not know when the keyboard was invented, but certain it seems that the organ keyboard was too cumbersome a contrivance to be applied to a stringed instrument for several centuries after the beginning of the Christian era. This application, in the form of interest to us, took place about the eleventh century, and the instrument to which keys were then applied was a scientific rather than a musical instrument. It was the monochord, which had been used in the mathematical determination of the relation of tones ever since the time of Pythagoras—that is, ever since the sixth century before Christ. As its name indicates, the monochord had but a single string. This was stretched over two bridges, on a sound-box. By stopping this string in the middle the octave of its fundamental tone was produced; two-thirds gave the fifth, three-fourths the fourth, and so on, the harmonic interval being perfect in proportion to the simplicity of the numerical ratio. It was a simple matter to add strings to the monochord to facilitate its manipulation in the comparison of intervals, and two theoretical writers in the second century A.D., Aristides Quintilian and Claudius Ptolemy, refer to an instrument having four strings tuned in unison which was used in the study of tonal ratios. It was once customary to attribute nearly all inventions in music to Guido d'Arezzo, the monk to whom we are indebted for our sol-fa syllables. He is credited, too, with having applied keys to the monochord which, on being pressed down, lifted a bridge against the string from below, simultaneously making it sound and dividing off the portion whose tone it was desired to hear. Whether or not he made this discovery is not proved, but that he was familiar with a keyed instrument is plain, from the fact that he left a writing for his pupils, counselling them to practise their hands in the use of the monochord.

II

Mediæval Precursors

WE have now before us the primary form of the instrument which, despite its simplicity, contested longest for supremacy with the pianoforte after the latter had entered the arena. The mechanism of the monochord of the eleventh century was to all intents and purposes the mechanism of the clavichord (*clavis*, key; *chorda*, a string), which might still have been seen occasionally in the music-loving houses of Germany in the middle of the nineteenth century.

The key was a simple lever, one end of which received the pressure of the finger, while the other, extending under the strings of the instrument, was armed with a bit of metal placed upright and at right angles with the string. When the key was pressed down the blow dealt by this bit of metal, called a "tangent," set the string to vibrating, and at the same time measured off the segment of the string which had to vibrate to produce the desired tone. The tangent also acted as a bridge, and had to be held against the string so long as the tone was to continue. On its release the tone was immediately muffled, or damped, by strips of cloth which were intertwined with the wires at one end.

Down to the end of the sixteenth century, though the strings were multiplied, the name monochord was still used, and, though the range of the instru-

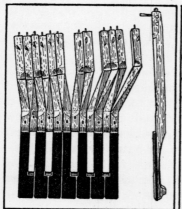

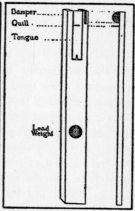

A Group of Clavichord Keys
(From an instrument owned by the author)

A Harpsichord Jack

ment had reached twenty-four notes, the strings were still tuned in unison. Gradually, however, the strings for the acuter tones were shortened by a bridge placed diagonally across the sound-board, this contrivance being borrowed, it is said, from another keyed instrument, called the clavicymbal, which was, in effect, a triangular system of strings to which a mechanical device had been applied which plucked or snapped the strings, somewhat in imitation of a harp player.

It is to instruments of this class that I now address myself, for it was for them that the earliest music was written which has survived in the repertory of the pianist, and it was upon them that the predecessors of the great virtuosi about whom I shall speak played. But it would be idle to attempt to explain all the differences between them. They were a numerous tribe and the members bore numerous names, of which those that have endured longest in the literature of music, and which, indeed, were spoken by our grandparents as glibly as we say piano now, were spinet and harpsichord. We shall be spared a lot of curious and vain brain-cudgelling if we look upon these names, as also clavicytherium, clavicembalo, gravicembalo, épinette, and virginal, as no more than designations in vogue at different times or in different countries, or at the most as names standing for variations in shape or structure of the instrument which filled the place before the nineteenth century that the pianoforte does now.

In all the instruments of this class the strings were picked with tiny points of quills (generally, though the material varied) held in bits of wood called "jacks," which moved freely in slots piercing the sound-board, and rested upon one end of the key levers. The quill was a tiny thing, not more than a third of an inch in length, thrust through a narrow tongue which moved on a pivot through a slot in the upper part of the jack. When at rest the quill point lay a trifle below the string and at a slightly acute angle with it. The key pressed down, the jack sprang upward, and the quill in passing twanged the string. When the key was released the jack dropped back to its place and the quill slipped under the string, ready for a repetition of the movement. To enable it to do this was the mission of the little tongue in which it was set. This was held in place flush with the front face of the jack by a delicate spring of wire or hog's bristle. The tongue could move backward, but not forward, but, the quill being pointed a little upward, when it fell back upon the string the spring gave way, the tongue moved back a bit, and the quill regained its position below the string. If you will read Shakespeare's 128th sonnet it will help you to keep in mind the action of these jacks, though at times the poet's description seems to confound them with the keys.

Two hundred years ago the perfection of instruments of the clavier class—that is, instruments with strings played upon by manipulation of keys—was thought to have been reached. This, at least, is the recorded judgment of writers of that period. From a mechanical point of view, indeed, some of these instruments were marvels; but as music became less and less mere pretty play of sounds, and gave voice more and more to the feelings of composer and player, the deficiencies of virginal, spinet, and harpsichord became manifest. Even the most elaborate and perfect of the quilled instruments, the harpsichord, was a soulless thing. It was impossible to vary the quantity and quality of its tone sufficiently to make it an expressive instrument, and it is very significant to this study in all its aspects that the greatest musicians of two centuries ago, while they were obliged to compose for the harpsichord and give it their preference in the concert-room, nevertheless, as we know from Bach's example (but of that more anon), used the crude and simpler clavichord as the medium of their private communings with the muse.

Imperfect and weak as it was, the clavichord had yet the capacity in some degree to augment and diminish the tone at the will of the player. The tone of the other instruments was not ineptly described as "a scratch with a note at the end of it." Efforts unceasing were made to increase and give variety to the tone, but in vain. The defect was fundamental. The earliest attempts at improvement seem to have been directed to the jacks. The quill-points had an unfortunate habit of wearing out rapidly, and when a player sat down to his instrument in a fine frenzy of inspiration he sometimes had to stop and put in new quills as well as tune it. So substitutes for goose and crow quills were sought for, and fish bone, stiff cloth, leather, metal, and other materials were tried. The principle, however, always remained the same, and the defect was never remedied: the jacks twanged the strings, and twanged them with uniform loudness. For the sake of variety in tonal effects dampers of various kinds were also invented to check and modify the vibration of the strings after they had been twanged; and, later, strings were added which could be plucked simultaneously with the original set by an additional row of jacks. These added strings were first tuned in unison with the others, so that just twice the amount of tone resulted from their use, but Ruckers, of Antwerp, the most famous harpsichord builder of his time, conceived the idea of adding an extra system of strings tuned in the octave above, which could be coupled to the original system at will. The front of the harpsichord, which was the instrument to which most of these improvements were attached, came in time to look something like the console of an organ, with its draw-stops, pedals, and knee-swells.

The builders also used different kinds of metal in their strings for the sake of added effects, and since the quantity of tone could not be varied by the touch of the player, the swell-box idea was borrowed from the organ, the entire sound-board of the instrument being covered with a series of shutters like the so-called Venetian blinds, which could be opened and closed by the player by pressure of his foot. All these mechanical contrivances were little better than makeshifts. They did not go to the real seat of the difficulty, and the inventive ingenuity which prompted them spent itself largely in the creation of fantastic contrivances whose worthlessness is demonstrated by the fact that they have long since ceased to occupy the attention of musicians. Devices which enabled the harpsichord player to imitate the voices of the flute, trumpet, bagpipe, bassoon, oboe, and fife, the rattle of drums and castanets, and even the noises of a rain-storm, were admired by the idle and curious, but to the serious musician they were mere mechanical curiosities only.

Several of the contrivances, however, were afterward utilized in the pianoforte for nobler ends. The shifting of the keyboard by means of a pedal, which is now used in the grand pianoforte to divert the blow of the hammer from one or two of the unison strings (*una corda*, or the "soft pedal," as it is commonly called), was first applied to the harpsichord for the purpose of transposition. Cloth dampers which were used to modify the tone of the harpsichord are interposed between the hammers and the strings of a square pianoforte for soft effects.

For many decades builders of spinets and harpsichords strove—their successors, indeed, are still striving—to overcome a deficiency which is inherent in the nature of the instrument. As I have said elsewhere,[1] despite all the skill, learning, and ingenuity which have been spent on its perfection the pianoforte can be made only feebly to approximate that sustained style of musical utterance which is the soul of melody and finds its loftiest exemplification in singing.

To give out a melody perfectly presupposes the capacity to sustain tones without loss in power or quality, to bind them together at will and sometimes to intensify their dynamic, or expressive, force while they sound. The tone of the pianoforte, like that of all its precursors, begins to die the moment it is created. The discoveries in the field of acoustics which have been made within the last century, and the introduction of the hammer-action in place of the jacks, have wrought an improvement in this respect, but the difficulty has not been obviated, and cannot be within the family to which the keyed instruments which we have been considering belong. A string plucked or struck in order to produce a sound is at once beyond the control of the player. To keep it within control the string must be rubbed. It is because of the importance which this truth assumed in the mind of one of the inventors of the pianoforte, and his experiments with an instru-

[1] See "How to Listen to Music," p. 158.

ment which combined the dulcimer and harp principles, that I shall tell the story of the German inventor, Schröter, at greater length than that of the Frenchman, Marius, or the Italian, Cristofori. To each of these I purpose to leave the credit of being an isolated inventor, though they worked at different times and brought forth their inventions in the reverse order of that in which I have presented their names.

One of the devices invented for the purpose of prolonging the tone of the harpsichord was incorporated in an instrument called Geigenwerk, which came from Nuremberg, famous for its inventions through many centuries. Properly speaking, it did not belong to the instruments of the clavier class at all, for, though it utilized tense strings, a soundboard, and keys, its fundamental principle was borrowed from the viol. It was, in fact, a highly developed and aristocratic hurdy-gurdy. In it, by means of treadles, wheels covered with leather and coated with powdered resin were made to revolve, and while revolving were pressed against the strings by manipulation of the keys.

Christopher Gottlieb Schröter was a musician and teacher in Dresden who became dissatisfied with the harpsichord because of the inability of his pupils to play on that instrument with the taste and expression which they exhibited when they practised on the clavichord. He went with a lamentation to the Saxon court chapelmaster, who advised him to get one of the Nuremberg hurdy-gurdy claviers. He did so, and the fact that it was possible to sustain the tones in a singing manner on the instrument pleased him much. But there was still a fly in the ointment. He was unwilling while making music to work with both his feet "like a linen-weaver," as he expressed it. While in this frame of mind he heard the performance of a famous virtuoso on the dulcimer, and from this performance conceived the idea of constructing an instrument on which, if it should not be able to sustain the tone like the Geigenwerk, should at least make it possible to play *forte* or *piano* at will. He went to work himself in a joiner's shop during the resting hours of the workmen, and succeeded in constructing two models for a hammer mechanism to be applied to the harpsichord. These, in February, 1721, he submitted to the King of Saxony, by whom the invention was heartily approved, as well as by the court chapelmaster. He had no means to build an instrument or exploit his invention, and though the king ordered one built it was never done. Soon thereafter Schröter left Saxony. Many years later, finding that every pianoforte builder in Germany was claiming the invention of the instrument, he printed his story, giving all the dates with the greatest care. He could do this because he had kept a diary all his life, and he even mentioned the time of day at which he carried his models to the royal palace.

The merit of having suggested the German invention of the pianoforte was due to a player on the dulcimer, and since we are concerned with a study of principles rather than mechanics it may be profitable to consider what it was in the performance of this man which so powerfully excited the imagination of Schröter. The player was Pantaleon Hebenstreit, for many years a chamber musician at the Saxon court. Although an excellent violinist, his favorite instrument was the dulcimer, on which he had acquired great proficiency as a boy. Not content with the simple form of the instrument as he found it, he increased its size, strung it with a double system of strings—one of brass and one of gut—and tuned it in equal temperament, so that it might be used in all the major and minor keys, following in this the way pointed out by the great Bach. He played it in the primitive fashion with a pair of hammers, and his music excited the liveliest interest wherever he went. He played before Louis XIV. in 1705, and the Grand Monarch honored him by giving the name "Pantaleon" to his dulcimer. A year later he became director of the orchestra and court dancing-master at Eisenach, and later still chamber musician in Dresden, at an annual salary of 2,000 thalers and an allowance of 200 thalers for strings.

It is in Hebenstreit's dulcimer that we are privileged to see the first instrument with some of the expressive capacity of the modern pianoforte. The interest created by his performances was not due alone to the effects of *piano* and *forte* which he produced by graduating the force of the hammer-blows and utilizing the two kinds of strings. Discerning musicians heard in his playing for the first time an effect whose scientific study of late years has done more to perfect the tone of the instrument and to influence composers and players than anything else in pianoforte construction. Kuhnau, who was Bach's predecessor as choirmaster of the Church of St. Thomas, in Leipsic, praised the great beauty of the tone of the pantaleon, the bass notes of which, he said, sounded like those of the organ; but, more significantly, he recorded the fact that on sounding a note its over-tones could be heard simultaneously up to the sixth. Helmholtz's determinations as to the influence of partials on the timbre of musical instruments have been of the utmost importance in pianoforte construction.

III

The Pianoforte of To-day

THE story of the German invention of the pianoforte cannot make for the glory of Schröter
as against the credit due to Cristofori, the earliest
inventor of the instrument. It has been told only
because it illustrates so luminously the principles
which we are trying to keep in view in this chapter
of musical evolution. Discoveries and inventions
of all kinds are growths; there was never anything
new under the sun.

The three men to whom I have left the honor of
being independent inventors of the pianoforte are
the Italian, Bartolommeo Cristofori; the Frenchman, Marius, and the German, Christopher Gottlieb
Schröter. It is in the highest degree probable that
efforts had been made in the direction in which
these men labored a long time before they came
forward with their inventions. The earliest use of
the word pianoforte (or, literally, *piano e forte*) as
applied to an instrument of music antedates the
earliest of these inventions by one hundred and
eleven years, but the reference is exceedingly vague
and chiefly valuable as indicative of how early the

minds of inventors were occupied with means for obtaining soft and loud effects from keyed instruments. Cristofori's invention takes precedence of the others in time. This has been established, after much controversy, beyond further dispute. In 1709 he exhibited specimens of harpsichords, with hammer-action, capable of producing *piano* and *forte* effects, to Prince Ferdinando dei Medici, of whose instruments of music he was custodian at Florence, and two years later—that is, in 1711— his invention was fully described and the description printed, not only in Italy, but also in Germany. It embraces the essential features of the pianoforte action as we have it to-day—a row of hammers, controlled by keys, which struck the strings from below. In the description, written by Scipione Maffei, the instrument is designated as a "New Invention of a Harpsichord, with the Piano and Forte" (*Nuova Invenzione d'un Gravicembalo col Piano e Forte*). In February, 1716, the Frenchman, Marius, submitted two models for a "Harpsichord with Hammers" (*Clavecin à Mallets*) to the Académie Royale des Sciences; one illustrated a device for hitting the strings from above, the other from below. It was a much cruder invention than Cristofori's, but it contained the vital principle which differentiates the pianoforte from its mediæval and later precursors. Marius's confessed purpose in devising the new mechanism was economy. He wanted to save musicians the constant trouble and cost of requilling the harpsichord jacks. Schröter's models also struck the strings from above and below.

There are only two pianofortes made by Cristofori known to be in existence. The older, made in 1720, was bought by Mrs. John Crosby Brown in 1895 and is now housed in the Metropolitan Museum of Art, in New York.[1] The other is the property of the Commendatore Allessandro Kraus and is preserved in his museum in Florence; it is pictured in Mr. A. J. Hipkins's "History of the Pianoforte."[2] The instrument bought by Mrs. Brown was long the property of Signora Ernesta Mocenni Martelli, of Florence, whose father bought it (according to family tradition) in 1819 or 1820 at a public sale of supposedly worthless furniture in the Grand Ducal palace at Siena. A sentimental feeling on the part of the Signora Martelli led to its preservation by her until her death. A father whose memory she revered had bought it, and she had learned to play upon it as a child. That it had value as an historical relic was not suspected until 1872, when Signor Cosimo Conti, a scholar and intimate friend of the Martelli family, discovered, on the board which serves as a hammer beam, an inscription as follows: "*Bartholomæus di Christophorus Patavinus, Inventor, faciebat, Florentiæ,*

[1] See Frontispiece.
[2] Novello, Ewer & Co., London and New York, 1896

MDCCXX." He communicated the fact to the Cavaliere L. Puliti, whose investigation finally and definitely established priority of invention for Cristofori. Puliti confirmed the authenticity of the instrument, which was restored in 1875 by Cesare Ponsicchi, of Florence, and described and pictured it in his monograph on the origin and evolution of the pianoforte, published in 1876.

The case of the instrument, which preserves the shape of the old-fashioned harpsichords, is seven feet and one-quarter inches long, three feet and three inches wide, and three feet high. It has a compass of four and a half octaves (fifty-four notes) from the second leger line below the bass staff to the fourth space above the treble staff. Its longest string is six feet and two inches; its shortest two inches. Its thickest string is seven-tenths of a millimetre in diameter; its thinnest four-tenths of a millimetre. There are only three thicknesses of strings, and those of the lowest six tones are uniform in length and thickness, the variation in pitch being occasioned by difference in tension.[1]

---

[1] "The strings of the pianoforte were originally of very thin wire. The difference between them and those now in use is very striking. As an illustration we may remark that the smallest wire formerly used for the C in the third space of the treble staff was No. 7; that now used for the same note is No. 16. The weight of the striking length of the first is five and a half grains; of that of the second, twenty-one grains. This is sufficient to account for the increased bracing in the modern pianoforte." ("The

The frame is of hard wood and the case rim is only half an inch thick. The sounding board is strengthened by belly-bars, and, unlike those of the modern pianoforte, the dampers extend through the entire register of the instrument. New hammers have been put in the action, which are modern in shape, though very light; but the action itself is Cristofori's, albeit showing improvements on the mechanism described in the account of Scipione Maffei printed in the "Giornale de' Litterati d'Italia," of Venice, in 1711. It is a marvel of ingenuity compared with the actions of half a century later. It allows repetition of the blow, though it lacks what is called the "double escapement."

Since I am not writing an exhaustive history of the pianoforte, nor a treatise on its construction, it will not be expected of me that I trace the development of the instrument through all its steps, or describe all its parts in technical phrase.[1] It will

Pianoforte," by Edward F. Rimbault, LL.D., London, 1860, p. 178.)

The contrast between old and modern stringing will be illustrated even more vividly when at the end of this chapter I bring the features of the Cristofori instrument into juxtaposition with those of a Steinway Grand.

[1] To those interested in the subject I would recommend the study of "The Pianoforte, Its Origin, Progress, and Construction, etc.," by Edward F. Rimbault, LL.D. (London: Robert Cocks & Co., 1860); "Geschichte des Claviers vom Ursprunge bis zu den modernsten Formen dieses Instrumentes," by Dr. Oscar Paul (Leipsic: A. H. Payne, 1868); and especially "A

suffice if I point out the changes which have taken place in the instrument from the time of its invention up to the present, in order to show, as I shall hope to do later, how these changes, in connection with other things, influenced the style of pianoforte composition and the manner of pianoforte playing. Also how the desires of composer and performer influenced the manufacturer. This is the kind of knowledge, it seems to me, which is of practical value to the music-lovers for whom this book is intended.

Speaking in round terms, the pianoforte had to reach the age allotted by the Psalmist to man before it achieved recognition from musicians as a successful rival of the harpsichord as an instrument for public performance. During this time it was, indeed, but a rudimentary affair, a mongrel; neither a harpsichord nor a pianoforte in the modern sense. It long remained, in fact, what its French and Italian inventors called it in the descriptions of their inventions: a harpsichord with hammers and, in consequence of these, possessing the capability to give out tones *piano* and *forte*. Up to 1820 wood only entered into the construction of its frame. The introduction of metal was a slow growth and, to judge by the printed record of the

Description and History of the Pianoforte and of the Older Keyboard Stringed Instruments," by A. J. Hipkins (London and New York: Novello, Ewer & Co., 1896).

patent offices and books, the causes which led to it were mechanical merely;—manufacturers wanted to utilize some of the space taken up by the wooden beams and trusses necessary to enable the frame to stand the strain imposed by the strings for silly contrivances, such as drums, cymbals, etc., which had won a large popularity as attachments to harpsichords; also to compensate for the expansion and contraction of the metal strings, and finally, and chiefly, to gain the greater strength and rigidity necessitated by a steady increase in the diameter and tension of the strings.

It appears to me, however, that a purely artistic influence must also have played its part in the introduction of a reform which in a few decades grew into a revolution. It is easy to imagine that the change from plucking the strings with quill-points to striking them with hammers would soon bring in a change in finger-action. In the music of the quilled instruments there was neither accent nor dynamic variety beyond that which could be achieved by such mechanical means as I have described in my account of the devices applied to the harpsichord for the purpose of mitigating its inherent imperfections. The effect of a slow pressure on the keys was much the same as that of a quick blow. Very different, indeed, was the effect in the manipulation of the hammer-action. A gentle blow—a caress—produced a soft tone, a sharp blow a loud one; and there were left at the command of the player all the gradations between. The fingers no longer walked monotonously over the keys "with gentle gait" like those of the dark lady apostrophized by Shakespeare in his sonnet, but pounced upon them smartly, and the weight of the hand came to play its part. Now it is not the weight of the hand alone, but the energy of the muscles of the wrist and forearm as well. We shall see, presently, when we come to review the development of pianoforte technique, how gradually this change in the style of playing took place, but there is little doubt in my mind that the emotionalism which strove against æsthetic conservatism from the earliest times down to Beethoven exerted a steady pressure along the line which has ended in the stupendous instrument and the Samsonian players of to-day.

With an increase in the weight and tension of the strings, due in part on the mechanical side to improvement in the manufacture of steel wire, there grew the need of greater solidity and strength in the parts of the instrument called upon to endure the strain of the strings. The frame was ingeniously trussed in various ways, but as the strain increased it was found that in spite of everything the fierce pull of the strings from the piece of timber holding the pins to which the further end of the strings was fastened, the wrest plank, into which the tuning-pegs were driven, warped the wooden structure so that in a comparatively short time it became distorted and so disorganized that the instrument would not stand in tune. It was a common thing two generations ago to interrupt a concert with an intermission, not so much to enable the player to rest and the listeners to unbend and refresh themselves with chatter, as is the case now, as to allow the tuner time to reset the tuning-pegs. This was due to three defects which have been largely remedied since—namely, want of rigidity in the frame, lack of elasticity in the strings and of firmness in the wrest pins. I have known pianists to render a pianoforte discordant in our own day, but this was not so much because of the vehemence with which they belabored the instrument as a maltreatment of the pedals—shifting the hammer by means of the left pedal from one of each set of unison strings, and then pounding upon the others. Naturally the struck strings were stretched by the process, while the untouched unisons remained at the original tension.

The idea of obviating the defects due to an all-wood frame by the employment of metal seems to have haunted the minds of pianoforte makers long before it found realization. Prejudice, doubtless, played a rôle here. For a quarter of a century or more after its introduction metal was looked upon as a necessary evil. William Pole, quite as good an authority on music as on whist, in a book on "The Musical Instruments in the Great Industrial Exhibition of 1851," and Dr. Rimbault after him, expressed the opinion that the tendency to the use of too much metal in the construction of pianofortes threatened injury to the quality of the tone. Mr. Hipkins, a later and greater authority, writing thirty years after Pole and Rimbault, was not at all fearful of the modern steel frame, for he says:

> The greater elasticity of iron as compared with wood does not allow the lesser vibrating sections or upper partial tones of a string to die away as soon as they would with the less elastic wood. The consequence is that in instruments where iron or steel preponderates in the framing there is a longer *sostenente* or singing tone, and increasingly so as there is a higher tension or strain on the wire. Where wood preponderates, these vibrating sections die out sooner. The extremes of these conditions are a metallic whizzing or tinkling and a dull "woody" tone. The middle way, as so often happens, is to be preferred.

The three large steps from the all-wood frame to the modern frame of cast-steel, which now takes up in itself all the strain of the strings, were the use of bars and tubes between the hitching and wrest-planks, the addition of an iron hitching-plate, and the casting of an iron frame with all its parts in one piece. As in the case of the action, three men of three nationalities seem to have marked the steps independently of each other. They were John

Isaac Hawkins, an Englishman, who came to the United States toward the close of the eighteenth century and patented the upright pianoforte in 1800; William Allen, a Scotchman, who while working in London in 1820 introduced tubular braces of metal, and Alpheus Babcock, who patented an iron frame in a single casting in Boston in 1825. The application of the system to the three styles of the instrument, square (now practically obsolete), upright (Cottage, Cabinet, Piccolo, etc.), and grand, was only a matter of time, but it was again an American, Jonas Chickering, of Boston, who invented the complete iron frame for the concert grand. The structure, which three-quarters of a century ago buckled under the pull of the puny strings then in use, can now resist a strain of thirty tons.

The changes which have taken place in the stringing of piano-fortes have been quite as radical and extensive as those in the construction of the frame which they were chiefly instrumental in bringing about. The makers of the pianoforte's precursors were diligent in the search for metals which might ennoble the wiry, tinkling tone of their instruments. As the old organ builders sometimes mixed precious metals in the composition of their pipes, so the makers of clavichord and harpsichord wire sometimes turned to silver and gold. In the catalogue of the court orchestra of Philip II., 1602, mention is made of a clavichord of ebony, with cover of cypress, keys of ivory, and strings of gold. Experiments were made with gut, silk, and latten.

Gold and silver compounded [says Dr. Rimbault] and rendered elastic would undoubtedly produce beautiful tones. A gold string or wire will sound stronger than a silver one; those of brass and steel give feebler sounds than those of gold and silver. Silk strings were made of the single threads of the silkworm, a sufficient number of them being taken to form a chord of the required thickness; these were smeared over with the white of eggs, which was rendered consistent by passing the threads through heated oil. The string was exceedingly uniform in its thickness, but produced a tone which the performer called tubby.

The earliest pianofortes were strung with brass wire for the lower tones and steel for the upper. Seven or eight thicknesses of strings were used in the clavichords, spinets, and harpsichords of the seventeenth century, but the Cristofori pianoforte discloses but three diameters. The evidence adduced by this instrument, however, is not unimpeachable in this respect, since Signor Ponsicchi may have found it necessary, or thought it wise, to alter the stringing so far as diameters were concerned, when he restored it in 1875. In the modern instrument all the strings are of steel, though those for the lowest twenty tones (taking the Steinway Grand as a model) consist of a steel core wrapped about closely (like the G-string of a violin) with wire of a compound metal to give them greater weight and compensate for their disproportionate vibrating length. Irrespective of this covering, eighteen different sizes of wire are used, the development during the last century having been not only along the lines of elasticity, tenacity, and tension, but also diameter. The lowest eight bass tones are produced by single strings, covered; the next five, by double unisons, covered; the next seven by triple unisons, covered, and the remaining sixty-eight by triple unisons, of simple wire. In all 243 strings are employed to produce the eighty-eight tones of the concert grand. The average strain on each string may be set down in round numbers at 176 pounds. It was much higher before an agreement was reached some fifteen years ago among the principal pianoforte manufacturers of the United States to adopt a lower pitch than the old London Philharmonic, which had long been standard, and which many makers gave up grudgingly because of a belief that it was more brilliant than the French *diapason normal*.[1] Before the change a Steinway Concert Grand endured a strain of nearly 60,000 pounds; now the pull is the equivalent of 43,000 pounds.

The Cristofori pianoforte has a compass of four and one-half octaves, from C on the second leger line below the bass staff to F in the fourth space

[1] The exact Steinway pitch is still a trifle more acute than the *diapason normal*, viz.: $A = 438\frac{6}{10}$ as against $A = 435$.

above the treble. Very early the keys were extended downward to F, on the fourth leger line below the bass staff, so as to give the instrument five octaves. At the time of Haydn and Mozart five and five and a half octaves were in use, Clementi having added the half octave in 1793. The pianoforte which Broadwood, the English manufacturer, sent to Beethoven in 1817 had a compass of six octaves, but six and a half had already been reached in 1811, and the practical extreme of seven octaves in 1836. I say the "practical extreme" because the three notes which have been added since are of no artistic value. This, I venture to say, will not be disputed by any honest maker, but commercial considerations have led to their preservation. Bösendorfer, in Vienna, however, has made an "Imperial Concert Grand" with a compass of eight octaves, from sub-contra F, in the eighth space below the bass staff, to E *in altississimo*, in the eleventh space above the treble.

Pianoforte strings increase in thickness as the tones proceed down the scale in obedience to a law of acoustics which teaches that when strings have the same length and tension, but differ in weight (that is, thickness), their vibrations are in inverse proportion to their weight. Two other canons of the stretched string are also of validity, one of which teaches that as a string is lengthened it vibrates more slowly, as it is shortened more rapidly, the tension remaining the same; in the former case the tone produced is graver (lower is the popular definition); in the latter more acute (higher) than the fundamental. According to the second canon the tighter a string is drawn the higher the tone; the looser the slower its vibrations and the lower the tone, the length remaining equal. All three canons find their application in the stringing of pianofortes. The old rule, still prevailing in some houses, like that of Erard, in Paris, and their imitators, is to dispose the strings parallel with each other. The majority of manufacturers the world over, however, have taken a leaf out of the book of American practice and carry the overspun bass strings of the lowest octave across a number of the strings immediately adjoining. The disposition is thus fan-shaped and greater length is obtained for the strings of the lowest octave. This is the so-called overstrung scale, the combination of which with the solid steel or iron frame is the distinguishing feature of the American pianoforte, a feature that has been extensively adopted in European countries.

The principle exemplified in the overstrung scale, like the other features of construction the invention of which has been discusssed, had long been in the air before it was successfully applied. The device was employed in clavichords of the eighteenth century, and it seems likely that the idea was fermenting simultaneously in the minds of the American inventor of the solid iron frame for a square pianoforte, Alpheus Babcock, and Theobald Boehm, the German who revolutionized the flute by his new boring and system of keys. Cabinet and square pianofortes are now made in London after Boehm's design in 1835, but overstrung squares were exhibited in New York two years before, and the patent of Babcock for "cross-stringing pianofortes" (his meaning is vague and the original record is lost) was taken out in 1830. In 1859 Henry Engelhard Steinway, grandfather of the present president of the corporation of Steinway & Sons, combined an overstrung scale with a solid metal frame, thus taking the last really radical step in the development of the American pianoforte. What has been done since is in the way of development of the system in details.

The mechanism by means of which the hammer is made to strike the string and set it to vibrating is a marvel of ingenuity. Its simplest form was that shown in the tangent of the clavichord—by depressing the key a short tongue of metal was thrust against the string. The key was a simple lever, and the metal tongue, the tangent, had to be held against the string as long as it was desired that the tone should sound. The next step in the way of improvement was to hitch the handle of a small hammer to a rail with leather hinges and to replace the tangent with a bit of stiff wire with a leather button at the end, placed upright on the further end of the key. A slow pressure on the key lifted the hammer-head to within a short distance of the string; a blow impelled the hammer away from the key with its metal spine and against the string, from which it fell by its own weight. This device was imperfect, in that the blow necessary to the

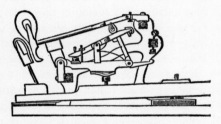

Hammer-Action of a Grand Pianoforte

production of a tone had to be so strong that very soft playing was impossible. Then came the device which in various forms and modifications has remained in use till now. The key raises a hopper which exerts a thrust against the hammer-shank with an energy corresponding to that exerted by the finger of the player. The hammer is thrown against the string, and on its recoil is caught by a check which prevents its rebounding and holds it in readiness for a repetition.

45

The fact that the hammer does not need to travel over the entire distance from its resting place to the string makes extremely rapid repetitions of the blow possible. As the key acts upon the hopper it also raises a damper of wood lined with felt, which in its normal position lies against the string from above. The release of the key brings this damper back to its place of rest and checks the vibrations of the string, thus preventing the discordant confusion of tones which would be heard if they were permitted to die by the gradual cessation of the vibrations. When it is desired that the tones shall continue through a series of arpeggios or a repeated harmony all the dampers are raised simultaneously by means of a pedal, the one to the right—the damper pedal, commonly spoken of as the loud pedal, though its use for the purpose of increasing the volume of tone is the cheapest to which it can be put. The left pedal shifts the action sidewise so that the hammers strike only one of the double and two of the triple unisons, leaving the others untouched to vibrate sympathetically. This is the action of the left pedal in the grand pianoforte; in the upright it moves the hammer-action nearer to the strings so that the hammer describes a smaller arc in reaching the strings and its force is lessened; in the obsolete square it interposed a strip of felt between the hammers and the strings and thus softened the tone.

The soft pedal movement of the grand does more than diminish the volume of tone; the tone emitted by the strings which have not felt the impact of the hammer but vibrate sympathetically—that is to say, in response to atmospheric waves sent forth by their unisons—is of an æolian sweetness and lends a color of wonderful charm to the music. It is the desire to combine this tint with sonority that tempts pianists to the abuse of the instrument discussed in connection with the difficulty of keeping pianofortes in tune before the introduction of the metal frame. On some pianofortes there is a third pedal between the other two, called the Tone Sustaining Pedal, the action of which is to withhold the dampers from the string or strings struck just before the depression of the pedal.

The actions which have been in use for many decades are modifications of three models:—the English perfected by Broadwood, the French repetition invented by Sebastian Erard, and the Viennese invented and perfected in Vienna. These models have been modified in particulars but not in principles by different manufacturers to suit the requirements of their instruments.

A comparison of some of the details of the Cristofori pianoforte in the Crosby Brown collection at the Metropolitan Museum of Art, in New York, and a modern concert grand made by Steinway & Sons will help to illustrate the tremendous progress made in the art of pianoforte construction from the time of the invention of the instrument till now. The Steinway concert grand pianoforte is 8 feet and 10 inches long and 5 feet wide. The weight of its metal plate is 320 pounds, which probably is more than the weight of the Cristofori instrument in its entirety. The total weight of the Steinway is 1,040 pounds. It has a compass of seven and a quarter octaves (eighty-eight keys), against the Cristofori's four and a half octaves (fifty-four keys), its range extending nineteen keys above the top note of the Cristofori instrument and fifteen below the bottom note. The longest string of the Steinway is six feet seven and one-half inches in length, its shortest two inches; the longest string of the Cristofori is six feet two inches, the shortest four and one-half inches; but the longest string of the Steinway consists of a steel core two millimetres thick, wound with wire thicker than the thickest strings of the Cristofori, so that the Steinway string is in all five millimetres thick. One or two octaves of these bass strings contain enough metal to string the Cristofori pianoforte throughout. The thickest string on the Cristofori is smaller in diameter than the thinnest string on the Steinway. The triple unisons on the Steinway which produce the lowest note of the Cristofori are wound and two millimetres thick. The highest note of the Cristofori has a string five and one-half inches long on the

Steinway and exerts a strain of 170 pounds for each of its three unisons. A few such strains would crush the frame of the Cristofori pianoforte like an eggshell, but it is not much more than the hundredth part of what the Steinway frame is called upon to endure.[1]

[1] For assistance in making this comparison I am much beholden to Mr. Henry Ziegler.

Part II

The Composers

IV

The Earliest Clavier Music

THE period of musical composition which falls naturally and properly within the scope of this book is coextensive with the period within which stringed instruments with keyboards were developing into significant factors in the economy of music. If we were to confine ourselves strictly to the period which has elapsed since the invention of the pianoforte we should not be able to extend our inquiries further back than the earliest known publication embracing the name or a description of the instrument in its title. This publication, according to Mr. Hipkins, is a set of sonatas (the word sonata used in a sense less determinate than it possesses now, as will presently appear in this study) composed by D. Lodovico Giustini di Pistoia, and printed in Florence in 1732. The pieces are described on the title page as being *Da Cimbalo di piano e forte detto volgarmente di Martellatti*—that is, "for the harpsichord, with soft and loud, commonly called with little hammers." The repertory of the modern pianist extends back of the date of this publication more than a century, however, and in its earlier portion shows so interesting a phase of musical evolution that it would be a grievous error to omit it from consideration.

I cannot include in this part of my study, however, such a genesis of principles as I allowed myself in the promenade toward the avenue in the first part. Speculation, the study of poets' utterances and the legends of ancient peoples, the inspection of ancient sculptures and mural paintings, may help us to conceptions of the appearance and even capacity of early instruments, but they can teach us nòthing of the music practised during the eras in which they arose. For us the history of instrumenal music does not begin until the fourteenth century, and it is a fact of profoundest significance that we find the instrumental art still in its dawn when the vocal art reaches its meridian. The reasons are not far to seek. Though more instruments were used in the secular practice than now, most of them were scarcely more developed than their precursors which are to be found in a state of arrested development in the Far East to-day. The influence of the taboo which the church had placed on the instrumental art while the musical law-givers were exclusively churchmen had not yet worn off. As late as the fourteenth and fifteenth centuries secular musicians were vagabonds in the eye of the law. Like strolling players

Beggars they were with one consent,
And rogues by act of Parliament.

The organist enjoyed an honorable exception, but it was not until the mechanism of the organ keyboard had been developed so as to permit of something like the modern facility of manipulation that music more fluent than the mediæval church chants could be performed upon the instrument. In the preceding centuries the key-mechanism was so cumbersome that a heavy pressure of the hand or a blow of the fist was required to force a key down. For a long time in Germany organists were called *Orgelschläger*—that is, "organ beaters"—because of the action of their hands in playing. The similarity between the keyboards of the organ, clavichord, and the various quilled instruments (which I shall frequently allude to generically as claviers) turned the attention of organists to them as soon as the effect of the ecclesiastical taboo began to wear off, and other than ecclesiastical music began to be admitted to polite habitations; but there was a long controversy between the artistic and the popular practice. Even after compositions for keyboard stringed instruments began to appear in print it was not uncommon to find them described as pieces translated from "music" to notation for instruments—organ, lute, and clavier sometimes being specified, sometimes not. "Music" was still so dignified a term that it had to be protected from association with the agencies which had no employment in the service of the church.

It was the organ that played the part of interceder and advocate of the instrumental company for their admission into the province of art, and it was in Venice that instrumental music began to flourish in the fourteenth century. The skill of a long line of organists in the fourteenth, fifteenth, and sixteenth centuries shone pre-eminently among the contemporaneous glories and magnificence of the City of the Doges. The Cathedral of St. Mark was the magnet that drew organ players to Venice, as the Sistine Chapel drew composers and singers to Rome. These organists gave pomp and brilliancy to the services, to which kneeling thousands listened, by their improvisations upon church melodies and the set pieces which they played at times when the choir was silent. There were two organs in St. Mark's, each generally in the hands of one of the world's greatest masters, and they were employed antiphonally at times for preludes, interludes, and postludes before, between, and after portions of the choral service. The service (such is the force of conservatism) remained exclusively vocal for the two hundred years in which the musical glory of Venice was most resplendent. It was not until a new era had been ushered in by purely secular activities that the organ was permitted to lift its voice along with the voices of the singers.

During these two hundred years the organists of

Venice and other art capitals gradually worked for the emancipation of instrumental music from the thraldom of the church. Of the pioneers of this movement in Italy we know little more than their names, preserved for us in the stories of their fame. Francesco Landini, the hey-day of whose celebrity fell in the seventh decade of the fourteenth century, was poet as well as organist. He was a Florentine, and blind, yet one of the brightest ornaments in the festivities given by the doge in honor of the King of Cyprus and the Archduke of Austria. Petrarch stood by at one of these festivities and saw the Florentine Homer crowned with laurel for some of his poetic effusions. Nevertheless, the laureate suffered defeat on the organ bench at the hands of Francesco da Pésaro, an organist of St. Mark's. Almost simultaneously another blind man brought glory to Munich and won tributes from royalty by his marvellous skill. This was Conrad Paulmann, or Paumann, a native of Nuremberg, born sightless, yet a sort of universal genius in music. Of him, it is recorded that the Emperor Frederick III. gave him a sword with blade of gold and a golden chain. He died in Munich in 1473, and was buried in the Church of Our Lady. His tomb shows him in effigy seated at the organ, and the inscription proclaims him to have been *Der Kunstreichest aller Instrumentisten und der Musika Maister.* So, too, a bust in the cathedral at Florence testifies to the fame of Antonio Squarcialupi, organist of the cathedral about 1450.

Of other Italian musicians distinguished in the instrumental field in the fourteenth century the names, but not the works, of Nicolo del Proposto and Jacopo di Bologna are preserved; of the sixteenth, a long list culminating in men of the highest importance in the development of the science and art of music—Claudio Merulo, Andrea Gabrieli, and Cipriano di Rore. To this list I add the names of a few men who, though not of Italian birth, were yet instrumental in the development of Italian music, viz., a German whose name was obviously Bernhard Stephan Mürer, but who was called Bernardo Stefanio Murer (and also Bernard the German) by the Italians; Jacques Buus, who was organist of St. Mark's for ten years, from 1541 to 1551 (in which latter year he left Venice), and Adrien Willaert, founder of the Venetian school and chapelmaster of St. Mark's for a period beginning in 1527. To Bernard is credited the invention of the pedal keyboard for the organ. Willaert and Buus were Netherlanders.

Instrumental music, having begun after the unaccompanied style of vocal music had been perfected, was, naturally enough, written in the contrapuntal style of the church. Monophonic music—that is, a melody supported by harmonies in solid or broken chords—being all but unknown till toward the end of the sixteenth century, solo music except that in the church service (*i. e.*, the chanting of the priest at the altar) was also unknown. When various instruments were grouped so as to form a band, each instrument sang its part precisely as the individual singer in the choir sang his. All these parts were melodies, and all were equally important in the musical fabric. There was no subordination of three or more of the contrapuntal voices to one to bring out the beauty or sentiment of the tune carried by that voice. Strictly speaking, there was no tune in the modern sense any more than there was harmony in the modern sense. Compositions were built up on Gregorian melodies, and the melody, which became the *cantus firmus* of a piece, was allotted to one voice (generally that called the tenor); but it was not importunate in the manner of the modern melody. On the contrary, it was frequently less assertive than the voices consorted with it, being merely a stalking-horse on which the ingenious fabric of interwoven melodies was hung. It is a mistaken impression on this point which has led to the wholesale and irrational condemnation of mediæval composers for using secular tunes in their masses. The popular notion, created and nourished by the vast majority of writers on musical history, is that when the old Netherlandish composers wrote masses on the melody of "L'Homme armé" (an extremely popular subject), or "Dieu quel mariage," the effect upon the hearers was something like the effect would be upon worshippers of to-day if *Credo in unum Deum* or *Gloria in excelsis Deo* were to be sung to the tune of the first of the "Beautiful Blue Danube" waltzes. Nothing could be further from the truth. Many a critic who writes glibly about the "secularization of the mass" in the fifteenth century would be hard put to it to write out the theme of a "L'Homme armé" mass from an old score even if it were laid before him in modern notation, while to distinguish by ear the naughty secular tune moving through the contrapuntal mass would tax the ability of many of our professional musicians.

When the orchestra took its rise the music set down for the different instruments differed in nothing from vocal music. Compositions were published with titles indicating that they were to be sung or played as one wished. Equally vague during this period was the terminology of the instrumental art. There were *Sonate, Canzone, Ricercare, Toccati, Contrapunti, Fantasie,* and so on; but the names were but obscure indices to the form and contents of the compositions. Willaert seems to have distinguished between his *fantasie* and *ricercare* on the one hand and his *contrapunti* on the other by employing themes of his own invention for the former and church melodies for the latter. The only difference between a *sonata*—the term originally meant no more than a "sound piece" as distinguished from a "song piece"—and a *canzona per sonar*, which Michael Praetorius could point out in his "Syntagma musicum," published in 1620, was that sonatas were grave and majestic in the style of the motet, while canzonas were written in notes of shorter duration, and therefore fresh, lively, merry. The themes, whether original or borrowed from the church chants, were varied in the different compositions, no matter what they were called. They were worked fugally, bedecked with ornamental passages, transferred from part to part, and motives drawn from them were treated in imitation. The composers for the church having sought for basic melodies in secular fields, it is not to be wondered at that the composers for instruments did the same. The songs and dances of the people were now taken as themes, and in Italy there appeared *Canzone Villanesche*, *Canzone Napolitane*, and *Canzone Francese*, which were varied in like manner as the church melodies. Dance tunes (galliards, corantos, and chaconnes) also came into use, and when the jig (*giga*) was consorted with them the time was ripe for their combination into a *partita*, or suite—a form which pointed the way to the cyclical compositions culminating in the modern sonata and symphony. The employment of folk-tunes stimulated accompaniments in chords, and under the inspiration of the reformatory movement begun by a group of amateur musicians in Florence as a protest against the artificiality and lifelessness of the church style, also dominant in the theatre— a movement which brought about the invention of the opera—instrumental music was slowly emancipated from the vocal yoke.

V

The English Virginalists

ALREADY in the sixteenth century England had taken the lead in the creation, and probably also in the performance of clavier music. In view of her comparative sterility since, it would be interesting in many ways to know where to go to find the explanation of England's pre-eminence in one department of music before and during the reign of Queen Elizabeth. There are evidences enough that England drew her fashions in music as in other forms of artistic culture from Italy and France; but in her handling of the borrowed forms she was as forward, fresh, vigorous, and energetic as in the fields in which she created her own models, namely, poetry, the drama, and that higher type of statecraft which makes for human liberty. Perhaps the explanation of any one phenomenon which shone luminous in England's Golden Age is also the explanation of the other, and may not lie hidden any deeper than in the moral, physical, and intellectual amalgam which resulted from blending the rugged virtues of Briton, Saxon, Norman, and Dane with the gentler graces lent by Latin culture.

To my readers who are more desirous to know something of the musical culture growth of England at this time than to follow the growth of the technical elements in composition, I advise a course at once more profitable and more pleasurable than that prescribed in the handbooks. It is to look at the musical taste and practices of Shakespeare's people through the eyes of Shakespeare. The poet wrote for all the people of his day and nation, and his use of words and phrases appertaining to music becomes an index to the state of musical culture during the reign of Henry VIII., Elizabeth, and James I., which is frequently luminous. In this respect as in so many others, he shows "the very age and body of the time, his form and pressure." As he wrote for the whole people and made copious use in his dramas of the popular music of the day by introduction as well as allusion, it is to be assumed that the people who were called upon to understand and enjoy his many fleeting allusions to the art and the songs which he took out of their mouths were near to him in musical taste and knowledge. Like him they were nimble-minded, up-to-date, and fearless of anachronisms. There was nothing to give pause to the fancy or judgment of the patrons of the Globe Theatre in the circumstance that the poet's Frenchmen, Italians, Greeks, and ancient Britons were all sixteenth century Englishmen; that they thought, talked, sang, acted, and danced like the people of Elizabeth's court or her simpler subjects.

What manner of people, then, were they to whom Shakespeare could talk blithely, without need of oral gloss or foot-note, of "discords," "stops," "rests," "dumps," "diapasons," "burdens," "descant," "divisions," "frets," "concords," "base," "sharps," "pricksong," "broken music," "gamut," "A-re" (and so on through the notes of the mediæval scale), "plainsong," "minims," "means," "virginalling," "jacks," and a score or more of similar terms belonging to the vocabulary of music? Without calling for evidence outside of the fact that Shakespeare did so write we must conclude that they were not a commonplace people; else there would have been no Shakespeare to write for them. He sprang from their loins. From many sources we know that they were a strong people. Rather rude; having those physical, mental, and moral qualities dominant which marked out a large portion of the world for their possession. Stout eaters and most courageous drinkers. Contentious. Fond of show, and fickle of taste in dress as the devotees of fashion are to-day. Somewhat given to swashbuckling, I fear. Heedful of the laws of courtesy and gallantry, yet plain-spoken. Not tender-hearted. Kindliness and pity held possession of only a small portion of their souls; even the Virgin Queen delighted in bear-baiting. The women not prudish, either in the playhouse or at home, but frank in their recognition of natural appetites. Frank, too, and amiable in the exercise of the social amenities. The hostess or her daughter might greet the gentleman visitor with a kiss—"a custom never to be sufficiently commended," said the gentle Erasmus; and the gentleman might ask the tribute from his fair partner after each dance—or even before, to judge by King Henry VIII.'s remark on first seeing Anne Bullen:

> Sweetheart,
> I were unmannerly to take you out
> And not to kiss you.[1]

Foreigners were amazed at the beauty of the women and their learning. "The English challenge the prerogative of having the handsomest women, of keeping the best table, and of being the most accomplished in the skill of music of any people," wrote the same Erasmus.[2]

Many of the gentlewomen had "sound knowledge of Greek and Latin and were skilful in Spanish, Italian, and French." The ladies of Elizabeth's court translated foreign works into Latin or English, and for recreation practised "lutes, citherns, pricksong, and all kinds of music." "Argal" the people were familiar with and fond of music. The

[1] King Henry VIII., Act 1, Scene 4.
[2] *Britanni, præter alia, formam, musicam, et lautas mensas proprie sibi vindicent.* (Erasmus, *Enconium Moriæ.*)

professional practitioners outside of the church were still looked upon as vagabonds, more or less, but all classes, from royalty down to mendicancy, were devoted to music. Henry VIII., being a younger son, was first set apart for holy orders (his youthful eye already on the see of Canterbury), and in the course of study which he pursued music was obligatory. Nevertheless, his inclinations carried him far beyond training in church music merely. He played the recorder, flute, and virginal, and composed songs, ballads, and church services. Anne Bullen "doted" on the compositions of Josquin des Prés, whom Luther, no mean authority, esteemed higher than all the composers that had ever lived. Edward VI. made personal record of the fact that he had played upon the lute in order to display his accomplishments to the French ambassador in 1551. Elizabeth was so vain of her skill as a performer upon the virginal that she planned to be overheard by Mary Stuart's ambassador, Sir James Melvil, in order that he might carry the news to the Scottish queen. She played "excellently well," says Sir James—but read the pretty and ingenuous story in his memoirs.

Gentlemen with a polite education were expected not only to be able to sing pricksong (*i. e.*, printed or written music) at sight, but also to extemporize a part in harmony with a printed melody or bass. This was the art of descant. A bass viol, like the "viol de gamboys" on which Sir Toby boasted that his friend Aguecheek could play, hung in the drawing room for gentlemen visitors to entertain themselves withal; and, if called upon, they, too, must play divisions to the pricksong which my lady played upon the virginal. The cithern and gittern hung on the walls of the barber shops, and the virginal stood in the corner, so that customers might pass the time with them while waiting, or the barber find solace in his idle moments. "Tinkers sang catches," says Chappell, "milkmaids sang ballads, carters whistled; each trade and even the beggars had their special songs." In his "Sylva Sylvarum" Bacon left a scientific discussion of music, its psychological effects, the nature of dissonance and consonance, and the character of the instruments most in use in his day; Michael Drayton gave a complete list of the instruments in use at the time in his "Poly-Olbion" (1613); Shakespeare did nothing so prosaic, but having the whole field of musical culture before him—the practice of the people as well as the art and science of the professional musicians—he opened up a much wider and clearer vista than did my Lord Verulam or the cataloguing poet.

The era in question was the most brilliant in the history of England, but Shakespeare has preserved no tribute to the polite art of the day comparable with that which he pays to the popular art in the introduction of allusions to the people's songs and dances in his plays or the songs and dances themselves. These songs and dances were the staple of the group of organists and virginalists who form the brightest gem in England's musical crown. Though clavier music was composed on the continent as early as it was in England—the historical record going much further back, indeed—it was nevertheless in England that the earliest known collections of compositions for keyboard-stringed instruments were made. These compositions were nominally written for the virginal, and I have, therefore, called the men who wrote them virginalists rather than harpsichordists. It may have been only an amiable affectation which made the English composers of the sixteenth century name the virginal as the instrument for which their music was intended, but since their music makes no demand for the mechanical contrivances applied to the harpsichord to increase its expressive capacity, it seems likely that the composers really had in mind the instrument which was most widely diffused among the people. In Pepys's diary, under date September 2, 1666, one may read, in his description of the scenes attending the Great Fire: "I observed that hardly one lighter or boat in three that had the goods of a house in but there was a paire of virginals in it." Plainly, in proportion to population, virginals were as plentiful in London two hundred and fifty years ago as pianofortes are to-day.

This would be in harmony with the belief that I have expressed in the universality of musical culture in England during Shakespeare's time and also with the sentimental inclination which led some writers to suppose that the virginal had received its name from the circumstance that it was the favorite instrument of the Virgin Queen. Unhappily for this pretty theory the virginal, commonly spoken of at the time as "virginals" or "a pair of virginals," was known by the name before Elizabeth was born.

It is only within a recent period that study of a large body of English virginal music has been open to students. Until the publication of the "Fitzwilliam Virginal Book," in 1899, students were restricted practically to the few pieces printed in the histories and the collection edited by E. Pauer and published under the title of "Old English Composers." The scholarship of Mr. J. A. Fuller Maitland and Mr. W. Barclay Squire has now given one of the most famous of musical MSS. to the world in modern notation. The manuscript figured in musical literature for a century as "Queen Elizabeth's Virginal Book," this title having been given to it under the belief that it had once been the property of the Virgin Queen. Historical investigation, however, dealt harshly with this amiable delusion, and since its publication it has borne the name of the Fitzwilliam Museum, in which it has long been housed. It is a veritable thesaurus of the best clavier music that the world produced in the sixteenth and the first quarter of the seventeenth centuries. The manuscript is a small folio volume of 418 pages, gilt edged and bound in red morocco, elaborately tooled, ornamented with fleurs-de-lis, and otherwise embellished. It contains 219 compositions copied by the same hand. The editors are inclined to the belief that the compiler and transcriber was one Francis Tregian, who did the work between the years 1608 and 1619, while an inmate of Fleet Prison, to which he had been committed for recusancy. He was a Papist, like his father, who sat in prison twenty-four years on account of his religious beliefs. It was the discovery that some of the compositions in the book were not composed until seventeen years after Elizabeth's death which spoiled the pretty story that the book had belonged to that queen. Among the composers whose works figure in the book are Dr. John Bull, William Byrd, Thomas Morley, John Munday, Giles Farnaby, William Blitheman, Richard Farnaby, Orlando Gibbons, and Thomas Tallis.

Other valuable manuscripts collated by Dr. Rimbault with the Fitzwilliam manuscript in the preparation of his "Collection of Specimens Illustrating the Progress of Music for Keyed-Stringed Instruments," printed in his history of the pianoforte, are the Mulliner Virginal Book, the Earl of Leicester's Virginal Book, Lady Neville's Virginal

Book, and two manuscript collections which I judge to belong to the latter part of the seventeenth century, now preserved in the New York Public Library, Lenox Foundation, having been bought by the late Joseph W. Drexel at the sale of Dr. Rimbault's library in London in 1877. The music in these manuscripts is written on staves of six lines, like that of the Fitzwilliam book. Among the composers repesented are Orlando Gibbons, Christopher Gibbons, Dr. Bull, Dr. Rogers, Albert Byrne, Matthew Locke, Thomas Tomkins, J. Cobb, and P. Phillips. The chief source of knowledge touching English virginal music outside of the manuscript collections in the seventeenth century was a work printed in 1611, entitled "Parthenia." It contained music written by Byrd, Bull, and Orlando Gibbons, and went through six editions within forty-eight years, during which time (according to Anthony a Wood) it was "the prime book used by Masters in Musick." In 1847 it was reprinted under the auspices of the Musical Antiquarian Society, Dr. Rimbault being the editor.

The variation form was almost exclusively cultivated by the English virginalists, though there are evidences of novel strivings in manner as well as content in some of the pieces called fantasias. Thus, the first composition of John Munday (died 1630) in the Fitzwilliam book is a fantasia in which an effort is made to delineate a series of meteorological changes. Its sections, rhythmically varied and without thematic connection, bear the inscriptions "Fair Weather," "Lightning," "Thunder," three times; finally there comes a slow concluding movement section marked "A Clear Day."[1]

So, too, there is an early specimen of another style of programmatic composition, once so admired

[1] It may interest the curious to note that the device with which Munday attempts to suggest lightning is not unlike in idea that which Wagner invented for the same purpose more than two centuries later, as will appear from a comparison of the two phrases:

Musical Lightning in Munday's Fantasia.

Musical Lightning in Wagner's "Walkure."

that the echoes of it have come down quite to our
own day, in a piece by William Byrd, which is
found transcribed in Lady Neville's virginal book
and twice in one of the manuscripts in the New
York Public Library, where it is annotated (evidently by Dr. Rimbault) as having been collated
with Dr. Burney's MS. This, which seems to have
been as popular a piece in its day as its successor,
Kotzwara's "Battle of Prague," was a century and
a half later, was called "A Battaille," sometimes also
"Mr. Byrd's Battle." It is a compages of separate
pieces bearing descriptive titles, as follows: "The
Soldiers' Summons," "The March of Footmen,"
"The March of Horsemen," "The Trumpets,"
"The Irish March," "The Bagpipes' Drone,"
"The Drums and Flutes," "The March to the
Fight," "The Battles Joined," "The Retreat,"
"The Victory," and "The Burying of the Dead."

Melodies from the popular songs of France and
Italy (corresponding to the *canzone Napolitane* and
canzone Francese of the Venetian organists) were
also utilized by the English virginalists, as well as
church melodies; but the bulk of their thematic
material was drawn from the popular songs and
dances of the day. In the Fitzwilliam book we find
that peculiarly winsome song sung by the clown
in the roistering scene in Shakespeare's "Twelfth
Night" (Act III., Scene 3), beginning "O Mistress
Mine," set by Byrd; the tune called "Hanskin" to

which Autolycus sings "Jog on, jog on," in "A Winter's Tale" (Act IV., Scene 2), set by Richard Farnaby; and "Bonny Sweet Robin," one line of which poor, distraught Ophelia sings to Laertes before going to the brook, where she was pulled

> from her melodious lay
> To muddy death,

set by Giles Farnaby. There, also, is Byrd's setting of "The Carman's Whistle," the song which, in all likelihood, was in Shakespeare's mind when, in having Falstaff descant on the early life of Justice Shallow, he made the knight say:

He always came in the rearward of the fashion; and sung those tunes to the over-scutched huswifes that he heard the carmen whistle and sware they were his "fancies" or "his "good nights." [1]

[1] Scant justice has been done to this music by the German historians, as a rule, and it is therefore the greater pleasure to note the laudable exception made by Dr. Oscar Bie, who waxes enthusiastic over Byrd's setting of "The Carman's Whistle" and "Sellinger's Round":

"'The Carman's Whistle,'" says Dr. Bie, "is a perfected popular melody, one of those tunes which will linger for days in our ears. At the beginning of the third and fourth bars Byrd sets the first and second bars in canon, in the simplest and most straightforward style. Next come harmonies worthy of a Rameau, with the most delicate passing notes. In the variations certain figures are inserted which are easily worked into the canonic form, now *legato* with the charm of the introduction of related notes, now diatonic scales most gracefully introduced, now *staccato* passages which draw the melody along with them like the singing of a bird.

Among other songs I mention the following as figuring more or less extensively in the writings of the poets, dramatists, and essayists of the time, the melodies of which are preserved for us in the music of the virginalists, viz.: "Walsingham," "Quodling's Delight," "Packington's Pound," "Malt's Come Down," "Why Ask You?" "Go from My Window," "John, Come Kiss Me Now," "All in a Garden Green," "Fain Would I Wed," "Peascod Time," "Tell Me, Daphne," "Mall Sims," and "Rowland." The popularity won on the continent by the last tune is quite irreconcilable with the notion of the historians, a notion shared with his

Finally fuller chords appear, gently changing the direction of the theme. From first to last there is not a turn foreign to the modern ear.

"The 'Sellinger's Round' is more stirring. Its theme is in a swinging 6-8 rhythm, running easily through the harmonies of the tonic, the super-dominant and the sub-dominant. It strikes one like an old legend, as in the first part of Chopin's Ballade in F major, of which this piece is a prototype. The first variation retains the rhythm and only breaks the harmonies. Its gentle fugalization is more distinctly marked in the third variation, which at the conclusion adopts running semi-quavers, after Byrd's favorite manner, anticipating at the conclusion of the one variation the motive of the next. The semi-quavers go up and down in thirds, or are interwoven by both hands, while melody and accompaniment continue their dotted 6-8, in a fashion reminding us of a Schumann. In the later variations the quaver movement is again taken up, but more florid and more varied, with runs which pursue each other in canon. This piece, perhaps the first perfect clavier piece on record, which had left its time far behind, was written in 1580."

predecessors, even by Dr. Bie, that the influence of the English school of virginalists was short lived and confined to England. Not only did the English comedians who introduced farces sung to popular tunes in Germany and Holland set the fashion which created the German Singspiel, they also habilitated there the melodies of their native land. "Rowland," which is called "Lord Willoughby's Welcome Home" in Lady Neville's virginal book, became the *Rolandston* to which scores, probably hundreds, of erotic, historical, and religious songs were written in Germany and the Netherlands. So the "Cobbler's Jig," "Fortune My Foe" ("The Merry Wives of Windsor," Act III., Scene 3), "Greensleeves" ("The Merry Wives," Act II., Scene 1, and Act V., Scene 5), "Packington's Pound," "Mall Sims," and other English tunes were known all over the continent, where in the seventeenth century a dozen or more English musicians were employed in high positions at different courts. Richard Machin was at the court of the Landgrave of Hesse; Thomas Simpson at that of Count Ernest III. of Schaumburg; Walter Rowe, and after him Walter Rowe, his son, were in the service of the Elector of Brandenburg; Valentine Flood was active in Berlin and Dantzic; William Brade in Berlin and Hamburg; John Stanley in Berlin, and John Price in Dresden. All these men published their compositions in Germany.

Part of a page from "Parthenia." (See page 72.)

The English school was known and respected on the continent and its influence felt. Dr. John Bull (born about 1563, died 1628) amazed the *cognoscenti* by his playing at the courts of France, Spain, and Austria, and died in service as organist of the Cathedral of Notre Dame at Antwerp. In the course of his career, which began when he was nineteen years old, he was organist of Hereford Cathedral, member of the Chapel Royal, recipient of the degree of Mus. Doc. from both Oxford and Cambridge universities, professor of music at Gresham College (for which post he was recommended by Queen Elizabeth herself and by special dispensation was permitted to read his lectures in English instead of Latin), travelling virtuoso and court musician on the continent, and organist at Antwerp. He was unquestionably the greatest of the musicians who extended the repute of England abroad, but he was not without companions. Evidence of his digital fluency, which may be looked upon as the equivalent in that day of technical proficiency in this, is found in his proneness to write difficult passages for both hands and to indulge in profuse ornamentation. He was considered a marvel of learning, and of skill in composition also, as is illustrated by the tale that he added forty new parts to a composition already containing forty. The tale sounds fantastic and mythical to modern ears, but it must be remembered that though the infancy of the instrumental art failed to show the fact in anything like the measure disclosed by the vocal, the age was an ingenious and scholastic one when, as William Mason, precentor of York Cathedral and biographer of the poet Gray, has said—

there were Schoolmen in Music as well as in Letters; and when, if learning had its Aquinas and Smeglecius, music had its Master Giles and its Dr. Bull, who could split the seven notes of music into as many divisions as the others could split the ten Categories of Aristotle.

We are as little concerned with the works which Dr. Bull wrote for the church as with like compositions by his great predecessor, Tallis; but if we wish to observe him in a wholly amiable mood we need only hear his "King's Hunting Jigg," a composition in which, with the jubilant vitality of its first part paired with the jocund, out-doorsy flourish of its second, I find more of the modern spirit than in any score of the programmatic and characteristic pieces written by the French masters who came a hundred years after him. Harsh and crude are many of the progressions in some of these English pieces, monotonous the repetition of rudimentary passage-work in the variations, but their value as clavier music becomes luminous when compared with the bulk of the music written for the harpsichord in the same period on the continent.

Thomas Tallis (perhaps more properly Tallys, 1527–1585) plays his most important rôle as "the father of English cathedral music" and the teacher (and business associate in a monopoly of music printing and the sale of music paper) of William Byrd (1544 or 1546–1623). Orlando Gibbons (1583–1625) was one of three brothers who were eminent in their day in the cathedral service, and the father of Dr. Christopher Gibbons (1615–1676), who was organist of Winchester Cathedral, the Chapel Royal, Westminster Abbey, and private organist to Charles II. Byrd seems to have been the most popular writer of virginal music in his time, and his pieces outnumber those of any of his associates in the "Fitzwilliam Virginal Book." His closest competitor, as evidenced by that standard, was Giles Farnaby, who bridged over the sixteenth and seventeenth centuries, but of whom next to nothing is known. Giles Farnaby is represented in the collection by fifty-one pieces to Byrd's sixty-eight; Dr. Bull follows with forty-four, Tallis with twenty-two, and then comes Peter Phillips with nineteen. Phillips was a Catholic cleric of English birth, evidence of whose sojourn in Italy and on the continent is found in his arrangements of melodies by such Italian masters as Orlando Lassus, Luca Marenzio, Alessandro Striggio, and Giulio Romano. With Dr. John Blow (1658–1708) and Henry Purcell (1658–1695) the list of epoch-making English composers may be said to have ended, though Mr. Pauer has included pieces by Dr. T. A. Arne (1710–1778), in his "Old English Composers." The finest fruit of Purcell's creative genius, itself the finest product of England's capacity, was given to the church and stage. By the time that Purcell won the headship the element which gave the English school of virginalists its most national and striking characteristic—that is, English folksong melody—had been abandoned and the suite of dance forms had taken its place. John Playford, in his "Introduction to the Skill of Musick," said:

> Our late and Solemn Musick, both Vocal and Instrumental, is now justled out of Esteem by the New Corants and Jigs of Foreigners, to the grief of all sober and judicious Understanders of that formerly solid and good Musick: nor must we expect Harmony in People's minds, so long as Pride, Vanity, Faction, and Discords are so predominant in their lives.

This deprecatory comparison of the present with the past is a familiar phenomenon in the history of music. It can easily be traced back as far as the time of Aristotle, whose pupil Aristoxenus could find little or no merit in the music of his age, when he pondered on what music had been when the popular taste was reflected in the compositions of Æschylus, Pindar, and Simonides; and I shall not be surprised if this review, too, runs out into plaints against the hollowness of composers of this latter day.   In the case of Playford, however, it marks the transfer of the sceptre of supremacy from his people to another, and this change seemed to him as woful in its consequences to music as did the change in the style of dancing (which not only accompanied but conditioned it) to morals and decorum to John Selden.   In his "Table Talk" that political moralist found time to deplore the change which had come over court dancing when he remembered how the gravity and stateliness which had prevailed during an earlier generation had given way to the boisterousness of "Trenchmore" (which, according to Burton, went "over tables, stoves, and chairs") and the "Cushion Dance," which might best be likened to a rural kissing game of the present day.[1]

The dance music written down in the books of the old English virginalists belongs to the period when the court dance, at least, was still full of "state and ancientry."   It consisted chiefly of pavans, galliards, and allemands.   The form and movement of these stately dances invited the florid figuration and canonic imitations which had been invented for the *ricercare* and *toccati* of the Venetian organists.   The pavan in melody and movement was as solemn and even lugubrious as a covenant-

---

[1] "So in our court," says Selden, "in Queen Elizabeth's time, *gravity and state* were kept up.   In King James's time things were *pretty well*.   But in *King Charles's* time there has been nothing but Trenchmore and the Cushion Dance, *omnium gatherum, tolly polly, hoite cum toity*."—("King of England.")

er's psalm or a *Chorale* of the German church. The favorite dance tune of Charles IX. of France was the melody to which Psalm cxxix. was sung. Full court dress, with hat, cloak, and sword, was *de rigueur* with men, long trains with women. The dance was executed as a majestic procession, like the courtly Polonaise or Fackeltanz of a later period. It was a display of haughty carriage and gorgeous raiment. The solemn music changed from double to triple rhythm and, quickened in tempo, became a galliard, in which there was less show of dignity and composure and more of skill and agility. The galliard permitted, if, indeed, it did not require, more or less vigorous and fantastic caperings.[1]

"Every pavan has its galliard," says a Spanish proverb. In "Parthenia" and the manuscripts to which I have referred this intimate association of the two dances is illustrated in a melody for each

[1] A few lines from Shakespeare's "Twelfth Night" as an illustration:

Sir Toby. What is thy excellence in a galliard, knight?

Sir Andrew. Faith, I can cut a caper . . . and I think I have the back trick as strong as any man in Illyria.

Sir Toby. Wherefore are these things hid? . . . I did think, by the excellent constitution of thy leg, it was formed under the star of a galliard.

Sir Andrew. Ay, 'tis strong, and it does indifferent well in a flame colored stock. Shall we set about some revels?

Sir Toby. . . . Let me see thee caper; ha! higher! ha! ha!— excellent! (Act I., Scene 3.)

galliard, which is itself only a variation in triple time of the tune of the preceding pavan. "Pavan; Galliard to the Pavan"—this is the common formula. When Playford wrote, these solemn measures with their variations had given place to the suite consisting of a number of dance melodies, some stately as a saraband, some lively as a jig. In Purcell's music we find suites composed of a prelude, alman (the alman and almain of the earlier English composers, the allemande of the French and German); of a prelude, courante, saraband, chaconne, and siciliano; of a prelude, almand, courante, saraband cebell (gavotte), minuet, riggadoon, intrada, and march, and so on. Insular and continental tastes are met, and the people who by taste and training are best fitted to set the pegs for the new fashion become the arbiters for the time being of the polite world. With the instrumental art secularized in tone and purpose and emancipated from the vocal forms, the French naturally acquired great importance in its practice.[1]

[1] I yield to the temptation to offer here a curious contribution to a vexatious problem in musical terminology. In the country districts of the eastern portion of the United States a figure in a lively square dance is variously "alleman," "eleman," and "alement," the pronunciation evidently depending much upon the taste and fancy of the pronouncer. The question raised by this is whether or not we have here a survival of a dance which long ago fell into disuse in the Old World. The allemande was a popular dance in the sixteenth century, and also found favor in the court of Louis XIV., because, it is said, being little else in its

performance than a German waltz with figures, it was supposed to symbolize the union of Alsace with France. But as a popular dance the allemande, which survived in a musical form in the partitas and suites of the eighteenth century, died in the seventeenth. According to Arbeau's "Orchésographie" (1588) it was a dance of German origin, as its name implies, which was a sort of procession of couples holding hands. Steevens, in a note on "Hamlet," quotes some one as saying: "We Germans have no changes in our dances. An almain and an upspring, that is all." In portions of New York State the command, "Alleman!" is carried out by the dancers "swinging corners."

VI

French and Italian Clavecinists

FOR two hundred years after dancing had become the most polite of polite arts it was swayed by the gay and gallant court of France. When Catherine de Medici came to Paris the influence of her native Italy—splendor-loving, pleasure-loving Italy—was already at work. It had long been nourished by the sun of the renaissance, which had revived the pantomimes and spectacular shows of the ancient Romans with all their gaudy paraphernalia. At the courts of the great ones of Italy, of the Estes and Medicis, in the palaces of popes and cardinals, there had grown up and been humored with extravagant generosity those pantomimic and musical entertainments in which the virtues of the noble patrons of art were celebrated by allegories and paraphrases of the beautiful fables of classical antiquity. In these entertainments music played an important part; but for long it was music which in form and spirit failed to meet any requirement of the dramatic art or to echo a single sound from the voice of romanticism which spoke in the songs and dances of the plain people.

The predominant position which the dance occupied among the polite diversions of the aristocracy of Italy and France during the sixteenth, seventeenth, and eighteenth centuries must be kept in view if the significance of the French school of clavecinists and its successors in Germany is to be understood. Three hundred years ago nobody thought the dance beneath his dignity. The most august members of the Council of Trent, the princes of the church, cardinals, bishops, abbots, and priests danced at the ball given in honor of Philip II. of Spain, in 1562. Dancing in the churches (a custom of vast antiquity) endured in France until prohibited by decree of the Paris Parliament, in 1667. It still survives in Seville. It was a priest, Jehan Tabourot, who wrote that famous treatise on the dances of the sixteenth century known as Arbeau's "Orchésographie." Cardinal Richelieu tricked himself out like a merry andrew, with green velvet breeches and bells on shoes, rattled his castanets as he danced a saraband for the delectation of Anne of Austria. It is written that for twenty years Louis XIV. took a daily dance lesson from Beauchamps. Under a ministerial decree issued in his reign (1669), members of the nobility were permitted to perform at the opera for hire without loss of dignity, and even to follow dancing as a means of livelihood.

Don Juan of Austria, when Viceroy of the Neth-

J. PH. RAMEAU

Né à Dijon le 25 septembre 1683.
Mort le 12 Septembre 1764.

JEAN PHILLIPPE RAMEAU.

erlands, went *incognito* from Brussels to Paris to see
Marguerite of Valois dance a minuet. Molière,
Lully, and Quinault devoted a portion of their
genius to the invention of ballets, a species of entertainment so popular, even before female dancers
had been admitted to the stage, that no fewer than
eighty of them were brought out at the Opéra in
the year 1610. Catherine de Medici not only introduced heroic, comic, gallant, and allegorical
ballets in which the princes and nobles of the French
court masqueraded as apes, bears, ostriches, and
parrots; she also supplemented the grave and solemn low dances (*danses basses*), like the pavan and
branle, with brisk Italian dances, like the galliard
and volta. In the old dances modesty of apparel
was paired with decorum in bearing, but in the new
the gentlemen had to caper, the ladies wear skirts
short enough to permit the movements of their feet
to be seen and allow themselves to be swung
bodily over the hips of their partners.

A love for variety of movement, rhythm, melody,
and color having been created, it was stimulated by
the introduction into the ball-room and on the stage
of the people's dances. The saraband was im-
ported from Spain, the passepied from Bas Bre-
tagne, the bourrée from Auvergne, the tambourin
and rigaudon from Provence, the gavotte from
Dauphiné. These dances were performed in the
costumes habitual to the various provinces, and to

the music of provincial instruments. At one of Catherine's balls hautboys played for the dances of Burgundy and Champagne, violins for those of Brittany, the large Basque drum marked the time for the Biscayans, the tambourine and flageolet for the Provençals, and the bagpipe for the people of Poitou.

Here we have a picture of French music and manners to place face to face with our English picture. The French school of clavecinists which grew up under the influences of the court of Louis XIV. reflected the spirit and the manners of that court. It was characterized by the gayety, the grace, and the rhythmical incisiveness of the dance. It led to the perfection of the suite, the highest formal expression of the clavier art down to the close of the old régime by the German giants, Bach and Handel. It came a full century after the English school, and reached its culmination within a single generation; whereas the English school compassed over a hundred years. It marked the climax of a tendency without illustrating the steps in its development. It was gentle, gracious, and affected where the English was rugged, virile, and straightforward. For our purposes it may be said to have begun with Jacques Champion (called de Chambonnières, after the estate owned by his wife), and culminated in Couperin (surnamed "the Great") and Rameau. Its fashions were followed by François Dandrieu (1684–1740), Jacques André Dagincourt (1684–175—?) and Louis Claude Daquin (1694–1772). Chambonnières was clavecin player to Louis XIV.; so, too, was François Couperin (1668–1733), whose father, Charles (died 1669), and uncles, Louis (1630–1685) and François (1631–1701), had preceded him in the post of organist at the Church of St. Gervais.

The chief importance of Jean Philippe Rameau (1683–1764) rests on his having laid the foundations of the modern system of harmony; but his operas and ballets made him the idol of the French people, and a few of his compositions for the harpsichord have come over into the pianoforte repertory of to-day. He is, indeed, oftener heard than Couperin, who is generally set down in the books as the head of the old French school. Rubinstein paid a much higher tribute to Rameau than to Couperin in his historical lecture recitals given in St. Petersburg in 1888 and 1889. In fact, Rubinstein was disposed to value the Couperin who is called "the Great" less highly than the Couperin, his uncle, who was plain Louis. Rameau is more modern than Couperin—much more modern than is indicated in the difference between their birth and death dates. Couperin's pieces are predominantly two-voiced; Rameau's predominantly three. Rameau, moreover, indulges freely in chords and arpeggios, and betrays an appreciation of broad effects. "Many of his modulations are as profoundly conceived as those of Beethoven and Schumann," says Rubinstein. Conscious of the awakening demand for sonority and richness of tone, he sought to supply it even at the cost of pure consonance.

Comparatively a small number of compositions written by the French clavecinists other than Couperin are open to the study of ordinary amateurs. Among those which have lived in the affections of musical antiquaries because of their puissant beauty are Rameau's "Le Rappel des Oiseaux," "La Poule" (a fascinatingly ingenious piece built on a theme which imitates the cackling of a hen), "Les tendres Plaintes" (most gracious and winning in its melody), "L'Egyptienne," "La Timide," "Les Soupirs," "La Livri," and "Les Cyclops"; Dandrieu's "Les tendres Reproches," and Daquin's dainty "Le Coucou" and "L'Hirondelle." Couperin is in a vastly different case. Between 1713 and 1730 he published four books of "Pièces de Clavecin," containing no less than 236 compositions; and all but a trifling fraction of these have been edited with painstaking care by Brahms and Chrysander and published in London (Augener) as well as in Germany. Couperin did not call his sets of pieces suites, but *ordres*. He did not confine himself to the conventional sequence—I., allemande; II., courante; III., saraband; IV., gigue, with the occasional interjection of a gavotte, passepied, branle, minuet, bourrée, etc.—but, preserving key relationship (changing from major to relative or parallel minor and *vice versa*), as an external tie between the members of his sets, he cultivated contrast and interchange of mood.

Mixed in with pieces bearing the simple names of the different orders of dances were others to which he gave all manner of fanciful titles. Here, for instance, is the list of pieces which make up the first *ordre* of his first book: Allemande l'Auguste, première Courante, seconde Courante, Sarabande la Majestueuse, Gavotte, Gigue la Mylordine, Menuet, Les Sylvains, Les Abeilles, La Nanette, Sarabande des Sentimens, La Pastorelle, Les Nonnettes, Gavotte la Bourbonnoise, La Manon, L'Enchanteresse, La Fleurie, Les Plaisirs de St. Germain en Laye.

He has a whole gallery of portraits: Nanette, Manon, Antoinine, Babet, Angelique, La Couperin; another of temperaments, moods, and characters: La Prude, La Diligente, La Voluptueuse, La Ténébreuse, La Flateuse, La Dangeureuse, L'Insinuante, La Seduisante; an Olympian stageful of mythological creatures: Sylvains, Bacchantes, Graces, Corybantes, Diane, Terpsichore, Hymen, Amor. Bees and gnats buzz and hum in some pieces, butterflies flutter and birds sing, even an amphibian drags his slow length through a solemn passacaille. Nuns, shepherds, pilgrims, sailors, harvesters, and spinners are delineated, so far as may be, by imitative hints at the sounds made by them in the pursuit of their vocations. Nothing, in fact, is too insignificant so its name awaken an image in the fancy which may be associated with the movement or mood of the music—not even a scarf with flying ends ("Le Bavelet flottant").

The court allegories and ballets provide hints for further bits of musical delineation, as, for instance, in "Les Folies Françaises, ou les Dominos," where we find impersonations of Maidenhood, Shame, Ardor, Hope, Fidelity, Perseverance, Languor, Coquetry, Jealousy, Frenzy, and Despair dancing in dominos of appropriate colors—a premonition of the "Carnaval" which was to come with Schumann. But, however the little piece might be intituled, it was a dance in form and movement—its periods and sections rigorously measured off, its melody and bass moving along in gracious union and with many a pretty courtesy, one to other, linked together by an occasional chord. Adorned like the ladies of Louis's court are these pieces, overcrowded with embellishments, full of "nods and becks and wreathèd smiles"; and when the harmonies spread out at the cadences we cannot but yield to the fancied image of a *grande dame* in Louis's court sinking low with ineffable grace as she receives the *congé* of the King:

To erect a platform of observation which may prove useful it can now be said, broadly, that down to the beginning of the eighteenth century all composers for keyed stringed instruments were church musicians. The traditions of the fifteenth century were enduring until the emancipation of instrumental music from the vocal style was complete. It is, therefore, not surprising that when we take up the story of Italian clavier music where it was left when the English school appeared upon the scene we find ourselves back again among the great organists of the land that has been called the cradle of music. The most brilliant achievements of the old organists of St. Mark's, in Venice, were eclipsed by Girolamo Frescobaldi (1588–1645?), a native of Ferrara who, after he had studied in his native land and practised his art in Antwerp, found that so wondrous a renown had preceded him to Rome that twenty-five thousand persons attended his first performance in St. Peter's. This was in 1614, and the next year he was appointed organist at the great church.

In the course of the twenty years following several collections of his works were published in Rome and Venice. They were, like the works that had preceded them, *ricercare, canzone, fantasie, capricci,* etc., and some of them were stated to be equally adapted for voice or instrument or to be played on the organ or cembalo. The meaning of this is that they preceded the invention of a real clavier style. This began to disclose itself in the compositions of Bernardo Pasquini (1637–1710), a Tuscan. He had studied with Antonio Cesti, an opera writer, and the effect of the monodic school's use of the keyed stringed instruments in the harmonic support of the airs in the *dramma per musica* may have had something to do with his advancement of the art of clavier composition. Rubinstein thought that Pasquini's significance was not less than that of Couperin's and Rameau's. He was the recipient of great honors in Florence, Vienna, and Paris, and the classic legend "S. P. Q. R." was carved on his tombstone to testify that he had been organist to the senate and people of Rome.

The Italian school of this period found its culmination in Domenico Scarlatti (1683–1757), son of Alessandro Scarlatti (founder of the Neapolitan school of opera) and pupil of Pasquini in organ and harpsichord playing. Scarlatti was so great an admirer of Handel that he followed him from Venice to study his methods. He stayed ten years in Rome, where he became chapelmaster of St. Peter's, and there was no corner of Europe to which his fame as composer and player did not penetrate. In 1720 he was cembalist at the opera in London and saw the production of his opera "Narcissus." He was a voluminous writer of pieces for the organ and clavier, and is frequently spoken of as the inventor of the sonata. The works which he wrote under this title (the Abbate Santini collected 349 of them) are, however, not sonatas in the sense of to-day, though they foreshadow the modern form in the contrasting mood of their principal themes and the key relationship in which the themes are presented. They are modern, too, in the firmness with which the major and minor modes are kept in view, as distinguished from the old ecclesiastical modes, their brilliant passage work, broken chords in contrary motion, repetition of single notes by different fingers, and other indications of virtuosity. The two sonatas in G and E major adapted for the pianoforte by Carl Tausig, entitled "Pastorale" and "Capriccio," have much grace and animation, but are as purely objective, formal, and soulless in their musical content as any other compositions of their epoch. Scarlatti, indeed, did not aim at emotional expression. "Amateur or professor, whoever thou art," said he in the preface to a collection of his sonatas, "seek not in these sonatas for any deep feeling. They are only a frolic in art, intended to increase thy confidence in the clavier."

Apropos of Scarlatti's sonatas I find a singular blunder in Rubinstein's St. Petersburg lectures. "Scarlatti wrote many sonatas for the clavicembalo, as well as the less *cantabile* clavichord. He probably played two instruments. He played the *Andantes* on the clavicymbal, the brilliant movements on the clavichord." The names of the instruments should, of course, be reversed. The clavichord was capable of a singing tone; the harpsichord was not, for reasons which I have tried to point out. It seems strange that Rubinstein should have erred here, but even Dr. Oscar Paul seems to have been ignorant of the mechanism of the clavichord when he wrote his "Geschichte des Claviers."

For most of the music of the Italian composers of this period students are thrown largely upon historical works. Scarlatti's sonatas are plentiful enough; Haslinger published two hundred of them, edited by Czerny, in 1839; Breitkopf & Härtel's

LES CLAVECINISTES

DOMENICO SCARLATTI
Né à Naples en 1683 — Mort à Madrid en 1751

DOMENICO SCARLATTI.

catalogue contains sixty and Kistner's thirty. An excellent collection of a later date contains twenty-four pieces in eight suites, edited and fingered by Alessandro Longo. Of Frescobaldi's works a capriccio is published in Rimbault's history and a *canzone in sesto tono* in Weitzmann's "Geschichte des Clavierspiels." Weitzmann also prints sonatas by Pasquini, Francesco Durante (1684–1755), and Pier Domenico Paradies (1710–1792). In his "Alte Claviermusik" (Leipsic, Bartholf Senff) Pauer publishes a canzona and corrente by Frescobaldi, two fugues by Antonio Nicolo Porpora (1685–1767), a sonata by Baldassare Galuppi (1706–1785), a gavotte and ballet by Giovanni Battista Martini (1706–1784), and a sonata by Paradies. "The Golden Treasury of Piano Music," five volumes, published by Schirmer, New York, is a fine and serviceable collection of harpsichord pieces of the sixteenth, seventeenth, and eighteenth centuries.

VII

The German School—Bach and Handel

IT is not easy to form a clear idea of what the domestic element in instrumental music—the element which springs first to mind when we think of pianoforte music to-day—was like in the Middle Ages. To us the pianoforte represents the whole world of music *in nuce;* stage and choir-loft are charmed by it into the intimacy of the home circle. But the clavier, in its two forms of tangential (clavichord) and quilled (spinet, virginal, and harpsichord) instrument, did not assume this position until long after the work of developing an instrumental art had begun. The pioneership of England in this work has already received recognition in these studies; its significance lies chiefly in the fact that in that country the supremacy of the lute as the domestic instrument of music *par excellence* was overthrown by the virginal before the clavier had gained dominion on the Continent.

That there should have been a greater number and variety of instruments in popular use at a time when instrumental music was struggling to come into existence than now, when it has forced purely vocal music out of the churches and suffers only the mixed form to stand beside it on the concert platform, is anomalous. The vast majority of these instruments, however, had not the slightest influence upon musical composition, and were not designed for domestic enjoyment. Prätorius catalogues and describes a hundred of them in his "Syntagma Musicum," but it needs only a glance at his plates to see that most of them were din producers, against which private doors had to be shut. With all their number and variety, moreover, they did nothing to advance the orchestral art, which returned to the principle of a combination of kind ("consorts of viols" and the like) as soon as the instrumental language had been freed from the vocal idiom.

In a twofold manner the organ was the intermediary between the music of ecclesiastical or courtly functions and the home circle. Constructed on a small scale, the instrument itself, under the names "positif," "regal," and "organo picciolo," made its way into cultured houses. Its keyboard being identical with that of the clavier, music composed for it was easily transferred to that instrument, whereas the lute necessitated the employment of a notation belonging to it alone. So it came by the operation of the law of survival that the favorite domestic instrument of generations of musical amateurs, *omnium instrumentorum Princeps*, the *nobilissimo stromento*, the *Regina instrumentorum* upon which, by the exercise of an incomprehensible skill, all the demands of home music were gratified, was practically supplanted by the clavier when the time for clavier music was come—that is to say, toward the close of the sixteenth century. It remained in use a century longer, but not as a potent influence.

There are a number of German names which may be added to the list of church musicians who became famous while the musical current flowed out of Italy in all directions. Hans Leo Hasler (1564–1612) won such renown in the service of Rudolph II. that that emperor ennobled him. Christian Erbach, Hieronymus Prätorius, Adam Gumpeltzhaimer, Melchior Franck, and Samuel Scheidt may be written down among the distinguished musicians of the early period on the testimony of their contemporaries. Now we reach the first name of large import—that of Johann Jakob Froberger (1637–1695). He carried his fame and activities as far westward as Dr. Bull had done toward the East. As a youth he was sent by the Emperor Ferdinand III. to Rome to receive instruction from Frescobaldi. He remained three years in the Holy City, went thence to Paris, thence to Dresden, and then returned to the service of the Emperor of Germany. In 1662, according to the accepted story which has only himself for authority, he got a leave of absence and set out for England *via* France. The tale of his adventures is worth telling, if for no other reason than that it throws a certain amount of light on a kind of music which he and his contemporaries cultivated in a degree not appreciated in this latter day. He says he was robbed before he reached Calais. There he set sail across the Channel, but fell into the hands of pirates and had to save his life by swimming.

He reached the English shore and begged his way to London. Tattered and torn, he found his way to Westminster Abbey, and, loitering in the church after the service, met the organist—it must have been Christopher Gibbons—who discovered him while locking the doors, and hired him to blow the organ. At the wedding of Charles II. and Catherine of Portugal, so the story goes, awed by the pomp of the function, he neglected his duty, and the organ stopped, breathless. Dire were the imprecations poured out upon the head of the luckless blower by the organist, who promptly disappeared into an adjoining apartment after he, too, was breathless. Then Froberger saw his opportunity. Filling the bellows he rushed to the keyboard and began to play. A lady of Charles's court who had been in Vienna recognized the artist's manner. He was summoned into the presence of the king, told his story on his knees, was bidden to rise, a clavier was hurriedly brought, and for an hour by the dial he improvised on the instrument to the delight of king and court. Charles gave him a necklace, and he became the lion of the hour. He returned to Vienna loaded with gifts and distinctions; but calumny had preceded him, and he vainly sought an audience with the emperor, whose mind had been poisoned against him.

This is the story, and it is surely worthy of a modern theatrical press agent. An organist playing long enough with a single inflation of the bellows to impress his individual style upon a casual listener —that detail might alone have served to arouse suspicion; but if it did not why have not the English critics called attention to the fact that Charles II. was not married in state at Westminster, but privately at Portsmouth? However, Froberger in all likelihood did visit London, and failing of rehabilitation at the imperial court of Germany on his return to Vienna, went to Mayence, where he perished miserably years later. Obviously, he was a brave *raconteur* who essayed to be as entertaining in his musical anecdotes as in his verbal; for Mattheson, who reports the London story, also tells of hearing one of Froberger's allemandes, which purported to describe in musical tones incidents, to the number of twenty-six, of an eventful Rhine journey—among others how a passenger, in attempting to hand his sword to the skipper, fell overboard and was struck on the head with a pike while struggling in the water.

The German School—Bach and Handel

We shall hear more about this kind of music presently.

Froberger was the first distinctively great German clavierist. In his other musical activities he had a colleague, contemporary and compatriot in Johann Kaspar Kerl (1625–1690 or 1628–1693), who, like him, was sent by Ferdinand III. to Rome to study; but though it is suspected that he, too, availed himself of Frescobaldi's skill and learning, his direct purpose was to study under Carissimi. Some of Kerl's compositions have been preserved for the modern student, but to English readers his name is likely to be best known as the author of the melody of "Egypt was glad when they departed," which Handel borrowed for his "Israel in Egypt" from one of Kerl's toccatas. George Muffat (died in 1704) spent six years in Paris under the influence of Lully and Couperin, and is said to have transplanted the latter's *agrêmens* to Germany. His son, Gottlieb Muffat (born about 1690), was clavier teacher to the family of Emperor Charles VI. and, like Kerl, an involuntary contributor to Handel's oratorios.

There now sprang up in the north of Germany a group of organists who found inspiration in the Protestant Church service akin to that which had so long come from Rome. In this service there had existed from an early period an element of romanticism borrowed from the folksong which had bound itself up intimately with German hymnology. Luther, though far from being an iconoclast, was desirous from the beginning of the movement which he led to give a national trend to the music of the new church—to have all the features of the service German in spirit and German in manner. It was a tendency embodied in him which brought it to pass that in Germany contrapuntal music based on popular tunes, like that of the Netherland school, soon developed into the chorale in which the melody and not the contrapuntal integument was the essential thing. In the hymns and psalms which Luther himself sang and heard the borrowed secular melody was almost as completely buried as in the masses which the books would have us believe scandalized the church before the coming of Palestrina. The people were invited to sing the paraphrases, it is true, and to sing them to familiar tunes (later in France they did so, and with a vengeance, sometimes using the melodies of popular dances with the versified psalms of Marot), but the choir's polyphony practically stifled the melody.

Soon, however, the free spirit so powerfully promoted by the Reformation prompted a manner of composition in which the admired melody was lifted into relief. Now the monophonic style entered so that the congregation might join in the singing—a distinctly romantic step. The musicians who fell under this influence were the direct predecessors of

the great Bach, in whom the polyphonic style culminated.   Diedrich Buxtehude was a Dane who
attracted so much attention with a series of concerts that he gave for years at Lübeck that Bach,
then nineteen years old, walked from Arnstadt to
Lübeck—more than two hundred miles—to hear
them.   When Buxtehude grew old both Mattheson and Handel went from Hamburg and reported
themselves as candidates for his position as organist; they fled incontinently, however, when they
learned that one of the conditions attached to the
post was that the new organist must marry the
daughter of his predecessor.   Some of Buxtehude's
organ music may yet be heard, but what were probably the best of his clavier compositions seem to be
irrevocably lost.   They were a set of seven suites,
in which, according to Mattheson, "the nature and
properties of the seven planets were agreeably
expressed."

Johann Pachelbel (1653–1706) was native of Nuremberg, and died there as organist of the Church
of St. Sebaldus, having spent three years of his
early career in Vienna as organist of the venerable
Church of St. Stephen.   He wrote many variations
on chorale melodies, publishing a group of four in
Erfurt in 1683 under the title, "Musical Death
Thoughts."   In six Bible sonatas by Johann Kuhnau (1667–1722) we find the programmatic tendency, which is daintily illustrated in the little

dance pieces of Couperin and Rameau, carried to an extreme which would be laughable were we not compelled to recognize a latter-day reversion to the type with all its absurdities in the symphonic poems of Richard Strauss and his disciples.

Kuhnau was Bach's predecessor at Leipsic, and had a high opinion of the expressive capacity of music—if words were brought to its aid. Sadness or joy in the abstract, he held, could be expressed by music alone, but he enlisted words when he wished a distinction drawn between the lamentations of a sad Hezekiah, a weeping Peter, or a mourning Jeremiah. He was a stanch believer in the helpful potency of a verbal commentary, and ingenious in his defence of a composer, "a celebrated Electoral Chapelmaster," whose name has not got into the records, but who seems to have been almost as subtle as Richard Strauss. This composer had written a piece which he called "La Medica," in which he described the groans and whines of a sick man and his relations (not forgetting to indicate the sex of the latter), the chase for a doctor, and the great grief of all concerned. The piece ended with a gigue, under which the composer had written: "The patient is making favorable progress, but has not quite recovered his health." "At this," said Kuhnau, "some mocked, and were of opinion that had it been in his power the author might well have depicted the joy of a perfect recovery. So far as I could judge," he goes on, "there was good reason for adding words to the music. The sonata began in D minor; in the gigue there was constant modulation toward G minor. At the final close the ear was not satisfied, and expected the closing cadence in G. Therefore the patient was not quite well."

Could anything be clearer? Certainly not to Kuhnau, who was quite as clever as the composer of "La Medica" in the invention of devices to make music explicit. One of his "Biblische Historien" tells the story of Gideon, the saviour of Israel. In this story Gideon asks God to give him a sign that He would save Israel by his hand; he would put a fleece upon the floor, and if on the morrow it should be found to be wet with dew and the earth dry, then would he accept it as the desired sign. And it was so. But Gideon was unsatisfied and wanted another test; let it be dry now only upon the fleece, and upon all the ground let there be dew. And God did so that night, for it was dry upon the fleece only and there was dew on all the ground. The composer of the "Pastoral Symphony" might have been stumped by the task of setting such a complicated phenomenon to music; not so Kuhnau. He introduced a theme to represent the dewy fleece and the dry ground, and then wrote it backward to represent the dewy ground and the dry fleece; and the thing was done.

I have now reached the two men in whom the polyphonic school found its culmination and in whose lifetime the pianoforte came to the fore, though too late and too timidly to influence the style of writing or the manner of performance. They are Georg Friedrich Handel (1685–1759) and Johann Sebastian Bach (1685–1750). Before recording their labors, however, or commenting on the character of their compositions, I shall venture to bring them into juxtaposition for comparison in order to make it plain why two men whose names are so intimately associated in musical history and who, in common and simultaneously, mark the highest achievements of their time, yet differ so greatly in the value of their contributions to the art whose story we are tracing. All creative artists are the product of their environment. The national traits of the people among whom and for whom Bach and Handel labored had much to do with fixing the character of their music, as well as the degree and nature of the influence which their compositions have exerted. Both were Germans by birth, but before they reached mature manhood their paths in life were widely divergent. Handel fell into the current of Latinized culture which dominated the larger cities of Germany two and a half centuries ago as completely as it did Paris and London. He was the son of a surgeon, went to a university, and became familiar with the humanities. He met the grandees of various courts and was patronized by them as a prodigy in music. Their influence was thoroughly Latin. When he began composing, it was in a style to fit the taste of the polite society of the period. He connected himself with the opera at Hamburg. Everywhere save in Italy, opera was at the time a monstrosity. It had sprung from the efforts of Florentine amateurs to revive the classic drama. The Germans had tried to suit the entertainment to their ruder tastes and harsher language. The vernacular came to be used, and the discovery was made that German words lent themselves but ill to Italian music. The opera-books were built on classic stories, such as were utilized in Italy. These German poetasters worked over into mongrel books, half German half Italian, and the composers had to set them according to rigid formularies. Handel's first opera, "Almira," contained fifteen Italian airs and forty-four German songs.

The artistic culture which tolerated such anomalies was assuredly debased compared with that which would have been the normal outcome of purely German tendencies. The Prince of Tuscany heard "Almira" with admiration, and offered to take the composer with him to Italy. Handel declined the generous offer, but soon after set out for the home of the arts on his own responsibility. He produced an Italian opera, "Rodrigo," in

Florence and "Agrippina" in Venice. His triumph was complete. Alessandro Scarlatti became his devoted friend and sincere admirer, and the nobility, resident and visiting, showered honors and attentions upon him. He went to London, composed operas, managed a theatre, bankrupted himself over and over again, and finally, compelled by sheer force of circumstances and in the bitterness of disappointment, struck out a new path and became the master of the fashion to which thitherto he had been a slave.

In many respects the career of Bach was the very opposite to that of Handel. He was a child of German simplicity. He came into the world the repository of the feelings, beliefs, and aspirations of a line of musicians extending over more than a century. His ancestors were church and town servants who had provided sacred and secular music for Thuringia so long that the family name became a generic term. He never went to a university and never enjoyed the privilege in his youth of drawing on such a clearing house of the world's knowledge, beliefs, and speculations as had honored the intellectual drafts of Handel. He travelled little, and seldom came in contact with the class of society whose tastes determined the early career of Handel. At eighteen he was organist at Arnstadt, at twenty-two organist at Mühlhausen. He accepted a post at Weimar, made a few visits to neighboring towns and cities to give organ concerts, was for five years chapelmaster at the court of Anhalt-Cöthen, and thence went to Leipsic, and became cantor of the St. Thomas school and director of the music in four of the churches of the old city.

Thenceforward his activity was confined to the promotion of music in a sphere which, while it was restricted in many respects, nevertheless left him free to develop his ideals without concern touching his livelihood. He could build on the solid ground of German feeling, and was not obliged to watch the shifting whims of an artificial and unnational culture. If we had not the works to prove the accuracy of the deduction, we could yet safely argue from the character of Bach's domestic and artistic surroundings that his compositions would show greater ideality, greater profundity of learning, greater boldness in invention, and greater variety of form than those of Handel. In the things which were dearest to him he could work either with complete indifference to the caprices of the public or in harmony with its most intimate feelings.

Bach remained a German; Handel became a cosmopolite. Handel went to Italy to learn how to write for the human voice. He went to London, and under stress of circumstances abandoned dramatic writing and took up oratorio. His style in the former was conventional; in the latter, not wholly divorced from convention, it was yet original. In the former he composed, as we now know, chiefly for the day in which he wrote; in the latter he composed, as the phrase goes, for all time. In both forms the human voice was the chief vehicle of expression.

Bach came of a race of instrumentalists. He was unequalled as an organ and clavichord player; a master of the technical part of violin playing; he knew thoroughly the structure of the organ; was the inventor of the viola pomposa (an instrument which occupied a place midway between the viola and violoncello); he combined the clavier and lute into an ingenious keyed instrument, and if he did not invent a method of tuning the clavier in equal temperament, he at least demonstrated that it could and ought to be so tuned, and fixed his demonstration for all time with one of his most charming and vital works, "The Well Tempered Clavichord." The men were contemporaries—born in the same year. The period in which they lived was still dominated by the vocal art. Handel followed the tendencies of the time without hesitation; Bach, impelled by inherited inclination and genius, worked to bring in the new era, the instrumental era of music. We are in the midst of that era to-day; it has taken possession of the art. Nothing has yet happened to check a progress the march of which in the space of a century and a half is unparalleled in any one of the other arts. Naturally and inevitably that composer exerts the most puissant influence now who, something less than two centuries ago, pointed out the line along which Mozart, Beethoven, and Wagner were to hew a road. That composer was Bach.

So we find Bach's clavier music more varied, more voluminous, more significant, and more vital by far than that of Handel. Of Handel's music specifically written for the harpsichord, very little is to be found upon the programmes of to-day. The air and variations popularly known as "The Harmonious Blacksmith" appears in the concert lists most frequently, and is the most generally admired of his compositions. Originally it constituted the last movement of a harpsichord suite. Aside from the charm of its melody (the origin of which has caused large discussion which may be said to have failed of definite result) the piece has interest as illustrating a brilliant style of variation which Handel introduced into the suite form. Tradition has added to the interest by wrapping an ample cloak of fiction around it. The familiar story runs that Handel was once caught in a rainstorm while walking through the village of Edgeware on his way to Cannons. He took refuge in the shop of a blacksmith, who sang a song while at work, keeping time to the music with his hammer on the anvil. Handel remembered the tune, and on reaching home wrote variations on it. It was thus that the tune acquired the name of "The Harmonious Blacksmith." A vast deal of labor has been spent in investigating the story, even the hammer and anvil which figure in it having been hunted up and preserved and the observation made that the anvil (reverentially written in the books with a big A) when hit by the hammer (spelled with a big H) gave out the tones B and E, dominant and tonic respectively of the key in which the air stands; but, unhappily for the lovers of musical romance, nothing has been found to substantiate the story. In the early editions of Handel's suites the movement has no other designation than "Air et Doubles."

As for the rest, Handel's name is oftener seen nowadays bracketed with that of Brahms as the composer of the latter's Twenty-six Variations (Op. 24) than alone on the programmes of pianoforte players. In the complete edition of Handel's works, published by the German Handel Society (the title is little else than a euphemism for Dr. Friedrich Chrysander) the clavier pieces are included in a single volume, which, in four divisions, contains sixteen suites, three chaconnes (one with sixty-two variations), two capriccios, six fugues, a fantasia, a prelude and air with variations, a lesson, a coranto and two minuets, a prelude and allegro, two sonatas and a sonatina. His fugues, like his concertos, were for either organ or harpsichord. A light-hearted, glad devotion to simple, sensuous beauty, the dower received in Italy and husbanded among the English aristocracy, characterizes this music. Everything is clear, everything natural, everything plastic, everything shows the typical physiognomy of the period.

Were I discussing Bach's church compositions it would be an easy and a delightful task to show how the influence of the German Reformed service, to which I have referred in connection with his predecessors of the North German school, made Bach's music in a peculiar degree an expression of true, tender, deep, and individual feeling—the hymning of a sentiment, sprung from a radical change in the relative attitude of church and individual accomplished by the Reformation in Germany. Bach was a supreme master in the treatment of the *Chorale*, in which the secular folksong was in a manner sublimated, and the romantic elements found in their melodies, coupled with the vast freedom allowed to him in their treatment (as hymns, organ preludes, the foundation of cantatas, motets, oratorios, etc.), emancipated him from nearly all conventional shackles. Polyphonist he was of a necessity, but with what a wondrous prescience of the future is shown in his "Chromatic Fantasia and Fugue."

This composition is one that has held musicians in wonder and admiration as long as it has been known. Forkel, who was practically Bach's first biographer, got a copy of the work from Wilhelm Friedemann, the great Bach's son. Accompanying it was a bit of paper containing the following doggerel, written by a friend of the biographer:

> Anbey kommt an
> Etwas Musik von Sebastian.
> Sonnst genannt: *Fantasia Chromatica*
> Bleibt schön in alle Sæcula.

In this monumental work the treatment of a purely vocal element—the recitative—is such as to bring it a century nearer us than it was in the works of Vivaldi and the Northern organists from whom Bach borrowed it. Tendencies toward homophonic writing may be found in his instrumental pieces, as in Handel's, but in the interweaving of voices he found a more eloquent means of expressing emotions than the Italians commanded, with their fondness for melody *quâ* melody. The seriousness of his nature is shown in the fact that the clavier pieces in which his individuality is most pronounced are those written for the instruction of would-be players and composers, chiefly of his own household. His French and English suites are written in the manner of the time, and his Italian concerto shows his appreciation of the sensuous beauty which was the be-all and end-all of Italian music at the time. The simplest form of his clavier music is found in his two and three part "Inventions," whose supplementary title confesses that they were composed to help players to attain to a *cantabile* style.

His loveliest work, the forty-eight preludes and fugues in all the keys, major and minor, known as "The Well Tempered Clavichord," not only had the educational purpose already assigned to it, but was also a tribute to that one of the clavier instruments which was most capable of expression. Its melodies, whether treated freely, as in the preludes, or strictly, as in the fugues, are full of the charm of spontaneous song, and are in a spiritual sense as eloquent a voice of romanticism as the recitatives in the "Chromatic Fantasia" and the efforts at the expression of set ideas in the "Capriccio on the Departure of a Beloved Brother" are in a material. It pleases me when I hear the C-sharp major fugue to think that Bach probably found the inspiration for such themes on those Sunday excursions which, he tells us, he used to make in order to rejoice and refresh himself at popular merry-makings with the songs and dances of the folk. In further explanation of the title and purpose of "The Well Tempered Clavichord" it may be said that it was composed to illustrate the practicability of equal temperament. In claviers tuned according to the system approved by Bach all the twenty-four keys in chromatic succession are equally in tune, whereas in the system formerly employed certain keys had to be avoided. For instance, B major and A-flat major were rarely used; F-sharp major and C-sharp major never. Bach gathered the first twenty-four preludes and fugues together in 1722 and the second set in 1744. Of the first set three copies are extant in Bach's handwriting; of the second there is no complete autograph. The work was not printed until 1800.

By Bach's four duets for two claviers, his variations for clavier with two keyboards, echo-effects in other works and the compositions specified as written for clavicembalo (harpsichord), as well as other works in which the clavier figures in association with other instruments, the student should be warned that the notes as written down and afterward printed by no means represent the music as it was actually heard in Bach's time. The mechanical construction of the harpsichord, with its several sets of strings and its couplers, placed at the command of the player a much greater variety and volume of sound in proportion to the normal voice of the instrument, than can be obtained from the pianoforte to-day. Since the name of Bach is so frequently bracketed with that of Liszt, it seems also well to explain that six of Bach's preludes and fugues for the organ were transcribed for the pianoforte by Liszt. The transcriptions were an experiment, Liszt desiring to see what effect could be produced on a pianoforte with works which their creator intended to be played upon the organ, with its multiplicity of keyboards—two or three for the hands and one for the feet. In reducing the mechanism which was at Bach's service to its lowest terms, so to speak, Liszt, anxious not to sacrifice any of the original polyphonic fabric, produced a set of virtuoso pieces which long remained his private property. He made the transcriptions in 1842, and it was more than ten years later that he yielded to the pleadings of Dehn and gave them to the public.

VIII

Classicism and the Sonata

IN a peculiarly intimate manner the pianoforte, which superseded the other instruments of the clavier family about the close of the period illustrated by the men last discussed, is bound up with classicism and the sonata. I use these terms arbitrarily, intending that they shall serve as observation points, and to this end I must attempt a definition of them. Such a definition ought to be general and comprehensive rather than specific. Strictly speaking, the dividing lines commonly considered as existing between periods, schools, and artistic forms do not exist. These things are overlapping and gradual growths. We recognize them, note their elements, give them names, and employ these names in broad characterization after a man of strong individuality has arisen and stamped them with the hall-mark of his genius. Such a man the people of a later day are prone to look upon as an innovator or inventor, when, in point of fact, he is only a continuator, and, at the best, a perfecter. So Palestrina; so Bach; so Haydn; so Beethoven; so Wagner. All these are but products of an evolution of vast scope and antiquity, and were surrounded by men who worked with them on the lines which they drew, broad and luminous, across the pages of musical history. That fact explains why it was that some of them seemed less great to their contemporaries than to those who came after them. They were not so pre-eminent in their day, because they were surrounded by composers whose learning and skill satisfied the critical demands and the popular taste of their times. Not even the greatest of these men would loom up in the historical vista as he does were the works of his predecessors and contemporaries intimately known and his relationship to them properly appreciated. The history of every art is full of pretty fictions—too much occupied with biography. When musical history shall be revised (as it will be when the labors of the critical antiquaries now active are completed) it will have lost some of its romance, but it will better disclose the processes of musical evolution.

But to the definitions. Classical music is music written by men of the highest rank in their art— men corresponding with the *classici* of ancient Rome. It is music written in obedience to widely accepted laws, disclosing the highest degree of perfection on its technical and formal side, but preferring æsthetic beauty to emotional content, and refusing to sacrifice form to poetic, dramatic, or characteristic expression. In this definition I have embraced the notion of rank and also the antithesis between classicism and romanticism which will have to be borne in mind when we proceed to a discussion of the music of the nineteenth century.

A pianoforte sonata is a piece of music designed for the instrument, consisting of three or four movements, which are contrasted in tempo and character, and, in the best specimens, connected by a spiritual bond. Strictly speaking, the model, or design, which distinguishes the sonata from other compositions is found in the first movement. This is tripartite. In the first section the subject-matter of the movement (generally two themes, which are contrasted in mood but related in key) is presented for identification; in the second it is developed, worked out, illustrated, exploited. The third section is recapitulatory; it is made up of a repetition of the first part, with modifications and a close.

The sonata became the dominant form in all kinds of instrumental music in the middle of the eighteenth century, and has remained the dominant form ever since. Like everything else in this world, it was a growth. Its name existed centuries before the thing itself as we know it now. If my readers will think back upon the story of the pianoforte as I have sketched it they will note that it illustrates the first, the simplest, and the most pervasive principle in the law of evolution. Each step, from the savage's bow to the grand pianoforte of to-day, shows a development from the simple to the complex, from the homogeneous to the heterogeneous. So, too, does the history of the sonata. When the term was first used it served only to distinguish pieces that were sounded—*i. e.*, played— from pieces that were sung. Sonata was the antithesis of cantata, and nothing more. The orchestral pieces of the Gabrielis, in the sixteenth century, were called sonatas; so were the instrumental preludes, interludes, and postludes in mixed pieces. A century later the term was applied to compositions in several movements for combinations of viols, for violin alone, and for violin solo with *continuo* for the clavier. Essentially there was no difference between the sonata and the suite of this period, a relic of which fact is still seen in the inclusion of such dance forms as the minuet and rondo in the sonata of to-day. The sonata form, with its triple division into expository, illustrative, and recapitulative sections, moreover, is itself little else than an expansion of a device found in some of the oldest printed dances. The repetition of the first section, the modulatory nature of the second section, and the reprise in the third may be seen in the following

branle (Shakespeare's "brawl"), from a book of
French dances published in 1545:

A Bach closed the epoch last described; a Bach
opened the new. The greatest master of the fugue
was succeeded by a son who laid broad the foundations upon which the structure characteristic of the
new century was to be reared. The contrapuntal
style gave way to the free, polyphony to homophony,
counterpoint to harmony. The change was not
abrupt, but gradual. The achievements of Johann
Sebastian Bach had long been presaged, and his
son, Carl Philipp Emanuel Bach (1714–1788), had
many forerunners. There were Rameau and Couperin, in France; Domenico Scarlatti and Paradies,
in Italy, and Kuhnau, in Germany. Nevertheless,
his immediate successors, Joseph Haydn (1732–
1809), and Wolfgang Amadeus Mozart (1756–1791),

looked upon him as the real fashioner of the form which each of them took a hand in perfecting. "He is the father, we are the boys," said Mozart. The form was a purely arbitrary one. Unlike the suite, it owed nothing to the dance; nor was it beholden to any type or types of folksong. Yet it proved to be a marvellously efficient vehicle for beauty, an inviting playground for the fancy. It promoted a love for symmetry, furthered unity between the parts, and at the same time increased the opportunities for contrast in moods not only between the movements, but in the movements themselves. Varied expression, flux and reflux of sentiment, wide and fruitful harmonic excursions, richness in modulation—all were invited by it. The way was broadened for the exercise of the imagination and opened to the play of the emotions. German music in especial lost some of its seriousness and sober-sidedness and took on some of the careless gayety of its French and Italian sisters. The sonata was a convenient formula for composers, and stimulated them to vast productiveness. Carl Philipp Emanuel Bach wrote 146 sonatas for clavier alone, 52 concertos with accompaniments, besides a mass of other works; Haydn wrote 34 sonatas and 20 concertos, and employed the form in his 125 symphonies and many chamber pieces; Vanhal composed 23 sonatas and 106 sonatinas; Clementi, 64 sonatas; Cramer, 105, and so on.

The laws of the sonata were less rigid than those of the polyphonic forms, yet it permitted the exercise of any amount of skill and learning. Logic was not excluded, but its demands were no longer tyrannous. Originality and ingenuity were expended chiefly in the invention of themes—that is, the discovery of material. This material, once found, was easily poured into the mould waiting to receive it. But there was scope for all the known styles of writing—for thematic development, which, along new lines, is become the be-all and end-all of music since Beethoven; for homophony and polyphony, for fugue, for recitative, for variety of rhythm, and, as appeared later, for dramatic expression as well as lyric.

C. P. E. Bach has suffered at the hands of modern criticism because he stands in the shadow of his father. He was Johann Sebastian's third son, and after he had abandoned the law became chamber musician and cembalist at the Prussian court. There it was his special duty to accompany the tootling of Frederick the Great's flute at the court concerts, of which Dr. Burney gives us so delightful an account in his "Present State." He was accounted less gifted than his elder brother, Wilhelm Friedemann (who inherited his father's genius in a large measure, but squandered it in an aimless and dissolute life), but he did a great service to music in strengthening and improving the

lines of the sonata, and also in laying the foundations of pianoforte playing in his book, entitled
" Versuch über die wahre Art das Clavier zu spielen,
mit Exempeln und 18 Probestücken in 6 Sonaten
erläutert." [1] This book was an authority in its
field for generations, and is still sought by students
of pianoforte pedagogics. Its first part was published by Bach himself in 1753, the second part in
1761. It discusses methods of fingering, embellishments (*Maniren*), style (*Vortrag*), accompaniment,
and thoroughbass. Bach printed much of his
music in periodical publications and otherwise, and
thus enjoyed an opportunity to reach the public ear
vastly greater than did his father, who ruined his
eyes copying and engraving his compositions.
Adolf Prosniz, in his "Handbuch der Clavier-
Literatur," [2] describes his music as predominantly
melodic, vivacious, and varied in rhythm; at times
full of feeling, and anon humorous; rich in conceits and modulations which occasionally run out
in *bizarrerie*. Flowing cantabile alternates with
lively figuration and passage-work calculated to
develop the capacity of the instrument. As in
Domenico Scarlatti, two-voicedness prevails; wherefore the music frequently sounds empty. In only a
portion of his works did this Bach utilize the com-

[1] "Essay on the True Manner of Playing the Clavier, Illustrated with Examples and 18 Trial Pieces in 6 Sonatas."
[2] Vol. I.   Published by Carl Gerold's Sohn in Vienna, 1887.

plete sonata form as he handed it over to Haydn. Couperin and Scarlatti seem to have influenced him more than the great father who begot and taught him, though this may have been largely due to his surroundings. There was nothing German about Frederick the Great's court except the people. The great soldier's tastes in art and literature were French; he had no patience with German ideals. Bach followed his French predecessors in writing little dance pieces, to which he gave titles supposed to be suggestive of their contents. Sometimes the titles were proper names (of his friends, doubtless); sometimes they were fancifully delineative of character, like those of Couperin which I have cited— "La Journalière," "La Complaisante," "La Capricieuse," and the like. The French excess of ornament also remains in Emanuel Bach's music.

Scan the programmes of the pianoforte virtuosi of to-day and you shall occasionally find the name of Haydn connected with the "Andante varié" in F minor. It is an exquisite musical blossom, standing far from its companions and redolent of romanticism. Supposing the recital to be an historical one, you may also look for a sonata, even two sonatas, in E-flat major, and a fantasia in C. Is this, then, the great Haydn, "the father of modern instrumental music"? It is. So far as this study goes, we are concerned with Haydn in the least significant aspect that he occupies in musical history. On this promenade we can only glance at him who established the string quartet and crystallized the symphony, and make obeisance in passing. Some of his sonatas live in the class-room, and the teachers are not few who prefer a few of them to most of the sonatas of the greater Mozart. "Indeed, in some of them he seems to step beyond Mozart into the Beethoven period," remarks C. F. Pohl in the article on the master in Grove's "Dictionary of Music and Musicians." Haydn does not mark so wide a stride beyond his immediate predecessor as C. P. E. Bach marked beyond his in the mere structure of his pianoforte pieces, but there is a great advance in the firmer, clearer modelling of his material, the greater depth and beauty of his melodies (especially in the slow movements), and the development of the spiritual bond of unity between the parts. Artificial elegance has given way to that ingenuous winsomeness which mirrored the composer's happy disposition in all that he did. There is less of salon courtesy and more of out-of-doors geniality in the new music. The largest groups of Haydn's music for the pianoforte consist of the thirty-four solo sonatas, the thirty-one trios for pianoforte, violin, and violoncello (also denominated sonatas when first published), the sonatas for pianoforte and violin (eight in number in the edition of Breitkopf and Härtel), and the concertos for pianoforte and orchestra. The groups are here put down in the order of their artistic value. The concertos have long been in the limbo of oblivion; the duet sonatas and trios live modestly in the home-circle of musical folk; the sonatas survive in the class-room. The order is reversed in the case of Mozart, the best of whose concertos still possess vitality and charm enough to engage the attention of public performers.

Though I have associated the pianoforte with the perfection of the sonata in its classic state the instrument did not become a dominant influence in composition until the advent of Mozart. The invention of Cristofori had practically been forgotten and had to be revived in Germany by Silbermann. That manufacturer produced instruments and brought them to the notice of Bach. It is a familiar story in the books how the great man visited Potsdam in 1747 on the invitation of the great Frederick, arriving at the palace while a court concert was in progress. "Gentlemen, old Bach is come," said the royal flautist, and closed the entertainment at once. Then the company went from room to room to hear Bach play "on the forte-pianos of Silbermann," and to listen with amazement and delight to that improvisation on a theme set by the king, which, when elaborated at home, became the "Musikalisches Opfer." Silbermann was extremely anxious to win the good opinion of Bach for his new instrument, but though he consulted him, profited by his advice, and eventually received his compliments, he never weaned him from his preference for the clavichord over all its rivals. Forkel said of Bach: "He liked best to play upon the clavichord; the harpsichord, though certainly susceptible of a very great variety of expression, had not soul enough for him, and the piano was in his lifetime too much in its infancy and still much too coarse to satisfy him." His son saw the pianoforte come into favor, but he, too, preferred the clavichord for his own communings with the muse, and brought forth that instrument when he wished to give Dr. Burney an evidence of his skill as a player.[1] There is nothing in the music of Haydn to suggest the need of the new instrument. He was not a virtuoso, like Mozart, and his public use of the harpsichord was probably confined to its employment as an accompaniment instrument in connection with the orchestra. But the advent of the gracious sonata style, the development of musical culture among amateurs, and, probably, also the growing popularity of the *Hammerclavier* led to the employment of keyed instruments in the manner exemplified in the duo sonatas and trios of Haydn. The old *continuo* gave way to a part which was of something like equal importance with that of the violin or the violin and violoncello; then to a part

[1] See the account of Burney's visit to Bach in his "Present State."

which might hold its own with an orchestral accompaniment.

The road to the modern trio, quartet, quintet, and concerto, in which the pianoforte shares the work of developing the thematic material with its companions, was thus blazed by Haydn, though it was not fully opened until a little later. That opening needed the coming of Mozart and the impetus which he, a public performer from the very outset of his career, received in the concert-room. When the wonderful child made his trip down the Danube, to play before the emperor and climb into the lap of the empress at Vienna, he carried his little clavichord with him. When he called for Wagenseil, in order that his playing might have the appreciation of "one who knew," he performed upon the harpsichord. Before the end of his career the pianoforte had won his love and entered upon that progress which, in our day, enables it to cope with an army of strings, wood-wind and brass. One of the items in the inventory of the property which he owned when he died was a pianoforte "with pedal," valued at eighty florins. A pianoforte is preserved among the relics housed in the quaint little museum, in the Getreidegasse, in Salzburg; as also is a clavichord, which, however, is generally and incorrectly set down in the catalogues as a spinet. A letter which he wrote to his father from Augsburg in October, 1777, tells of the pleas-

ure which he derived from playing upon a pianoforte made by Stein. In it he praises the equality
of the key action and the promptness of the escapement as something new, and lauds the superiority
of the damper-action, which was still worked with
the knee, like the swell of a harmonium.

As to the qualities of Mozart's pianoforte music,
they cannot be described better than Prosniz has
described them in the book already referred to:

> That beauty of form, purity of tone, and carelessly easy in-
> vention which were native to Mozart mark his clavier music.
> In his ideas noble expression alternates with innocent tone-
> play full of childlike ingenuousness. In the workmanship
> pellucid harmony is predominant, and that chaste temperance
> which permeates modulation as well as polyphony and never
> loses itself in *baroque* conceits and whimsicalities. Mozart
> widened the sonata form by an extended middle section in the
> song style. Some of his sonatas, as well as a number of his
> other pieces for pianoforte, are of lasting loveliness; but the
> centre of gravity in the music which he wrote for the instru-
> ment lies in the concertos. These are thoroughly novel in
> form and style. Though the pianoforte parts may appear
> puny in ideas at times, and faded in the passage-work, they
> are nevertheless ennobled by the symphonic and magical
> treatment of the orchestra which appears *concertante* with the
> solo instrument. Here we find veritable treasures of music.
> It was Mozart, too, who created the first important pieces for
> four hands in his incomparable sonatas.

It was Beethoven who breathed the breath of a
new life into that which had been little else than a
convenient formula for the expression of merely

sensuous beauty. Beethoven was at once the end of the old dispensation and the beginning of the new; the connecting link between classicism and romanticism; conservator and regenerator; historian and seer; master builder and arch destroyer. To him I purpose to devote a separate chapter. Grouped around, antedating and postdating him, influencing him and receiving influence from him, are the *epigonoi* who tilled the ground prepared by the classic composers. It is significant of the period and the style of their writing that the best of them were virtuosi whose influence was most enduring in the department of pianoforte technics. Manner rather than matter distinguished their compositions. They were vastly productive, for they found their models at hand, and lofty thought and deep emotion had not begun to assert themselves as essentials when they began their careers. They were a numerous band, and the burden of their importance lies in the department of study to which I hope to devote my final chapter. A few, however, must have mention here, and I have chosen Muzio Clementi (1752–1832), Johann Nepomuk Hummel (1778–1837), Johann Ludwig Dussek (1761–1812), and Johann Baptist Cramer (1771–1858) as representatives of the class. Two other men may first enlist our passing attention and sympathetic interest because of their relationship, one physical, the other spiritual, to the giant who was the culmination of the preceding order. Johann Christian Bach shared only the family name with his great father, Johann Sebastian. Like Handel, he went out into the world of fashion, yielded to its sway, and became an elegant musician. Italy set its seal on him when he became organist of Milan Cathedral, married an Italian prima donna, and set his heart on operatic compositions. He spent the last twenty-three years of his life in London, where he became music-master to the queen. There the boy Mozart sat on his knees and improvised duets with him.

The Bach traditions did not live in him as they did in one between whom and their creator there existed no ties of blood. Friederich Wilhelm Rust (1739–1796) was only eleven years old when "old Bach" died, but at thirteen he was already able to play all the Forty-eight Preludes and Fugues by heart. Bach's music was his delight. He went to the sons Friedemann and Emanuel for lessons in composition and organ and clavier playing. His son, Wilhelm Karl, enjoyed the friendship of Beethoven, and his grandson, Dr. Wilhelm Rust (1822–1892), who edited some of his works (with modern additions, as Mr. Shedlock regretfully chronicles), appropriately became a successor of Bach as cantor of St. Thomas's, in Leipsic. Dr. E. Prieger has hailed F. W. Rust as *Ein Vorgänger Beethovens*, a precursor of Beethoven.

"With the exception of Mozart's sonata in C minor, Haydn's 'Genziger' and 'London' sonatas, both in E-flat, also some of Rust's . . . there are, to our thinking, none which in spirit come nearer to Beethoven than some of Clementi's," says Mr. Shedlock in his admirable book on the history of the sonata.[1] "Clementi represents the sonata proper from beginning to end," is Edward Dannreuther's dictum in his article printed in Grove's "Dictionary." Scholars frequently hold such opinions touching works which to the mass of musicians in our eager, impatient, and self-sufficient age seem hopelessly antiquated. Haydn has not been spared, nor Mozart, nor Beethoven; so radical has been the change in taste accomplished by the romantic movement characteristic of the nineteenth century. It is meet and proper, therefore, in a historical review, that the excellences of the masters of the past which appealed to their contemporaries be pointed out as well as the things which are shortcomings from a later point of view. Pianists are not likely soon to forget what Clementi did in a pedagogic way in his collection of one hundred studies entitled "Gradus ad Parnassum,"[2] neither should they so

[1] "The Pianoforte Sonata; Its Origin and Development," by J. S. Shedlock, B.A., London: Methuen & Co., 1895.

[2] "Gradus ad Parnassum, ou l'art de jouer le Pianoforte demonstré par des Exercices dans le style sévère et dans le style élégant." The work is in three parts, the first of which appeared in 1817.

completely neglect his sonatas as to remain ignorant
of the fine sense of characterization as well as the
vivacity and variety displayed in them. Clementi's
sonatas were the admiration of Beethoven, who
knew how to keep a firm foothold on the past even
while sending his prescient glances far into the
future. Mr. Dannreuther's comprehensive praise
need not disturb us. Clementi's life covered a
greater stretch of the classical sonata period than
any one of its sons. He was born twenty years
after Haydn, but lived twenty-three years later;
born four years before Mozart and outlived him
forty-one years; was eighteen years old when Beethoven was born, and had still five years of life before him when that master went to his grave. He
was Mozart's rival in the concert-field, and met him
in artistic combat, as was customary at the time,
before Emperor Joseph II. in 1781, when he played
the sonata in B-flat, whose principal theme became
the chief subject of the overture to "The Magic
Flute," a decade later. Mozart once called him a
"charlatan, like all the Italians"; but it was plainly
in a moment of irritation, and the remark did not
reflect a dispassionate judgment. It was not given
to Clementi to go beyond Haydn; but neither was
it given to Haydn to go beyond Mozart, though he
antedated him twenty-four years and outlived him
eighteen. He was a phenomenal talent, not a great
genius.

It is written that Haydn was in the habit of beginning a composition by inventing a theme, selecting the keys through which he intended to make it pass, and then going to a little romance which he imagined for sentiment and color while he worked. It is not unlikely that Clementi's method was a similar application of rule of thumb and subjective impression. However mild the dose of subjectivity, it was yet an advance toward romanticism, as compared with the externalism which held sway in the intituled dance pieces of Couperin and the Biblical sonatas of Kuhnau. Titles and marks of expression and tempo helped to fix the attention and arouse the fancy, and it is quite as easy to detect the conflicting emotions which tore the heart of unhappy Dido deserted by Æneas in Clementi's sonata in G minor, Op. 64, as the long train of poetical and metaphysical conceits in some of the programmatic pieces which came a century later. His hints, at least, were direct, lucid, modest, and not impertinent; for instance: "Didone abbandonata, Scena tragica. I. *Largo-sostenuto e patetico;* II. *Allegro-deliberando e meditando;* III. *Adagio-dolente;* IV. *Allegro-agitato e con disperazione.*" Dussek was less temperate in his use of titles, or, perhaps, like Beethoven and Chopin, a greater victim of the insensate desire of publishers to put attractive labels on their wares.

Dussek was a Bohemian, and there is an occa-

sional outburst of something like the Czechish fire
to which Smetana and Dvořák have accustomed us
in some of his music.   He was enormously fruitful
in the sonata field, though only a small fraction of
his works have survived in print.   We count twelve
concertos with orchestra, a quartet, a quintet,
twenty or twenty-five pianoforte trios, forty or fifty
sonatas for pianoforte and violin (or flute—it made
little difference to the taste of that day), twelve
sonatinas for pianoforte and violin, twenty-six
sonatas for pianoforte alone.   For four years Dussek was a friend and musical mentor to that Prince
Louis Ferdinand whose highest encomium is to be
found in Beethoven's comment: "Your highness
does not play like a prince, but like a musician."
When the prince died Dussek wrote a sonata in
F-sharp minor (Op. 61) and called it "Élégie har-
monique sur le mort du Prince Louis Ferdinand de
Prusse, en forme de sonate," following it with an
andante in B-flat, which he dedicated to the memory of his royal patron and called "La Consolation."   He also composed a "Tableau de la situa-
tion de Marie Antoinette," and a sonata, "La morte
de Marie Antoinette."   Nor did he disdain to follow
a horde of predecessors in writing a battle piece.
He called it a "Battaille navale," and issued it not
only as a pianoforte solo, but in an arrangement
for violin, violoncello, and big drum.   We may
smile at this, at Kotzwara's "Battle of Prague,"

"Mr. Byrd's Battle," and Munday's meteorological fantasia, but we can scarcely do so in good conscience so long as we accept Richard Strauss's setting of Nietzsche's philosophy with sober faces. Mr. Shedlock courageously breaks a lance for Dussek and finds that in his last three sonatas he was influenced "by the earnestness of Beethoven, the chivalric spirit of Weber, and the poetry of Schubert."

Johann Baptist Cramer wrote no less than 105 sonatas, of which forty or fifty were for pianoforte solo, the rest accompanied; also eight concertos and many pieces of a miscellaneous character. To a few of his sonatas he gave titles in Dussek's manner: "La Parodie," "L'Ultima," "Les Suivantes" (the three sonatas, Op. 57, 58, and 59), and "Le Retour à Londres." The distinction between the old and new styles of playing, which grew up in his time and was actively promoted by the English manufacture of pianofortes, was illustrated by Cramer in a "Fantasie capricieuse." Other pieces which he issued with titles (he was his own publisher) were "Un Jour de Printemps," "Le Petit Rien" (a romance with variations), and "Les Adieux à ses Amis de Paris." The last composition, and the sonata in which he celebrated his return to London, probably owed their origin, or rather titles, to the fact that he spent a few years of his life as a resident of the French capital.

Cramer was taken to London when one year old by his father, a German violinist, who became a conspicuous figure in the musical life of the metropolis as teacher, player, and conductor. He was leader for a time of the Antient and the Professional concerts, and conducted two of the Handel festivals in Westminster Abbey. His son studied with him and other local teachers of minor importance, then with Clementi and Johann Samuel Schröter, who succeeded Johann Christian Bach as music-master to the queen. Schröter deserves to be remembered even in so cursory a review as this, for the authorities agree that he was among the first teachers to disclose the possibilities of the pianoforte as distinguished from the harpsichord. He married one of his aristocratic pupils, who soon tired of him and purchased a separation. She became a pupil of Haydn when he came to London and formed an attachment for that susceptible old gentleman which found rather amusing expression in the letters which I gave to the public in a little book published in 1898.[1] Like Clementi, Cramer combined a commercial with an artistic spirit; he founded the music publishing house of J. B. Cramer & Co., which still flourishes in London. Not his concert-pieces but his works of instruction have kept his name alive. In his compositions de-

---

[1] "Music and Manners in the Classical Period." New York: Charles Scribner's Sons.

signed for public performances he reflects the shallow taste of his time; but he was an admirable virtuoso and a still more admirable teacher. His études are classics and in vigorous use to-day. Henselt published fifty of them with accompaniments for a second pianoforte, and his example was followed by Henry C. Timm, an American pianist and one of the founders of the Philharmonic Society of New York. Dr. von Bülow also edited half a hundred of the studies. His "Pianoforte School" and the "School of Velocity" have been published over and over again.

Clementi, Dussek, and Cramer have disappeared from our concert-rooms, but Hummel still maintains a place there in despite of the radicals, with his concerto in A minor and his perennially lovely septet. "A classic, but a dull classic," remarks Mr. Edward Dannreuther; "Hummel's pianoforte music represents the true pianoforte style within pure and noble forms," says Prosniz, "uniting agreeable and solid elegance and glittering ornamentation with warmth of feeling, which, however, seldom swings itself up to passionate expression. . . . Trained in the school and style of Mozart, he thoroughly developed the peculiarities of the pianoforte—its beautiful tone, its elegant and pleasing effects. He cultivated gentle song and dainty, often coquettish ornament." So far as it was possible in one whose genius was of a subor-

FRANZ LISZT.
After a drawing by S. Mittag.

dinate order, Hummel was a continuator of Mozart, in whose house he lived, and by whom he was taught for two years as a lad. He recognized his inability to keep pace with the heaven-storming Titan, Beethoven, and so, according to his own confession, he resolved not to try. His thoughts were not those of a great tone-poet, but those of a devotee of the pianoforte. In a manner he was a worthy precursor of Chopin and Liszt. In developing the varied effects and euphony of his instrument he was remarkably successful; and he reared a monument to it in his stupendous school with its 2,200 examples.

IX

Beethoven—An Intermezzo

THE characterization of Ludwig van Beethoven (1770–1827) which I made in the preceding chapter (and which I should like to have accepted, not as mere rhetorical hyperbole, but as sober and very truth) justifies, if it does not demand, the setting apart of a special chapter for the consideration of his contribution to pianoforte music. The contribution is a considerable one, though in bulk it does not measure up with the product of some of his predecessors or the virtuoso-composers of his own period. He did not write one-quarter as many concertos as Mozart; he wrote only half as many solo sonatas as Clementi, and one-quarter as many sonatas with other instruments *obbligato* as Dussek; but *as music* his contribution surpasses theirs, as it also surpasses all that has been written by any composer since, in variety, artistic dignity and significance. In using the qualifying phrase "as music," it is intended to distinguish Beethoven's pianoforte compositions from works whose merit lies largely, if not chiefly, in their specific relationship to the instrument for which they were conceived.

The point of view, moreover, is that of to-day. No critical historian need hesitate to say this, or, saying it, beg pardon of the *manes* of Schubert, Schumann, Mendelssohn, or Chopin. Not only is the climax of eleven decades of pianoforte music, as of eleven decades of symphonic and chamber music, still to be found in Beethoven, but the best example in each of the categories into which pianoforte music may be divided are worthy of being classed with the best examples of the other departments in which the composer is acknowledged to be pre-eminent. Only the best examples, of course. In the large form of the symphony and the mass, in the aristocratic form of the string quartet, there was not the temptation which beset him, as it has always beset the great, to write much and print freely music which affords opportunities for the *dilettanti* to display their accomplishments. We cannot conceive the writing of symphonies or quartets as potboilers: but with a clamorous public and importunate publishers we can easily conceive such a thing in the case of pianoforte pieces even when the composer is a Beethoven, to whom writing on commission was always irksome and sometimes impossible.[1]

[1] What fate sometimes attended the writing of a work for an occasion we see in the history of the Solemn Mass in D, which was completed three years after the installation of the friend, patron, and pupil whom Beethoven wished to honor with it.

The difference in merit, therefore, as well as the limitations set for these studies, compel me to choose chiefly two classes of compositions from which to deduce Beethoven's large and unique significance—the solo sonatas and variations. Of the solo sonatas there are thirty-two, not counting three which were written when Beethoven was a boy of eleven years, a fragment found among his posthumous papers, and two sonatinas. Of the variations for pianoforte solo there are twenty-three sets. His other compositions in which the pianoforte enters may be summarized as follows: Seven concertos with orchestra (counting in one in E-flat written when he was fourteen years old, and a transcription of the concerto for violin made by himself); one concerto for pianoforte, violin, violoncello, and orchestra; a rondo with orchestra (found among his manuscripts after his death); a fantasie for pianoforte, chorus, and orchestra; a quintet with oboe, clarinet, horn, and bassoon (also published for pianoforte and strings); three quartets with strings, nine trios with strings, a set of variations with strings on a melody by Wenzel Müller ("Ich bin der Schneider Kakadu"); ten sonatas with violin, a rondo with violin, five sonatas with violoncello, three sets of variations with violoncello, a sonata with horn, seven sets of variations with violin (or flute); a sonata, three marches, and two sets of variations for pianoforte (four hands), a fantasia; an Andante Favori

in F, eight cadenzas for his own concertos and two
for Mozart's concerto in D minor, and two scores or
more of bagatelles, preludes, rondos, dances, etc.
Though monumental labor and devotion were expended on the "Complete Edition" (*Gesammt
Ausgabe*) of his works published by Breitkopf &
Härtel, of Leipsic, unpublished manuscripts are still
in the hands of private collectors, though none of
those known is of critical significance.

I have called Beethoven a master builder and
arch destroyer. He was, indeed, both; but he
built up and strengthened what is essential in art
and destroyed only that which is unessential. His
iconoclasm did not have the purpose, nor was it of
the kind which ill-balanced admirers no less than
ill-balanced detractors have proclaimed it to be.
The extremists of to-day attempt to justify by appeal to him, or his example, not only the vagaries
of their own compositions, but their strained read-
ings of his texts and the changes which they arro-
gantly make in his pages. When they appeal to
him as the destroyer of form they disclose crass
ignorance of one of his highest artistic qualities;
they have no understanding of his attitude toward
the most important element of artistic construction.
It was not form, but formalism, or formula, which
Beethoven antagonized. Nowhere is there a greater
master or profounder reverencer of constructive
form than he.

Why should the question be beclouded? There can be no expression, no utterance of any kind in art without form. Form is the body which the spirit of music creates that it may make itself manifest. It is impossible to conceive of a combination of the integral elements of music (melody, harmony, and rhythm) in a beautiful manner without form of some kind. In music more than any other art form is necessary to the existence of the highest quality of beauty, *i.e.*, repose; the quality which Ruskin eloquently describes as being "the 'I am' as contradistinguished from the 'I become'; the sign alike of the supreme knowledge which is incapable of surprise, the supreme power which is incapable of labor, the supreme volition which is incapable of change." Music is not ineptly spoken of in the books as the language of feeling; and there is nothing truer than that it gives voice to things for which we seek in vain for utterance in words. There is no beautiful speech without an orderly arrangement of words and phrases—without some kind of form. Now, if this degree of form is essential to speech, which deals with ideas, how much more essential must it be to music, which deals with states of the soul, with emotions, which is a language the need of which as a medium of expression in its highest estate does not arise until words no longer suffice us for utterance! Let me quote, now, some words of mine from an earlier writing; the thoughts are apposite here, and I do not feel that I could improve on the manner in which they were expressed twenty years ago:

When the composers of two hundred and fifty years ago began to develop instrumental music they found the germ of the sonata form—the form that made Beethoven's symphonies possible—in the homely dance-tunes of the people, which, till then, had been looked upon as vulgar things wholly outside the domain of polite art. The genius of the masters of the last century (*i.e.*, the eighteenth) moulded this form of plebeian ancestry into a vessel of wonderful beauty; but by the time this had been done the capacity of music as an emotional language had been greatly increased, and the same Romantic spirit which had originally created the dance-forms, that they might embody the artistic impulses of that early time, suggested the filling of the vessel with the new contents. When the vessel would not hold these new contents it had to be widened. New bottles for new wine. That is the whole mystery of what conservative critics decry as the destruction of form in music. It is not destruction, but change. When you destroy form you destroy music, for the musical essence can manifest itself only through form.[1]

Until Beethoven came the sonata was a beautiful vessel whose contents were pleasing to the ear, gratifying to the intellect appreciative of symmetry and the display of ingenious learning, and charming to the fancy. "We have now become acquainted with the fluency and humor of Scarlatti, Rameau, and Couperin, the earnestness of Bach and Handel, the grace, elegance, and heartiness of Haydn and

---

[1] "Studies in the Wagnerian Drama," by H. E. Krehbiel, p. 83.

Mozart," said Rubinstein at one of his historical lecture-recitals in St. Petersburg in 1888, "but we have not yet found the soul of music. The man who filled music with soul, with dreamings and dramatic life, was Beethoven. The music which before him had a heart had no soul. It is often asserted that Beethoven wrote his first sonatas under the influence of Mozart and Haydn. This I deny *in toto*. The form, the manner of expression, the style were inherited, it is true, but not as an imitation of Haydn and Mozart, but as the expression of the period"; and later Rubinstein attempts to account for the new contents and changed manner of expression on political grounds by what he calls his paradox: "So long as political life was so constituted that the state cared for all the needs of the people music was the region in which simplicity, joyousness, and ingenuousness spread their wings. When after the Revolution man had to care for himself music became dramatic. Then Beethoven came to be the interpreter of the soul's travail and suffering—the suffering not only of his own soul, but also that of his people. Every man takes on the color of his period. When political life is without pronounced character, when it becomes colorless, then music becomes characterless and pallid —*as it is now!*"

This analogy between politics and art has often been discussed and Beethoven held up as a striking

illustration of its correctness. He certainly was the
first great democrat amongst the representatives of
his art. Before his time the greatest musicians no
less than the least were house servants of the politi-
cally great. Mozart sat high at the table (above
the cook if I remember rightly) in the servants'
hall of his master in Vienna; Haydn, as an officer
of the household of Prince Esterhazy, was charged
with the responsibility of looking after the livery
of the men in his orchestra as well as their habits
and behavior. Beethoven would brook no mark or
suggestion of servitude of any kind. Whether true
or not, Bettina von Arnim's story of the rebuke
which he administered to Goethe when the two
encountered the Austrian emperor in the park is
illuminative and characteristic; and it is very
likely that once he remarked to a prince: "You
are what you are by accident of birth; I am what
I am by the grace of God!"

Now, such a man would as little accept the bondage of formula in his artistic utterance as the
bondage of caste in social life. "Listen to Beethoven's Sonata in F minor," says Rubinstein again:
"the old elegance, grace, and loveliness have given
place to dramatic and passionate expression. Here
we see the gloomy face, seamed with pain, which is
seldom lighted up by a careless or merry smile.
The Adagio, because of its sweetness and gentleness,
is nearer the old period, but it has a new spirit.

And is there an iota in the last movement to remind us of the eighteenth century or Haydn and
Mozart?" It is the individual note which Rubinstein emphasizes here; but Beethoven did not speak
for himself alone. He was the poet of humanity;
he sang all its present joys and all its sorrows; all
its aspirations, its tragedies, its earthly environment
and its glimpse of the celestial. "Dalliance with
tones here becomes tonal speech," says Prosniz,
"and in this speech it was given him to utter the
unutterable"—that is to say, that which is unutterable in words. To Beethoven music was not only
a manifestation of the beautiful, that is art, it
was also akin to religion. He felt himself to be
a prophet, a seer. All the misanthropy, seeming
rather than real (for at heart he was a sincere and
even tender lover of man), engendered by his deafness and his unhappy relations with mankind, could
not shake his devotion to this ideal which had
sprung from truest artistic apprehension and been
nurtured by enforced introspection and philosophic
reflection.[1]

Beethoven was a conservator of form always, and
even of formula whenever thought and the conventional manner of expression balanced each other;
but when the former refused to go into the old
vessel he exercised the right which belongs to creative genius—but only true creative genius—to

[1] See the author's "Music and Manners," p. 237.

widen the latter.[1]   He provided new bottles for the new wine.   Like Hans Sachs in Wagner's comedy, he stood between the apparently warring elements of classicism and romanticism as I shall attempt to define them in the next chapter, and bravely did battle for both—conserving the old, but regenerating it and adapting it to the new régime.

We have taken a glance at the impulses which prompted him to break down some of the conventional barriers; let us now look at some of the devices by means of which he adapted the enlarged vessel to the new contents.   Weitzmann in his "Geschichte des Clavierspiels" likens the Beethoven sonata to a trilogy, or tetralogy, in which the satyr play, as he calls the scherzo, has a part but as a middle instead of a final member.   The expository part of the first movement contains a principal subject with which are associated a second subject and one or more episodes or side-themes which are in harmony with the mood of the whole, and which, themselves organically developed, bind together the principal themes.   Whereas the second theme of this first movement formerly entered as a rule in the key of the dominant (or in the relative major in the case of minor keys), Beethoven practised the liberty of using other keys which bore relationship to the original tonality for the sake of modulatory con-

---

[1] Only true creative genius. *Quid licet Jovi non licet bovi* should never be forgotten.

trast. In the second division of the movement, which is concerned with the development of this material, Beethoven indulges in modulations of great daring, touching at times far distant keys, thus stimulating curiosity concerning the return of the principal subject, and by contrapuntal devices and otherwise stimulating interest and not infrequently building up his climaxes in this development portion which English writers call the "free fantasia." The coda, which presents the principal material of the movement compressed and intensified, also affords Beethoven a field for his marvellously fertile ingenuity. In it he likes to startle the hearer once again before bringing about the conclusion for which ear and fancy are waiting.

"Occasionally," says Weitzmann, "Beethoven arouses the highest degree of expectancy by unusual resolutions of dissonances and deceptive progressions. His rhythms, moreover, veiling the metre, create a feeling of tensity and excitement, but the resting places for the fancy and the emotions are not neglected, and we are never wearied by too long continued deceptions or too persistent withholding of that which is expected." The same writer also directs attention to the labor and care bestowed by Beethoven on the choice and development of his melodic material. His compositions always contain melodies which are complete in their expression and easily grasped. Sometimes they are even popu-

lar in style, and for that reason appeal to the many
who are able to follow the artistic treatment to
which the tunes are subjected. "The adagio, or
andante, in Beethoven has either the extended form
of the first movement (the sonata form), with a
recurring episode in the second part, or the song
form, with one or more contrasting themes, which
appear but once, or it constitutes the introduction
to the movement which follows. The movement,
lively, bright, good-humored, humorous, called the
minuet or scherzo, which had already received a
place in the sonata scheme, first received a contour
appropriate to the character of the composition as a
whole through Beethoven. In connection with this
it is edifying to compare the structures created especially to this end by Beethoven, such as the march-
like movement in the A major Sonata, Op. 101;
the Scherzo of the B-flat Sonata, Op. 106, and the
Allegro molto of the Sonata Op. 110."

The Scherzo, as everybody knows, is the offspring
of the minuet. It appears in the first three Sonatas,
Op. 2, dedicated to Haydn, under whose bewitching
hand, as may be seen in some of the string quartets,
the old-fashioned dance had already received the
impulse toward what it became under Beethoven;
but it was the latter who eventually gave it a stupendous import in his symphonies, such as Haydn
never could have dreamed of. How the strange
quality of Beethoven's humor affected this jocose

movement in the sonatas, and some of the sonatas
themselves, is thus pointed out by Selmar Bagge:
"As Beethoven was always the enemy of formula,
he sometimes introduced this element of humor into
the slow movement and then omitted the scherzo,
as in the Sonata in G major (Op. 31, No. 1); or he
gave the minuet the character of emotional contrast,
as in the E-flat Sonata (Op. 31, No. 3); or he
imbued the scherzo movement, despite its rapid 3-4
time, with a serio-fantastic spirit, in which case the
adagio was dispensed with, as in the Sonatas in F
major (Op. 10, No. 2) and E major (Op. 14, No. 1)."

The conventional finale before Beethoven was
either a rondo or a minuet. In Beethoven's sonatas
it is sometimes a rondo, in which a principal theme
appears three, four, or more times in alternation
with various episodes, side themes, and develop-
ments; sometimes it has the sonata form; sometimes the principal theme is treated as a free fugue;
sometimes it blossoms into a series of variations, as
in the Sonatas Op. 109 and 111. It is in the highest degree noteworthy that in the last five sonatas
there is a return to a multiplicity of movements
(though there are only two in the transcendent one
in C minor, Op. 111, the last of all) and that in
these there is less intimation of a drama playing on
the stage of the individual human heart than of a
projection of the imagination into the realm of
cosmic ideality. Beethoven was frequently trans-

figured, but never so completely as in some moments of these great works with which he said almost his last word on the pianoforte. In the finale of Op. 111 he soars heavenward like a skylark in the rapture of the variations. He is "in the spirit" like John on the isle of Patmos. With the first movement of this sonata he carries us to the theatre in which the last scene in Goethe's "Faust" plays— the higher regions of this sphere, where earth and heaven meet as they seem to do at times in the high Alps. There we hear the song of the *Pater Profundis*, and thence we begin the ascent to the celestial realms above. The variations are the songs of the *Pater Ecstaticus*, *Blessed Boys*, *Penitents*, and *Angels*, who soar higher and higher, carrying with them the immortal soul of *Faust*.

It would require a detailed analysis of a majority of the sonatas to point out all the significant instances in which Beethoven changed, extended, and enriched the sonata form as it had been handed down to him. There is no steadily progressive development to be traced in the sequence of the opus numbers, for they are not always chronological records; nor in the times of composition, for, as in the case of the symphonies, there is a rising and falling of the emotional waters, and a portrayal of either profound or exalted feelings may be followed by a composition in which amiable dalliance with tones is the be-all and end-all of the work. Moreover, Beethoven's activities were dispersed over too wide a field to permit that each new production should show such a step forward as we observe in the lyric dramas of Wagner and Verdi. Yet it ought not to be overlooked that as the quality of dramatic expression grew more and more dominant in Beethoven's art the element of unity was emphasized. Now the development of melodies gives place in a large measure to the development of *motivi* such as is also exemplified in the E-flat, C minor, and D minor symphonies. Also, as has been intimated, movements which might interfere with the psychological unity of all the parts are omitted. The familiar "Andante Favori" in F was originally written for the Sonata in C, Op. 53. So says Ries, who adds that Beethoven substituted the present slow introduction to the final rondo for it when it was pointed out to him that the andante would make the work too long. A much likelier explanation is that Beethoven felt that its association with two such movements as the allegro con brio and the allegretto moderato would be an artistic *mésalliance*.

As the poetical, or emotional, contents determined the number of movements, their relative disposition, and the modification of their forms, so also it led to the introduction of new or unusual forms. So the stories of the two sonatas, Op. 27, are told in a rhapsodical way (*quasi fantasia*) and in the slow movement of the great Sonata in A-flat, Op. 110, a fragment of recitative, such as had already been employed in the Sonata in D minor (Op. 31, No. 2) many years before, becomes an element in a vocal form. This *adagio* is a scena, an arioso with an introduction in which we may hear (if we wish so to exercise our fancy) at first an orchestral introduction, then a voice speaking in the declamatory style of the recitative, then the two flowing together as cantilena and accompaniment. Whatever the shape and dimensions of the vessel, however, it is to be kept in view that they were determined by the contents which Beethoven poured into it.

We have ample evidence that Beethoven permitted impressions made on his mind by external things to influence his music—by natural scenes, happenings, and sounds. Thus, the murmur of a brook prompted the observation in a note-book, "The deeper the water the graver the tone"; the clatter of a horse's hoofs, Ries says, suggested the theme of the finale of the Sonata in D minor, Op. 31, No. 2; he caught the *motif* of the C minor symphony from a bird. But in his sonatas he was not a programmist in the crude sense of an imitator of sounds or user of the device of association of ideas. The principle which he followed was always that expressed in the words which he inscribed on the score of the "Pastoral" symphony: "More an ex-

pression of feeling than delineation." He was
chary about giving even a hint of the ideas or
feelings which had prompted his music, either by
writing titles or by word of mouth. Schindler says
that in 1816 he was prevailed upon to make arrangements for the publication of a revised edition
of his sonatas for pianoforte, being influenced in
this determination by three considerations, viz.,
first, "to indicate the poetic ideas which form the
groundwork of many of those sonatas, thereby facili-
tating the comprehension of the music and determining the style of the performance; secondly, to
adapt all his previously published pianoforte compositions to the extended scale of the pianoforte of
six and one-half octaves, and, thirdly, to define the
nature of musical declamation."

There is plausibility at least in the suggestion
that Beethoven entertained the second and third
considerations; but the first not only flies in the
face of Beethoven's consistent conduct, but is at
variance with an experience which Schindler himself had, as we shall see presently. If Beethoven
ever felt disposed to give verbal interpretations to
his sonatas he must have given them to the pupils
and patrons to whom he dedicated them; and had
he done this we would surely have had the poetical glosses handed down to us. Sometimes when
directly asked about his meanings he replied enig-
matically. The "Pastoral" symphony is most in-

dubitably programme music, yet Beethoven's note-books contain almost pathetic evidence of his desire that it should not be thought that in it he had dropped into realism. "All painting in instrumental music, if pushed too far, is a failure," is a note found among his sketches; "People will not require titles to recognize the general intention to be more a matter of feeling than of painting in sounds," is another.

Much mischief has been made by titles which publishers and others have given to works without the sanction of the composer. It was not Beethoven who called the Sonata in F minor "Appassionata," or that in C-sharp minor (Op. 27, No. 2) "Moonlight," or that in D major (Op. 28) "Pastorale." There is some appositeness in the first and last of these designations, and in the case of persons gifted with healthy intellectual and æsthetic stomachs they do no harm; but others are led by them to think foolish things of Beethoven and to play his music in a silly manner. The Sonata in C-sharp minor has asked many a tear from gentle souls who were taught to hear in its first movement a lament for unrequited love and reflected that it was dedicated to the Countess Giulietta Guicciardi, for whom Beethoven assuredly had a tender feeling. Moonlight and the plaint of an unhappy lover—how affecting! But Beethoven did not compose the sonata for the countess, though he inscribed it to her. He had given her a rondo, and wishing to dedicate it to another pupil he asked for its return and in exchange sent the sonata. Moreover, it appears from evidence scarcely to be gainsaid that Beethoven never intended the C-sharp minor sonata as a musical expression of love, unhappy or otherwise. In a letter dated January 22, 1892 (for a copy of which I am indebted to Fräulein Lipsius [La Mara], to whom it is addressed), Alexander W. Thayer, the greatest of Beethoven's biographers, says: "That Mr. Kalischer has adopted Ludwig Nohl's strange notion of Beethoven's infatuation for Therese Malfatti, a girl of fourteen years, surprises me; as also that he seems to consider the Cis-moll Sonate to be a musical love poem addressed to Julia Guicciardi. He ought certainly to know that the subject of that sonata was—or rather, that it was suggested by—Seume's little poem 'Die Beterin.'" The poem referred to describes a maiden kneeling at the high altar in prayer for the recovery of a sick father. Her sighs and petitions ascend with the smoke of incense from the censers, angels come to her aid, and at the last the face of the suppliant one glows with the transfiguring light of hope. The poem has little to commend it as an example of literary art and it is not as easy to connect it in fancy with the last movement of the sonata as with the first and second; but the evidence that Beethoven paid it the tribute of his music seems conclusive.

As for the epithet "Moonlight," it seems to owe its existence to a comparison made by a critic (Rellstab) of its first movement to a boat rocking on the waves of Lucerne on a moonlit evening. Many years ago a picture on the title-page of an edition led the Viennese to call it the *Laubensonate* (Arbor Sonata), the picture evidently referring or giving rise to a story of its composition in an arbor.

Rubinstein was unwilling to accept "Moonlight" as a characteristic title, because, though the sonata is nominally in a minor key, its music is predominantly major, and he was glad that Beethoven was not responsible for the designation. He also objected to the title "Pathétique" for the Sonata in C minor, Op. 13, though this has the composer's sanction. "Only the adagio might be said to justify the title," says Rubinstein; "the other movements develop so much action, so much dramatic life, that the sonata might better have been called 'dramatic.'"

The Sonata in F minor has long been called "Appassionata." Is there any appositeness here? Passionate the music assuredly is; but in what direction? Is there a passion of contemplative prayerfulness? If not, how can the epithet apply to the second movement, with its transfigured resignation, its glimpse into the celestial regions, into which Beethoven's soul soared so often when its pinions took a slow and measured movement? Then, if shallow passions murmur "but the deep are dumb," as Sir Walter Raleigh said, are the passions which not only murmur but mutter and swell and roar in this sonata shallow? No one shall think it who hears the music. The epithet is misleading because it is inconclusive and vague, though it is not as harmful as its companion, "Moonlight," which term has not only given rise to a multitude of foolish interpretations, as I have intimated, but also to a multitude of apocryphal stories which in some instances have got into and disfigured biographies of the great composer.

Schindler relates that once when he asked Beethoven to tell him what the F minor and D minor (Op. 31, No. 2) sonatas meant he received only the oracular answer, "Read Shakespeare's 'Tempest.'" Many a student and commentator has no doubt since then read "The Tempest" in the hope of finding a clew to the emotional contents which Beethoven's utterance indicates had received expression in the two works so singularly brought into relationship; has read and been baffled. But are there no tempests except those created by the elements of nature? What else were those psychological struggles which Beethoven felt called upon more and more to delineate as he was more and more shut out from companionship with the external world and its denizens? Such struggles are in the truest sense of the word tempests.

> The tempest in my mind
> Doth from my sense take all feeling else
> Save what beats there.

And one shall scarcely attempt to find verbal symbols for the music of the first and last movements of the sonata without being thrown back on the familiar one of night and storm. The chief trouble caused by Beethoven's dark hint is that it invites us to find in the sonatas delineation of a sequence of events, external and internal, such as we see in Shakespeare's comedy of enchantment. But Beethoven sometimes liked to talk in riddles, and was so frequently lost in profound broodings that it is possible he did not mean his words to be accepted as literally and comprehensively as his Boswell wanted to accept them. It is even possible that the question merely brought up a fleeting memory of the mood of the last movement and the circumstances of its composition. Ries is authority for the statement that once (it must have been in the summer of 1804) while he was walking with Beethoven they wandered so far into the country that it was nearly 8 o'clock before they got back to Döbling, where Beethoven was living at the time. During the walk Beethoven alternately kept humming and howling up and down the scale without reference to any particular intervals. When asked the meaning of this he replied that the theme of the final allegro of his sonata had occurred to him.

His conduct indicated that he was in a state of emotional excitement—again a storm, a struggle, but one of the human soul, not of the earth.

It was only when saying farewell to the pianoforte in the last group of sonatas that Beethoven made large use of the polyphonic forms; but to another form he paid tribute all through his career. It is that of the theme and variations. He was ten years old when he wrote variations on a march by Dressler; he was fifty-three when he put the capstone on his creations in this form by his "Thirty-three Variations on a Waltz by Diabelli" (Op. 120). The variation form is old; it suggests reflection, technical skill, formalism; yet Beethoven made it as perfect a vehicle for soulful poetizing as he had made the free fantasias in his sonatas and symphonies. In the old conception of the form, one which left the theme after all its embellishments essentially what it had been at the beginning, it may be said to have reached its culmination in Bach. Beethoven breathed a new life into it and lifted it to a height which no composer has been able to reach since. Indeed, it may be said that only three of his successors have been able to apply his ideal methods—Mendelssohn in his "Variations sérieuses," Schumann in his "Études symphoniques," and Brahms in his variations on themes by Handel, Paganini, Schumann, and himself. Beethoven's purpose in his variations was not, like that of the composers who preceded and the majority of those who followed him, simply to present a theme in a series of structural metamorphoses: he aimed to exhibit it in its potential poetical phases, to give an exposition of the various moods which his penetrative mind and exuberant fancy saw latent within it. It was as if one having a beautiful diamond should successively present each of its many facets to view so that the changes in diffraction might reveal all the gem's wealth of beauty in the light best calculated to make that beauty evident.

It is the testimony of practically all of Beethoven's contemporaries who have left a record of their impressions of his pianoforte playing that it was in his improvisations that his genius shone most refulgent. In the friendly competitions which were a common feature of the artistic life of his time he again and again met rivals whose technical skill upon the keyboard was admittedly as great if not greater than his own; but he met no one who could improvise upon a given theme as he could. And it would appear as if sometimes something else than the mere beauty of a theme would fire his fancy. There, for instance, is the story, often told, of his meetings with the redoubtable Steibelt. It was at the house of Count Fries in Vienna in 1800. At the first meeting Beethoven produced his Trio in B-flat for pianoforte, clarinet, and violoncello (Op. 11), and Steibelt a quintet for a pianoforte and strings. After these set pieces Steibelt yielded to the requests of the company and won rapturous applause by an exhibition of a fetching trick in arpeggios which was one of the catch-penny specialties of this charlatan. Beethoven could not be persuaded to touch the pianoforte a second time that evening. A week later there was a second meeting, at which Steibelt surprised the company with a new quintet, and an obviously prepared improvisation consisting of variations on a theme which Beethoven had varied in the trio played at the first meeting. Such a challenge was too obvious to be overlooked and Beethoven's friends demanded that he take up the gauntlet. At length he went to the pianoforte, picked up the bass part of Steibel's quintet, set it upside down on the music desk, nonchalantly drummed out the first few measures of the bass with one finger, and began to improvise upon the *motif* thus obtained. Soon the guests were listening in wonderment, and in the midst of the performance Steibelt left the room and never again attended a soirée at which Beethoven was expected to be present.

It is impossible to imagine the marvellous music which must frequently have been struck out in this manner when Beethoven's imagination was at white heat; but the incident recalls not only his fecund skill in developing large and beautiful ideas out of apparently insignificant but really pregnant *motivi* but also his skill in writing beautiful basses. The theme of the variations which make up the finale of the "Eroica" symphony is also the theme of a set of variations for the pianoforte (in E-flat, Op. 35) and the melody of the finale of the ballet "Die Geschöpfe des Prometheus." In its original form it is a little contradance which Beethoven may have written as early as 1795. In the pianoforte variations, as in the symphonic, Beethoven begins with the bass and introduces the melody as a counterpoint upon it; thereafter it remains the theme with the bass as an ostinato. "A musician is known by his basses" might well be set down as an axiom. "In the Sonata Op. 7," said Rubinstein in one of his historical lectures, "the bass of the Largo alone is, in my opinion, worth twice as much as (many) a whole sonata."

Of the transporting effect of the variations in Op. 111 I have already spoken. In cherubic union with them stand the variations in the Sonata Op. 109. Both sets, though their flight into the upper ether is infinitely greater, may be said to have had their prototype in the variations which begin the Sonata in A-flat, Op. 26. "A Titanic creation without parallel," says Rubinstein, speaking of the "Thirty-three Variations on a Waltz by Diabelli," and he goes on: "What the Ninth is among the symphonies and the Op. 106 among the sonatas these variations are among all others." The origin of the composition is as singular as it is diverting. Diabelli, the publisher of many of Beethoven's compositions, conceived a happy idea for a stroke of business. He wrote a simple waltz melody and then asked fifty musicians whose names were familiar to his patrons to write variations on his bantling —Beethoven among them. It was 1823, the year which saw the completion of the Symphony in D minor with its choral finale on Schiller's "Ode to Joy." Imagine what must have been the amazement of Diabelli when he received from Beethoven not one variation but thirty-three, and when he recognized, as he did, that his inconsequential tune had become the germ of an unrivalled masterpiece.[1] On his last visit to America Dr. von Bülow played these variations in New York at his concerts in which he produced the last five sonatas. To his penetrative mind it had been disclosed that, as Dr. Bie says, the variations "constitute an inner drama" like the sonatas. He provided each with a title in the manner of Schumann's "Carnival." To con-

[1] In the publisher's announcement of the work occurred these words: "The most original forms and thoughts, the most daring turns and harmonies are exhausted in this work; all utilized for pianoforte effects based on a solid style of playing. The work is made especially interesting by the fact that it was created on a theme which no one else would have deemed capable of treatment in a style in which our exalted master stands alone among his contemporaries."

tinue with Dr. Bie: "The variations are a last will and testament as were the Goldberg Variations of Bach. From melody to canon, from gloom to parody, from archaism to anticipation of the future, from popularity to the philosophy of the hermit, from mysticism to dance, from technical glitter to the mystery of enharmonics, they lead us along three-and-thirty paths to different realms."

Something remains to be said about the influence of the mechanism of the pianoforte as it existed in his day on the music which Beethoven wrote for the instrument. Sketches have been found, dating from about 1785 to 1795, which indicate that he had it in mind to write a pianoforte method. In his childhood, no doubt, he studied on the clavichord, which was not only in common use among the poorer classes, but preferred to the harpsichord for purposes of instruction. In the Elector's chapel and the theatre at Bonn he played upon the harpsichord as well as organ. Carl Czerny, in his "Outline of the Entire History of Music" (*Umriss der ganzen Musikgeschichte*) published in 1851, says:

Until 1770 clavier music existed only for harpsichord and clavichord. About this time the pianoforte (*Hammerclavier*) gradually became known. Very imperfect at first, it soon began to excel the other keyed instruments, and in 1800 clavichords and harpsichords were already completely dispossessed. Clementi and Beethoven (between 1790 and 1810), by their demands on the performer, contributed much to the perfection of the pianoforte and, in London, Clementi took part also in its manufacture. The pedals, previously called mutations, came into use about 1802.

From Junker we know that Beethoven used one of the pianofortes made by Stein (which had received the approval of Mozart in 1777) before he left Bonn. These instruments had a damper pedal, though it was at first operated by the knee in the manner of the swell on a cabinet, or "American," organ. About 1800 Beethoven used an instrument made by Walther and Streicher. In 1803 he received an Erard from Paris and in December, 1817, a Broadwood from London. In his room at the time of his death stood an instrument specially built for him by Graf, a Viennese manufacturer. It had four unison strings throughout the scale, and Graf also built a resonator, shaped somewhat like a theatrical prompter's box, to enable the deaf man to hear himself play. This interesting relic is now the property of the Beethovenhaus Verein and is preserved in the museum established by that society in the composer's native city. The English instrument was the gift of Ferdinand Ries, J. B. Cramer, G. G. Ferrari, C. Knyvett, and Broadwood, in 1818. At the sale of Beethoven's possessions after his death it was bought by Spina, the publisher, who gave it to Liszt in 1845. It is now in the National Museum at Budapest, to which institution it was presented by Princess Marie

Hohenlohe, daughter of Liszt's friend, the Princess Sayn-Wittgenstein. The action of all these instruments was light, the dip of the keys shallow. All of them, it would also seem, had two damper pedals, one controlling the hammers of the upper half, the other those of the lower half of the keyboard. The manuscript of the so-called "Waldstein" sonata (Op. 53) contains this note in Beethoven's handwriting: "N. B. When 'ped' is marked all the dampers, both bass and treble (*Discant*), are to be raised. 'O' means that they are to be released." It was possible, therefore, at that time to play with dampers on in one part of the keyboard and off in the other, a device which must have been of assistance in the production of an effective *cantilena*.

Some of the instruments used by Beethoven contained two shifting pedals, or two movements of a single pedal, to move the hammers from the three unisons to two strings (*due corde*) or one string (*una corda*) at will. Beethoven seems to have been the first composer to appreciate the beautiful effect of the sympathetic vibrations of the unstruck unisons, as we see in the slow movement of the G major concerto, composed about 1805, where the *una corda* is of entrancing effect.

In a general way it may be said that all the clavier compositions which Beethoven wrote before he took up his permanent abode in Vienna (in

1792) are equally adapted to the harpsichord and pianoforte; they contain the conventional scale passages, figurations, etc., common to the Haydn-Mozart period. But the fact that many of his pieces for pianoforte solo up to 1803 were published as for "pianoforte or harpsichord" (*Clavier*) should not lead the student to think that Beethoven was for so long a time indifferent to the newer instrument. Here again composer, no less than publisher, may have had an eye to the commercial side of the matter. So long as the harpsichord continued to be found in the houses of the musical amateurs it was only a bit of worldly wisdom to let these amateurs know that their instrument was not excluded from the new repertory.

It is a charge frequently brought against Beethoven's music that it is not *claviermässig*, as the Germans say—*i.e.*, that it is not always adapted to the instrument. There is some truth in this statement, no doubt. I have already emphasized the fact that it is as music that his pianoforte compositions are supreme, not as the utterance of the instrument. But though he may have grown comparatively indifferent to his medium as he became more and more engrossed in the art which to him was an evangel, and as he withdrew from public gaze as a virtuoso, he yet strove till the end to keep the pianoforte eloquent. It is the testimony of visitors to his apartments in his later years that his pianofortes were in poor condition. In one of the note-books in which Mr. Thayer kept the memoranda of his conversations with persons who had come into direct contact with Beethoven I found this record: "Once Beethoven told Stein that some strings in his Broadwood P. F. were wanting, and caught up the bootjack and struck the keys with it to show." His deafness affected his playing, and led him to adopt some idioms which were strange to the formulas, just as it led him to ask impossible things of the human voice. But some of the things which fright the souls of fearful virtuosi to-day, and keep some compositions out of the hands of all but specially gifted amateurs, were not in the same degree difficulties, or even *unclaviermässig*, when they were written. The octave *glissandos* in the finale of the "Waldstein" sonata are an instance in point. Beethoven marked them to be played with thumb and little finger of one hand, both descending and ascending. Dr. von Bülow simplified the passages by permitting both hands to play them. Restore the light action and shallow dip of the old mechanism, and the music is at once as easy as it is idiomatic.

In the note reiterated twenty-eight times with *crescendo* and *diminuendo* in the introduction to the Arioso of the Sonata Op. 110 Rubinstein beheld a prescient demand upon the pianoforte and player of the future which he declared the modern virtuoso could only meet by the "beggarly devices" of pedals and a light, reiterated stroke. Dr. von Bülow set down the analogous effect in the coda of the Adagio of the Sonata 106 as an imitation of the *Bebung*, or *Balancement*, practised by the old clavichordists, and Dr. Frimmel thinks that here Beethoven was harking back to his studies on the clavichord. It is, of course, a daring and impertinent thing for a mere critic to do, but I nevertheless venture to say that had either of the two great players whom I have cited pondered but a moment on the structure of the so-called soft pedal on Beethoven's pianofortes they would have seen that the reiterated strokes upon the key as indicated by Beethoven's own fingering, were necessary, not to prolong the tone, as Rubinstein thought, or to produce the effect of the *Bebung*, as von Bülow asserted, but to achieve an emotional and dynamic effect only possible by means of the strokes in combination with movements of the shifting pedal —from *una corda* up to *tutti corde* and back again, as see:

But to reproduce this effect, which is impossible

on modern pianofortes because of the absence of the middle movement (*due corde*), we must again equip the instrument with a shifting mechanism like that in use in Beethoven's day. And why not? We are rapidly coming to an appreciation of the fact that all music sounds best when played under conditions like those which existed when it was composed. The present generation may yet hear a Mozart or Beethoven sonata for pianoforte and violin from instruments in angelic wedlock instead of destructive warfare.

X

The Romantic School

THUS Beethoven ended the old dispensation and ushered in the new. He was the last great classicist and the first great romanticist. The words are out and we are at once confronted by the need of further definition. We cannot go on without it, yet I despair of inventing one which shall be accepted as of general validity. The best that I can do is to set one down which shall be applicable to this study, and urge some arguments in its defence; let it be discarded by all who can find a better.

From every point of view the term classic is more definite in its suggestion than romantic, which in musical criticism is chiefly used for the purpose of conveying an idea of antithesis to classic. In literary criticism this is not always the case. Classical poets and prose writers are those of all times whose works have been set down as of such excellence that all the world that knows them has accorded them a place apart, has put them in a class, out of which, so far as we can judge from the history of centuries, they will never be taken. Here the term, as Archbishop Trench pointed out, retains a relic of a significance derived from the political economy of ancient Rome, in which citizens were rated according to their income as *classici* or as being *infra classem*.[1]

When the term romantic got into literary criticism it meant something different from, though not necessarily antithetic to, classic, and this difference enters also into the term as used in musical criticism. Romantic writings in poetry and prose were those whose subject-matter was drawn from the imaginative literature of the Middle Ages—the fantastical stories of chivalry and adventure which first made their appearance in the Romance languages. The principal elements in these tales were the marvellous and the supernatural. When these subjects were revived by some poets of Germany and France in the early part of the nineteenth century, they were clothed in a style of thought and expression different from that cultivated by the authors who thitherto had been looked upon as models. So not only subject-matter but manner of expression also entered into the conception of the term romantic which these writers affected.

We see romanticism of the first kind in the subjects of the operas of Weber and Marschner; but this element cannot be said to enter significantly into purely instrumental music, least of all into music

[1] See the author's: "How to Listen to Music," page 65.

for the pianoforte, to which I am trying to confine myself. In a way it is influential, it is true, in music which relies more or less upon suggestions derived from external sources—"programme music," as it is called. · It would be incorrect, however, to classify all programme music as romantic. Froberger's attempt to describe the incidents of an adventurous journey, Buxtehude's musical delineation of the celestial spheres, Kuhnau's Biblical sonatas, Bach's "Capriccio on the Departure of a Beloved Brother," Dittersdorf's descriptive symphonies, were all cast in classical forms; the titles in no wise affected the character or value of the music as such. No more did the titles which the virtuoso composers of a later date gave their sonatas and fantasias. They did no more than invite a pleasing play of fancy and an accompanying intellectual operation—the association of naturally musical ideas. By this I mean a correlation of certain attributes and properties of things with certain musical idioms which have come to have conventional significance, such as position in space and acuteness and gravity of tone; speed, lightness, and ponderosity of movement and tempo; suffering or death and the minor mode; flux and reflux and alternating ascent and descent of musical figures, etc. Music of this kind may be only one degree higher in the æsthetic scale than that which is crudely imitative of natural sounds, like the whistling of the wind, the rolling crash of thunder, the roar of artillery, the rhythmical clatter of horses' hoofs, etc.

It is only when these things become stimuli of feeling and emotion, with their infinite phases, that they become associate elements, with melody, harmony, and rhythm, in music. Now, we have programme music of a higher order, the order which, because it demanded freer vehicles of utterance than were offered by the classical forms (especially when they had degenerated into unyielding formulas), came to be looked upon as antithetical to the conception of classicism, and therefore was called romantic as the newer literature had been.

The composers whose names first spring into our minds when we think of the Romantic School are men like Mendelssohn and Schumann, who drew much of their inspiration from the young writers of their time who were making war on stilted rhetoric and conventionalism of phrase. Schumann touches hands with the Romantic poets in their strivings in two directions. His artistic conduct, especially in his early years, is inexplicable if Jean Paul be omitted from the equation. His music rebels against the formalism which had held despotic sway over the art, and also seeks to disclose the beauty which lies buried in the world of mystery in and around us, and gives expression to the multitude of emotions to which unyielding formalism had refused adequate utterance.[1]

Now, I think, we are ready for the tentative definition of romanticism; it is the quality in com-

[1] "How to Listen to Music," p. 67.

position which strives to give expression to other
ideals than mere sensuous beauty, and seeks them
irrespective of the restrictions and limitations of
form and the conventions of law; the quality which
puts content, or matter, over manner. The striving cannot be restricted to the composers of any
particular time or place. Evidences of it are to be
found here and there in the works of the truly great
composers of all times; but it became dominant in
the creative life of the men who drew their inspiration from Beethoven. The chief of these are to be
studied after a brief excursion demanded by historical integrity.

I have already called attention to the circumstance (not peculiar to music but shared with it by
all other creations of the human mind) that there is
no sharp line of demarcation between characteristic
periods of development, but that they overlap each
other. Every great artist, before he becomes the
forward man who strikes a new path, first travels
along the old and has company on his journey. It
is only after posterity recognizes his puissance that
his companions drop out of sight and he appears in
his solitary grandeur. It is this that gives us the
perspective of the great masters touching hands
with each other in an isolated line, though their
contemporaries may have walked with them,
thought with them, and worked with them along
large stretches of their progressive journey. Beeth-

oven looms a lonely figure before our fancy when we contemplate him amid the period which produced him, and he still stands alone as the preacher of his ultimate evangel; but there were brave men not a few who recognized his greatness and profited by his example, though they could not divorce themselves as completely from the spirit of their time as he did. Their feet, like those of the mortals, as the Hindu legend has it, were on the ground, while his, like those of the immortals, touched it only in seeming. The period which began with his youth and endured throughout his life and until his spirit bore its first vigorous fruit in the founders of the Romantic School was one of technical brilliancy. Its representatives, building on the foundations laid by Cramer and Clementi, developed pianoforte playing to a high degree of perfection and established pedagogical principles which have been transmitted without loss of vitality by a direct line of successors down to to-day; but as composers, they created little which has withstood the tooth of time except instructive material. Most of them live in history merely as virtuosi and teachers. These shall receive attention in the final subdivision of these studies. Special considerations call for the mention of a few here.

Dr. Burney, in his "Present State," bears testimony to the extraordinary love for music cherished by the natives of Bohemia and their skill as practitioners. Among Bohemian musicians of the period which overlapped that of Beethoven there were several who deserve to be singled out because of their dignified position in musical history. J. L. Dussek has been discussed in connection with the development of the classical sonata up to Beethoven. A predecessor, J. B. Vanhall (1739–1813), was a composer of church music, symphonies, and chamber music, but most popular among the dilettanti for his pianoforte pieces, his sonatas challenging special interest, no doubt, by the titles which he gave to some of them, such as "Sonate Militaire," "The Celebration of Peace," "The Battle of Würzburg," "The Sea Fight at Trafalgar," etc. Louis Kozeluch (1748–1818) was a music-master at the Austrian court in Vienna, and received the appointment of court composer after Mozart's death. He composed voluminously in the large forms, instrumental and vocal, and wrote from forty to fifty pianoforte sonatas, three concertos for four hands and one concerto for two pianofortes.

Though Johann Wenzel Tomaschek (1774–1850) found as a teacher that his devotion to the æsthetic principles of his age was incompatible with the erraticism of Beethoven, the composer, we are yet indebted to him for an illuminative account of the effect produced by Beethoven's playing on impressionable hearers. He was a man of education and broad culture, one who, like Schumann, was trained to the law, but who abandoned jurisprudence for music when his pupil, Count Bouquoy, offered him a salaried place in his household. His compositions, of which twelve "Eclogues" and the same number of "Rhapsodies" were noteworthy, and caused one enthusiastic critic to call him the "Schiller of Music," enjoyed great popularity among his countrymen. Ignaz Pleyel (1757–1831) was a pupil of Vanhall and Haydn, with whom he lived for a space. When Haydn went to London in 1791 on the invitation of Salomon the managers of the Professional Concerts engaged Pleyel, whom they intended to play off against his old master. The rivalry between the two concert organizations was extremely bitter, and an inspired newspaper article which told that negotiations had been begun with Pleyel said that Haydn was too old, weak, and exhausted to produce new music, wherefore he only repeated himself in his compositions. How little the two artists felt the rivalry is indicated in the memorandum which Haydn entered in his note-book:

Pleyl came to London on the 23d of December. On the 24th I dined with him.

In 1783 Pleyel became musical director of the Cathedral at Strasburg, whence he went to Paris and founded a music publishing house and a pianoforte factory (1807), which still survives under his name. All of his sonatas and other compositions, except those intended for the purposes of instruction, were modelled after those of Haydn. Yet he cut a brave figure in the concert life of the eighteenth century. Ludwig Berger (1777–1839), who, among many other things, wrote a "Sonata Pathétique" and a "Marche pour les armées Angl.-Espagn. dans les Pyrenées," deserves to be remembered as the teacher of Mendelssohn, Dorn, and Taubert. A similar title is that of the Abbé G. J. Vogler (1749–1814), a Bavarian theoretician and organist, who taught Weber and Meyerbeer, and showed some appreciation of a tendency into which pianoforte music was later to fall in a piece for pianoforte with quartet accompaniment, entitled: "Polymelos, ou caractére de musique de différ. Nations." Louis Spohr (1784–1859), violinist, conductor, composer of operas, oratorios, and symphonies, is more significant in the department of chamber music employing the pianoforte than as a writer for that instrument alone—a characterization which also fits George Onslow (1784–1853), who, although descended from a noble English family, was a native of France. However, two sonatas for four hands have received praise from modern critics.

A successor of Mozart, Hummel, Clementi, and Beethoven was Ignaz Moscheles (1794–1870), whom Edward Dannreuther in Grove's "Dictionary of

Music and Musicians" describes as "the foremost pianist after Hummel and before Chopin." Moscheles, who has many pupils among the older musicians of to-day, made the pianoforte score of Beethoven's "Fidelio" under the eye of the composer, taught Mendelssohn when the latter was a lad of fifteen, became an active spirit in the affairs of the London Philharmonic Society, and was called in 1846 to the professorship of pianoforte playing at the Conservatory of Music in Leipsic. He filled the post till his death. Moscheles composed eight pianoforte concertos, among them a "Fantastique," "Pathétique," and "Pastorale." He also added variations to the theme of "The Harmonious Blacksmith" and wrote a "Hommage á Handel" for two pianofortes, which he first played with Cramer in London and afterward with Mendelssohn in Leipsic; but the public of to-day has scarcely heard any of his music in the concert-room except the cadenzas which he wrote for Beethoven's concertos. Nevertheless, his studies still possess vitality.

A most efficient propagandist of the so-called Vienna school of pianists was Carl Czerny (1791–1857). As a lad he became Beethoven's pupil, and later was the transmitter of many traditions touching the interpretation of his master's works, and the teacher of such famous virtuosi as Liszt, Thalberg, and Döhler. He has left a name of enduring brightness despite his subservience in some things to popular taste. It nevertheless speaks for the solidity of his character as a lad that Beethoven was sincerely fond of him, volunteered to take him as a pupil and for a space contemplated making his home with the boy's parents. Czerny was a tremendously productive composer, his published pieces at the time of his death having reached the number of almost one thousand. Most of those which were not designed for instruction were of the simply entertaining order, and served that end by their showy effectiveness. He followed the classic forms in his sonatas, but they, like his variations, fantasias, potpourris, etc., were mere hollow glitter. He also followed the fashion of the salon composers of his day in giving titles to some of his pieces and, it is easy to see, with an eye to the sales counter. Compositions like "The Conflagration of Mariazell" and "The Ruins of Wiener Neustadt" were aimed at arousing interest through the civic pride of the Viennese. His enduring value rests on his pedagogical works (chiefly on the "Complete Theoretical and Practical Pianoforte School" and "The School of Velocity"), and the principles which he instilled into his pupils and which have been handed down by them.

The honor of receiving pianoforte lessons from Beethoven was shared by Czerny with a youth who, like his companion in later years, contributed much interesting knowledge about their great master to the world.   This was Ferdinand Ries (1784–1838), the son of Franz Ries, a musician of Bonn, who had been kind to Beethoven's parents when they were suffering from poverty.   A letter from his father opened Beethoven's door to the young aspirant for musical honors when, after considerable wandering, he reached Vienna.   Ries remained under the eye of Beethoven, who also persuaded Albrechtsberger to give him lessons in composition for three years. He spent ten years in the prime of his life in London, where he faithfully promoted the interests of his master in every way possible.   He wrote nine pianoforte concertos, saying "Adieu to London" in one and giving a "Greeting to the Rhine" in another. His writings, though of a serious cast, are gone into desuetude; among them were ten solo sonatas, three pianoforte trios, and five pianoforte quartets. Friedrich Kuhlau (1786–1832) was opera composer and flautist, who wrote sonatinas and sonatas which appealed to the best taste of his own time and a long period afterward.

Two men stand in the shadow of Beethoven on the borderland of romanticism.   As a composer of operas one of these, Carl Maria von Weber (1786–1826), sent his glance far into the "Mondbeglänzte Zaubernacht," and is almost as fresh in the hearts of the German people as ever he was.   As a composer of dramatic overtures all the musically cultured peoples of the world admire him beyond measure, but as composer of pianoforte music he lives chiefly by virtue of his Sonata in A-flat, his Polacca in the same key, his "Concertstück" in F minor, and his waltz-rondo, "The Invitation to the Dance"—once the battle-horse of virtuosi like Tausig and Liszt, now the abused plaything of boarding-school misses, who appreciate its merits as little as they do those of Chopin's nocturnes. It is Weber's masterpiece in the field of pianoforte music, and in it I find a most gracious manifestation of the new spirit—a manifestation which is much clearer and more convincing in the original form of the composition than in the disarrangements of it which virtuosi have made to lend technical brilliancy to their playing.[1] Prelude and coda of the "Invitation," with their dainty device of tender dialogue and their exquisite characterization of the young lovers, are of ineffable poetic charm. Weber gave a plain indication of the romantic conceit which underlies his music in a little-known letter, and Dr. John Brown wrote a delightful rhapsody upon it in a review of one of Sir Charles Hallé's concerts printed in "The Scotsman" and incorporated in his book of essays, entitled "Spare Hours." The "Invitation" is not the only one of Weber's pianoforte

---

[1] As for the orchestral transcription by Weingartner, obviously made only because that musician found that the two waltz melodies could be brought together in counterpoint, it is a piece of vandalism which I cannot discuss with patience.

compositions to which he provided a verbal commentary. By his own confession, in his sonata in E minor (No. 4) he attempted to portray the sufferings of a melancholiac: his despondency sometimes lightened by hope in the first movement; rage and insanity in the second; the effects of consolation in the andante; exhaustion and death in the final tarantelle. The "Concertstück" was Weber's last composition for the pianoforte. Sir Julius Benedict, in his little biography of the composer, who was his teacher, tells the story of chivalry as he heard it from the composer's own lips on the morning of the day on which he finished its composition and also saw the first performance of "Der Freischütz." Dr. Bie is as far from appreciation of Weber's pianoforte music as Sir Julius is extravagant in its praise. I like best the brief but comprehensive estimate of Prosniz:

Through his pianoforte pieces there runs a popular and natural vein. Here, too, we observe those melodic turns with which his operas have familiarized us. In fact, Weber's pianoforte pieces often remind us of his operas. They are full of fire and bravura, permeated with gracious and graceful elements, yet often superficial and empty and almost trivial. His sonatas, his "Concertstück," and his popular "Aufforderung zum Tanz" represent Weber, the pianoforte composer.

John Field (1782–1837), born in Dublin, was a pupil of Clementi, whom he accompanied on his concert tours as far as St. Petersburg, where he stayed long enough to get the sobriquet "Russian Field." He was the precursor of Chopin in the cultivation of the nocturne. His compositions in this compact and simple form numbered eighteen. They are sadly faded now, but were potent enough long after Field passed away to draw words of admiration from Liszt.

Field [said he] was the first who introduced a genre which traced its origin to none of the existing forms, a genre in which sentiment and song were absolutely dominant, free from shackles and free from the slack of an imposed form. He opened the way for all achievements which followed under the style of songs without words, impromptus, ballads, etc., and to him may be traced the source of all those pieces designed to give voice in tones to particular sensations and feelings.

If Field really deserves this characterization he was surely the first genuine romanticist. Besides his eighteen nocturnes he composed seven concertos, one of them with the flamboyant title "L'incendie par l'orage"; at least six solo sonatas, a pianoforte quintet, and a number of smaller pieces.

We now come to the group of composers whose names are by universal consent first in the minds of men when romantic music is the topic of discussion. Before their compositions are studied an effort ought to be made to point out wherein the characteristic elements of romantic expression consist. Any attempt to do this, however, is likely to be as inconclusive as that to formulate a satisfactory definition of the term. The attitude of man toward music is an individual one, and in some of its aspects defies explanation; and what is generally true of the art becomes specifically true of its particular phases. Pianoforte music is in a singularly difficult case because it must perforce forego helps enjoyed by other kinds. It cannot be aided by words as vocal music is, which draws one of its elements from literature; when words give expression to ideas associated with romanticism a fitting musical setting of them may also be said to be romantic music. In orchestral music the voices of the instruments and the color which they impart may inspire a feeling of mystery and thoughts of the supernatural and thus proclaim the romantic character of the music so far as mystery and supernaturalism are elements of romanticism. This pianoforte music cannot do; it is thrown back upon content and the musical elements which that content influences.

Having in mind the best pianoforte music to which Beethoven pointed the way, it may be said that the following are the principal elements introduced into music written for the instrument by the new spirit, it being prefaced that all of them are imposed upon music which answers the primary notion of classicism as an embodiment of excellence:

(a) Freedom in the treatment of structural forms—*i. e.*, a freedom which contracts or expands or otherwise modifies forms to adapt them to their spiritual contents;

(b) Invention of new forms;

(c) Extension of the harmonic scheme, harmony being in a high degree a vehicle of the emotions, occupying in this respect the place filled by rhythm in the musical system of the ancient Greeks. This brings us to

(d) Freedom in modulation—modulation being a factor in the old conception of form;

(e) Increase in the number and variety of rhythms, from which element comes life in the sense of movement or action, as illustrated in the peculiarly propulsive effect of syncopation.

(f) Adoption of poetical conceits as underlying and determining factors of the composition, either as a starting-point for the creative imagination of the composer or the recreative imagination of the performer and ultimately the receptive mood of the hearer.

All these things are summed up in the axiom that in romantic compositions matter determines manner, content the dimensions and shape of the vessel. They might exist in a greater or lesser degree in music which is properly called classic, or music which, for want of the quality of beauty, is not entitled to either of the epithets which we are applying. Hence it is that here, as in the appreciation of music generally, personal equation enters so largely and definitively. Each individual must for himself recognize the existence of what Rubinstein called the "soul" which came into the art with Beethoven, and the propriety and effectiveness of the habiliments with which in each case it has been clothed.

The names of the High Priests in the Temple of Music are to its votaries sources of spiritual refreshment and inspiration. Those who bore them seem ever near us. Though they have passed away, their lives are still intertwined with ours. We think of Bach, and admiration surges up within us for the greatest representative of musical science that the world has ever known—a myriad-minded artist to whom its severest laws were the most natural vehicles for the expression of a soaring imagination; a tender, simple, devout, domestic man, yet the repository of all the music that had been before him and the fountain-head of all that was to come. We think of Haydn, and our room is at once sunlit and "out-doorsy," a world full of cheer and happy laughter; of Mozart, and a lambent flame of divinity appears to us, playing about one of earth's most gifted children, inspiring him to utterances which now search our souls to their depths, and anon fill us with an uplifting sense of the delight of living; of Beethoven, and our voices sink into the key which publishes awe and reverence, for his is the Ineffable Name. We think of Schubert and our heart-strings grow tense; something draws out our affections with a warm embrace; now we not only marvel, respect, and admire, we also love. His music is the most lovable of all. Not all of it; only the best, and of the best unfortunately the smallest portion is in the music which he wrote for the pianoforte. Two great symphonies (one a torso so perfect in its incompleteness, like the Venus of Milo, that we are unwilling to think of it otherwise than as it is), a grand mass, a string quartet (that in D minor), a quintet for pianoforte and strings, a fantasia for pianoforte (which the present generation of concert-goers knows only as a concerto with orchestra into which it was expanded by Liszt), and songs numbering hundreds—these are the works upon which the great fame of Franz Schubert rests. The remainder of the legacy is touched with mortality. Melody is the life-blood with which these works pulsate, and the source from which it flows was finite only because his physical life was bounded by years. His soul was lyrical. His symphony in C sings on and on in an ecstasy of loveliness, until we feel its only imperfection in its excess. He gave too lavishly always to give wisely, for moderation must enter into all things, even into beauty. He was too prolific to be critical or even judicious. Variations on melodies which he had conceived for songs make up the slow movements of two of the compositions set down here among his masterpieces—the String Quartet in D minor and the Pianoforte Fantasia in C. The Adonic metre which flows through the Impromptu in B-flat (one of the few pianoforte pieces still to be heard in the concert-room) runs through the slow movement of his String Quartet in A major, in the theme of the variations of his String Quartet in D minor (the song "Tod und das Mädchen"), in one number of his between-acts music to "Rosamunde," and several of his songs, the finest illustration being the cradle-song beginning, "Wie sich die Äuglein." (Its gentle beat is heard throughout the *Allegretto* of Beethoven's Symphony in A.) The song "Der Wanderer" supplies the theme of the variations in the Fantasia; "Die Forelle" that of the Quintet with double-bass. On the melody of "Trockene Blumen" (of the "Müllerlieder") he wrote variations for pianoforte and flute.

The list of pianoforte pieces composed by Schubert (1797–1828) comprises seventy-three titles, the majority made up of groups of small pieces, scores of them dances of no significance in pianoforte literature. There are eleven solo sonatas, and a fragment of a sonata which L. Stark completed for publication; two sets of impromptus; a set of short pieces called "Momens Musicals" which, with some of the impromptus, are the shining gems of the entire collection; a fantasia in C (Op. 15), many marches and divertimenti, overtures, polonaises, and rondos for four hands, some of them of high importance in their department. His chamber music, in which the pianoforte is combined with other instruments, consists of a

quintet (Op. 14), two trios with violin and violoncello, a "Rondeau brilliant" with violin, three
sonatinas with violin, a fantasia with violin, a
sonata with violin, an introduction and variations
for flute, and a sonata with arpeggione, the last
written for the inventor of the instrument, which
was of the viol kind, with six strings and a body
and fretted fingerboard like those of a guitar.

There is a great wealth of melodic inventiveness
in the sonatas, but also excess of injudicious passage-
work in the development portion. Through the
decades Schubert-lovers among the pianists have
tried to habilitate them in the concert-room, but in
vain. They fail to satisfy the lover of technique,
and, despite their occasional moments of poetical
charm, they weary the cultured lover because of
their *remplissage*. Schubert's nature was too un-
critical to win success in the larger and higher
forms. This is not said in disparagement of the
small forms in which he was at his greatest, but in
justice to the masters in all forms. There is nothing more foolish in modern criticism than the disposition of unthinking admirers of composers like
Chopin and Grieg 'to depreciate the large forms
because Chopin and Grieg were not so successful
in them as they were in smaller or small forms, to
which the bent of their genius inclined them. As
if the great cathedrals were less magnificent and
beautiful because the Taj Mehal is lovely!

FRANÇOIS FRÉDÉRIC CHOPIN.

We have seen that Liszt credited Field with being the first composer who introduced a genre in pianoforte music "in which sentiment and song were absolutely dominant . . . free from the slack of an imposed form." Except for the want of seriousness in content I do not see why Beethoven's "Bagatelles" should not have precedence in history over Field's "Nocturnes." The latter, however, were contemporaneous in publication with Schubert's "Impromptus" and "Momens Musicals," which are the most perfect of that composer's pianoforte utterances. "Schubert's greatest achievement," says Dr. Bie, "was the 'Momens Musicals,' which appeared in 1828, the year of his death. The first of these is a naturalistic, free musical expatiation; the second, a gentle movement in A-flat major; the third, the well-known F minor dance—in which a dance became a penetrating and sorrow-laden tongue; the fourth, the Bach-like C-sharp minor Moderato, with its placid middle section in D-flat major; the fifth, a fantastic march with a sharply cut rhythm, and the sixth, perhaps Schubert's most profound pianoforte piece, that revery in still chords which only once are more violently shaken in order to lull us to sleep with its pensive and dainty sorrow, its delicate connections, its singing imitations, its magic enharmonics, and its sweet melodies rising like flowers from the soft ground. The close of the trio in the style of a popular chorale, with its harmonization in thirds, is (like many of his harmonic passages in octaves or sixths) exceedingly characteristic of the popular nature of Schubert's music."

One who loved Schubert ardently, in whom the romantic spirit burst into unparalleled efflorescence, and who represents it with more varied eloquence than any of his contemporaries or all of them combined, was Robert Schumann (1810–1856). "What he did to develop the expressive power of the pianoforte is all his own," says Richard Aldrich (in "The Musical Guide," edited by Rupert Hughes). "He wrote for the instrument in a new way, calling for new and elaborate advances in technique—not the brilliant finger dexterity of Chopin and Liszt, but a deeper underlying potency of expression through interlacing parts, skilfully disposed harmonies, the inner voices of chords, and through new demands as to variety of tone quality, contrasts of color, and the enrichment of the whole through pedal effects. It has been called a crabbed style, but it is no less idiomatic of the piano than the more open and brilliant manner that was developed at the same period by the virtuoso school of piano-playing and composition." Schumann's music is admirable as that of Beethoven is, because of its excellence as music irrespective of the vehicle chosen for its exposition. Yet, like Beethoven, he put a greater eloquence into the tones of the instrument than did the virtuosi who called forth the critical wrath of his Davidites, or even Chopin, whose unique genius he so generously praised. He was the ideal representative of romanticism in every one of its aspects. He turned the fantastics and the whimsicalities of E. T. A. Hoffman and Jean Paul Friedrich Richter into instrumental song, and wove their parti-colored threads into his polyphony. He remains, after half a century, the foremost representative of idealized programme music; proclaiming not things, but the moods and essences of things, applying titles which do not weight the fancy, but lift it into a buoyant atmosphere, removing all fetters of soul and mind, pointing the way in all directions except those which lead to the realm of the ignoble and the ugly. The most perfectly emancipated of all the tone-poets after Beethoven, the one in whom intellect and the emotions were most equably poised, and a priest in the Temple of the Beautiful who held his duty sacred. To her who became his wife Schumann wrote: "Everything touches me that goes on in the world—politics, literature, people. I think after my own fashion of everything that can express itself through music or can escape by means of it. This is why many of my compositions are so hard to understand—because they are bound up with my remote associations and often very much so, because everything of importance in the time takes hold of me, and I must express it in musical form. And this, too, is why so few compositions satisfy my mind—because, aside from all defects in craftsmanship, the ideas themselves are often on a low plane and their expression is often commonplace." To such a man music could not be mere "lascivious pleasings." It was a language to be used in the service of the true, the beautiful, and the good. Its utterances he believed might be helped along by verbal suggestion in the shape of a title; but he was far from believing that the title or its literary suggestion entered into the quality of the music itself. His creed on the subject of programme music was as brief as it was clear and comprehensive; a title might help to appreciation by stimulating thought and the fancy; it could not help poor music and would not mar good; but music which required it was in a sorry case.

The catalogues of Schumann's works show forty pieces for pianoforte solo, four for four hands, one for two pianofortes, three for pianoforte and orchestra, and twelve for chamber music in which the instrument is consorted with others. All of his numbered compositions from Op. 1 to Op. 23 are for the pianoforte and the majority of his works in this class are what I have called idealized programme music, whether or not the fact be indicated by a title. The "Carnaval," which lives in loving company with Beethoven's Diabelli variations, as well as Schumann's "Études symphoniques," presents the picture of a masquerade with the familiar figures of *Pierrot, Harlequin, Pantaloon,* and *Columbine,* associating with real persons like Clara Wieck (*Chiarina*), Chopin, Ernestine von Fricken (*Estrella*), and Paganini (all indicated by imitations of their musical styles), creatures of Schumann's poetic fancy, *Eusebius, Florestan,* the *Davidites,* and the *Philistines,* these last being the hurdy-gurdy virtuosi of the period. In a letter to Moscheles, written in 1837, Schumann told the story of the composition in brief and furnished a hint at his purposes. He says: "'The Carnaval' was written for an occasion, and is for the most part and with the exception of three or four movements entirely upon the notes A, S, C, H, which spell the name of a little Bohemian town where I had a musical friend, but which also, strange to say, are the only musical letters in my name. The titles I added afterward. Is not music always sufficient unto itself and does it not speak for itself?"

Eusebius and *Florestan* were names invented by Schumann to embody the two contrasting temperaments in his own nature. Their fanciful holders were members of the society of *Davidites,* which existed only in Schumann's mind, but who labored in his compositions as well as his criticisms to destroy the *Philistines* in art. The two are the ostensible authors of Schumann's first sonata (in F-sharp minor), in which we recognize music that is not only programmatic but also biographic. *Florestan* is all energy, passion, and eager fancy; *Eusebius* is the personification of simplicity, tenderness, and dreamy mysticism. Schumann had recognized the habitation within himself of these antagonistic elements long before he thought of giving them existence on a title-page or in his journal. Writing from Milan to a friend in 1829, he said: "For several weeks, or, rather, always, I have seemed to myself entirely poor or entirely rich, utterly feeble and utterly strong, decrepit, and yet full of life." It must have been because he recognized how completely he had given expression to this quality of feeling in his sonata that he conceived the idea of putting it forth, not as the composition of Robert Schumann, but of "Florestan and Eusebius," who had already met *Chiarina*, to whom the sonata is dedicated under her real name in the "Carnaval." We recognize the gentle *Eusebius* in the introduction of the sonata, with its sweetness and love; in the second melody of the first movement proper, and the aria, which is borne up as on angels' wings, while the *Florestan* ranges through every strong measure of the *Allegro vivace*, consistently dealing his rhythmical blows.

It was Schumann's manner to compose a piece of music, or a set of pieces, under the influence of emotions aroused by his own experiences or the reading of his favorite authors, and when all was

The Romantic School

finished to invent a title which should be characteristic and give a hint at the poetic contents of the
music. It frequently happened that years elapsed
between the writing of a work and its publication,
and during this time it continually occupied his
mind and became associated with many notions
which had nothing to do with it in the beginning.
The Fantasia in C (Op. 17) is a case in point. In
several letters written two years after the composition of the work he plainly indicates that the inspiration of its first movement, at least, was his love
for Clara Wieck and the misery which grew out of
her father's opposition to their marriage. In one
letter he says to Clara: "The first movement is
perhaps the most passionate thing I have written";
in another: "The first movement is a deep lamentation over you"; in another: "You can only understand the Fantasia if you shall think yourself back
in the unhappy summer of 1836, when I gave you
up." It may have been this last reflection which
suggested the superscription, "Ruins," which he
gave to the first movement after he had decided to
make a gift of the composition to the Beethoven
monument fund at Bonn. When the work was
printed this superscription (together with "Triumphal Arch" and "Constellation," which he had
in mind for the other movements) was abandoned
and the simple title "Fantasia" was supplemented
by a motto from Schlegel.

A letter to Clara Wieck, written a few months after he had composed the "Nachtstücke" (Op. 23), furnishes an interesting bit of evidence of the manner in which he hunted for illuminative superscriptions. The piece had not been given to the printer, and he was anxious to indulge his fancy for programmatic titles. So he writes: "I have quite arranged the 'Nachtstücke'—what do you think of calling them: No. I 'Trauerzug'; No. II, 'Kuriose Gesellschaft'; No. III, 'Nächtliches Gelage'; No. IV, 'Rundgesang mit Solostimmen'?" Here we see a hint at the contents of each of the first three pieces in the set, but only a fanciful title suggested by its structural form for the last. The first title is explained by the fact that while engaged upon the first nocturne he was oppressed by a presentiment. "While I was composing I kept seeing funerals, coffins, and unhappy, despairing faces; and when I had finished and was trying to think of a title the only one that occurred to me was 'Leichenfantasie' ('Funeral Fantasia'). I was so much moved over the composition that the tears came into my eyes, and yet I did not know why, and there seemed to be no reason for it. Then came Therese's letter, and everything was at once explained." The explanation lay in the fact that his brother Edward was dying.

Not only his devotion to form but his consummate mastery of it has marred the excellence of

Felix Mendelssohn (1809–1847) in the eyes of the self-elected champions of progress since his death, nearly two generations ago. Perfection in a god is tolerable, but in a mere human artist contemplation of it becomes a vexation and weariness of the flesh. In his lifetime Mendelssohn was idolized; after he was dead he was overwhelmed with critical contumely. Now, despite the irreverence of the age, the divine light is again recognized in his countenance. Reformers and revolutionists are prone to be image-breakers. It is more difficult for artists who are impressionists, because they lack the skill to be anything else, to admire impeccable perfection in execution, than for those whose impressionism is a fulfilment of all their desires.

Mendelssohn brought no sword into the world; he was a reformer of taste, but not a revolutionist. There is not a word in the technical vocabulary of pianoforte music which traces its origin to him. To the romantic content of music he added little more than a form and an idiom; and because the form was degraded to a formula by himself and his imitators and the idiom overworked, their value soon came to be underestimated. "It is a pity," said Rubinstein to his pupils at the Imperial Conservatory in St. Petersburg, "that I am to play Mendelssohn to you after Weber. If I had played him after Herz you would better understand why we must think of him so highly." The point was well taken. It is also something of a pity that in this discussion I have placed Schumann before him; but it was done so that I might the quicker reach the heart of this phase of our study. In reading a book one may, if he wishes, turn back and reread an earlier page, while at a recital one can revert to what has been done only by appeal to memory and the imagination.

Mendelssohn's life was contemporary with Schumann's, though its artistic activities began as many years earlier than his as they ended. He, too, made war on the Philistines, though his was the *suaviter in modo* rather than the *fortiter in re* of his friend and admirer. Herz and Kalkbrenner, Dreyschock and Liszt, yes, even Liszt, were filling the salons of Paris with the jingles of operatic fantasias while Mendelssohn in Germany and England was turning the minds of amateurs to a purer taste by compositions which combined perfection of form with marvellous clarity, purity, and unity of style, masterly counterpoint, graceful melody, euphony, and brilliancy. It is easy to smile at the mushy sentimentalism of the majority of the "Songs Without Words" now, but think of them back in their historical environment and you will not withhold from them honor due. How hackneyed are the "Spinning Song" and the "Hunting," "Spring," and "Gondolier" songs; but give your imagination a little flight: Mendelssohn sits playing them

in Leipsic, Berlin, or London, while in a whited
sepulchre in Paris Herz's pianoforte scintillates
with scales, arpeggios, trills, and pretty *broderies*
above, below, and around melodic echoes of Rossini
and Bellini and Donizetti. How do the "Songs
Without Words" sound now? Pianistic babes and
sucklings have mastered their difficulties long ago,
but virtuosi who think seriously of their art still
play them in public, and we must not think it is
only to ingratiate themselves with boarding-school
misses.

So much for Mendelssohn's most marked contribution to pianoforte literature in the department of form; as for the fairy idiom of his scherzos,
though it, too, has been greatly abused, by him as
well as his successors, it was an inspiration straight
from the world of sunshine and happiness in which
Mendelssohn lived and moved and had his being;
and it is as substantial and beautiful a contribution to the language of music as the plangent tone
of Chopin's nocturnes even to-day. It was not in
vain that Mendelssohn's mother named him Felix,
and we should not repine that there was no tragedy
in his life which he found it necessary to proclaim.
It is a singular fact that this idiom fell into the mind
of the glorious boy when he wrote his overture to
"A Midsummer Night's Dream" in the same year
in which Weber, sinking pain-racked into his grave,
found appropriate and similar delineation for his

fairy-folk in "Oberon." It proved to be service-able in many instrumental forms, and though it has been much abused, its charm remains perennial.

Mendelssohn's pieces for pianoforte solo num-ber a round hundred, nearly half of them "Songs Without Words," a too convenient and appealing appellation. There are three sonatas, but they do not mark high water; that is done by the "Varia-tions sérieuses," which even Dr. Bie, who is sar-castic and contemptuous because of the compos-er's too persistent perfection of utterance, says are "without a suspicion of triviality and filled with in-tellectual lines and harmonies—a splendid struct-ure," though he thinks that "they rest on all sides on Schumann." To him the "Songs Without Words" are "folksongs in evening dress." In illus-tration of what he considered the best in Men-delssohn as regards artistic content Rubinstein se-lected the third fugue, the first, third, seventh, seventeenth, twenty-second, twenty-third, and twenty-seventh "Songs Without Words," the "Ve-netian Gondolier's Song," and the "Variations sérieuses"; for his technical significance the "Ca-priccio" in F-sharp minor, "Rondo capriccioso," Scherzo in E minor, Fantasia in F minor, Étude in F, and the "Scherzo capriccio," which last he held to be the most valuable and individually char-acteristic of all of Mendelssohn's pianoforte pieces. For four hands he wrote an "Allegro brillante" and a "Duo concertante" (variations on the march in "Preciosa")—the latter with Moscheles. In the department of chamber music Mendelssohn wrote two sonatas for painoforte and violoncello, and one sonata for pianoforte and violin; "Variations concertantes" for pianoforte and violoncello; two trios, and a sextet for pianoforte and strings; a "Song Without Words" for pianoforte and violoncello, and a piece called "The Evening Bell" for pianoforte and harp, the bell in question being that of Atwood's gate. He joined the pianoforte with the orchestra in two concertos, a "Capriccio brillante," a rondo, and a "Serenade and Allegro giojoso." All of these were concert-room hobbies in the heyday of the composer's popularity, the vogue of the Concerto in G minor being so great as to provoke Berlioz's amusing skit in which he tells how the pianoforte at the Conservatoire at an examination of pupils began at last to play the concerto of itself at the mere approach of a pupil, and the hammers continued jumping about even after the instrument had been demolished and thrown out of the window.

If I were to consult only my own mental comfort I should omit all except a mere mention of him here and classify Frédéric François Chopin (1810–1849) with the representatives of national schools of composition in the next chapter; but he has so long been held up as an arch romanticist that such a step might prove disturbing. Chopin stands alone in musical history. Albert Lavignac in his "Music and Musicians" says: "Although France was the country of his adoption, and, indeed, his family were of French origin, I do not hesitate to class him by reason of his affinities in the romantic school of Germany." James Huneker says he remained aloof from the romanticists, "though in a sympathetic attitude," and was "a classic without knowing it," but immediately attributes to him one of the qualities which I have been pleased to think are determinative of romanticism: "With Chopin form was conditioned by the idea. He took up the dancing patterns of Poland because they suited his inner life." If these principles are dominant in his music then Chopin is a romanticist, though a national romanticist because of his use of folksong idioms, as we shall see hereafter. Then, too, we should find him well consorted in this chapter with Mendelssohn because of their common love for architectural symmetry, their attitude toward programme music, and their devotion to beauty, a quality which they impressed upon even the most native and characteristic of their utterances. Adherence to architectural structure was forced upon him by his adoption of dance forms for so many of his compositions; but he made free with form in the conception which is foremost in the mind of the pedagogue—the relative distribution of keys in a composition; and, therefore, if he was a classicist in one sense, he was a romantic-classicist, as Bach was at times, and Beethoven always.

Thus do our definitions rise up and seemingly try to plague us. But we shall not permit them to do so. They are, at least, like some of the so-called scientific laws, "good working hypotheses."

We are not yet at the end of the Chopin paradox. If it is difficult to deduce his artistic creed from his works it is impossible to do so from what we know of his musical predilections. He admired Mozart, but disliked Schubert; thought Weber's pianoforte music too operatic; seems to have believed that Beethoven's greatness was largely summed up in the C-sharp minor Sonata, and that Schumann's music (the "Carnaval," at any rate) was scarcely music at all. This apparently bears out Mr. Huneker's contention that he was unconsciously a classicist. But Chopin is a sentimentalist, despite the fact that some virtuosi have tried to make him appear otherwise by strenuous playing of his works; and how can one who is devoted to sentimental utterance be at heart a classicist? Dull a classicist might be, commonplace, monotonous, and uninspired; but a morbid publisher of poppy and mandragora, never. And Chopin is morbid, despite the fact that Schumann declared him to be "the boldest, the proudest soul of the time." Mendelssohn, with a calmer view than Schumann, thought his playing "a little infected by the Parisian mania for despondency and straining for emotional vehemence."

I do not know that Mr. John F. Runciman, who says many things only to startle his readers, ought to count when he classes Chopin among the "inheritors of rickets and exhausted physical frames"; but he has many among the composer's admirers who believe with him that his music is "sick, unhealthy music." Dr. Niecks, his greatest biographer, confesses that there is seductive poison in the nocturnes, and prescribes Bach and Beethoven as antidotes. Heinrich Pudor is a greater extremist than Runciman, one who affects at least to despise all modern tendencies. "No less decadent," he writes, the reference being to Wagner and Liszt, "is Chopin, whose figure comes before one as flesh without bones—this morbid, womanish, slipslop, powerless, sickly, bleached, sweet-caramel Pole." Dr. Bie is more discriminating. An enthusiastic admirer of Chopin's music, he yet utters a protest against putting it in the hands of the young.

We know that the extreme of culture is closely allied to decay, for perfect ripeness is but the foreboding of corruption. Children, of course, do not know this, and Chopin himself would have been much too noble ever to lay bare his mental sickness to the world, and his greatness lies precisely in this: that he preserves the mean between immaturity and decay.

His greatness is his aristocracy. He stands among musicians in his faultless vesture a noble from head to foot. The sublimest emotions toward whose refinement whole generations had tended, the last things in our soul whose foreboding is interwoven with the mystery of judgment day, have in his music found their form.

This is rather extravagant, but Chopin enthusiasts are prone to hyperbole, and as we have permitted Runciman and Pudor to have their say we can only in justice give the other side a hearing. Thus Huneker:[1]

Chopin neither preaches nor paints, yet his art is decorative and dramatic—though in the climate of the ideal. He touches earth and its emotional issues in Poland only; otherwise his music is a pure æsthetic delight, an artistic enchantment, freighted with no ethical or theatric messages. It is poetry made audible, the "soul written in sound."

Rubinstein:

The piano bard, the piano rhapsodist, the piano mind, the piano soul is Chopin. Tragic, romantic, lyric, heroic, dramatic, fantastic, soulful, sweet, dreamy, brilliant, grand, simple—all possible expressions are found in his compositions and all are sung by him upon his instrument.

And Tappert:

If ever a composer deserved the title tone-poet, it was Chopin. He set chords to vibrating which had never been

---

[1] "Chopin, the Man and His Music," p. 116.

touched before, and have not been touched since. He asked little about rule and formula, and what he learned is of minor importance in his works. He dipped his transporting melodies and harmonic combinations out of an original and brimming fountain of invention. Unlettered in the sense of any particular pedagogic tendency, he handles his natural gifts with the utmost freedom. In the matter of the pianoforte, its technic, and all that relates to the two, Chopin must be set down as the greatest and most skilful genius. Even the tiniest leaf of his graceful arabesques can be traced from a poetic impulse. He never aimed merely at vain bravura. . . . The once homeless stranger has everywhere found a home. In life the suffering exile won a crown of thorns; a grateful posterity crowned him with laurel. He passed into the land of eternal harmony. He came, charmed, and—died!

Like many of the virtuosi-composers who preceded him, Chopin wrote almost exclusively for the pianoforte. Among his compositions are seventeen settings of Polish poems for voice and pianoforte, and these, together with five works for pianoforte and orchestra, four chamber pieces in which the instrument is used in combination with strings, and a rondo for four hands, make up the sum of his compositions which are not pianoforte solos. The entire list of published works, including a polonaise of doubtful authenticity, numbers close on to two hundred. For pianoforte and orchestra there are two concertos, a "Fantasia on Polish airs," a "Krakowiak," and a set of variations; for pianoforte and violoncello a sonata, an "Introduction and Polonaise," and a "Grand Duo Concertanto" on a Theme from "Robert le Diable." His solos embrace 56 Mazurkas, 27 Études, 25 Preludes, 19 Nocturnes, 15 Waltzes, 13 Polonaises, 4 Rondos, 4 Ballades, 4 Scherzos, 3 Sonatas, 3 Impromptus, 3 Ecossaises, 3 sets of Variations, 2 Fantasias, 1 Tarantelle, 1 Berceuse, 1 Barcarolle, 1 "Concert Allegro," 1 "Marche funébre," and 1 Bolero.

Though some of the most friendly analysts of Chopin's music have fallen foul of his two concertos and denied them a place among his greatest and most characteristic works, both have maintained a place in the active lists of concert pianists for two generations. If Chopin's genius were generally recognized as the loftiest that his century saw in music, this fact would not be calculated to cause so much wonder. Then his concertos would themselves create the standard by which they would have to be judged, and one might think them inferior to all his other compositions and still hold them to be without a rival so far as the concertos of others are concerned. But that is not the case, and the admiration and love with which they are regarded, though confessedly faulty, is a beautiful tribute to their winsomeness and subtle charm. They date back to the early manhood of the composer, having been composed in the reverse order of their publication when he was still in Warsaw and before he had won fame outside of his native land. Yet they are full of the unmistakable individuality of his genius, not only in the exquisite gracefulness of the figuration and melodic ornament, but also in the character of the melodies themselves. This is particularly true of the slow movement of the second concerto (in F minor), which is the imperishable monument which the composer reared to an early love, that for Constantina Gladkowska, a singer. A great drawback to the popularity of the concertos has been found in the ineffectiveness of their orchestral parts; wherefore these have been rewritten— whether successfully or not critical opinion has not yet determined. It was Mr. Edward Dannreuther's opinion that the concertos were most effective when played on two pianofortes.

The Études have a purpose indicated by their title, which is to develop the technique of pianoforte playing along the line of the composer's discoveries—his method of playing extended arpeggios, contrasted rhythms, progressions in thirds, octaves, etc.—but some of them breathe poetry and even passion. The title "Préludes" can scarcely be considered as more than a makeshift, adopted in default of a better one. It indicates nothing of the character of the pieces which have aptly been compared to sketches in an artist's portfolio—notes, memoranda, impressions, studies in color, light and shade, contrasts and contours. Schumann said of them: "They are sketches, beginnings of studies, or, if you will, ruins, single eagle-wings, all strangely mixed together." Some of the most strikingly beautiful of the composer's inspirations are gathered under this head in Op. 28. The prototypes of the Nocturnes, dreamy, contemplative, even elegiac pieces, we have met in the principal compositions of John Field. The term "Ballade," however, is an invention of Chopin's, who applied it to four compositions written between 1836 and 1843. These works have in common that they are written in triple time and belong to the composer's finest inspirations. Schumann said on the authority of Chopin himself that they were prompted by Mickiewicz's poems, and that a poet might easily write words to them. They are moody and passionate, and may be said to have correspondence with Schumann's "Noveletten" and Liszt's "Sonnets." Byron could find no good in a waltz, which was to him only "a damned seesaw, up and down sort of tune." Evidently he knew only the poorest waltzes of the ball-room, or was, like Lamb, organically unmusical. Chopin's waltzes are salon music of an aristocratic kind. Ehlert called them "dances of the soul, not of the body," and Schumann, in his guise of *Florestan*, declared that he could not play the one in A-flat for a dance unless at least half of the women dancers were countesses.

The term "scherzo" which Chopin gave to four of his compositions has struck some writers as being just as arbitrary as prélude and nocturne, and even more anomalous. "How is gravity to clothe itself if jest goes about in dark veils?" asked Schumann, commenting on the first scherzo. We have since learned, as Schumann might have learned from Beethoven, that the emotional content of a symphonic scherzo need not always be jocose; that the term, indeed, may sometimes stand only for the form of a composition. There is more madness than merriment, more tragedy than comedy, in the forced and desperate gayety of many Slavic scherzos, and the struggle between the human and the divine which is reflected in Beethoven's C minor symphony is carried on as grimly in the third movement as in the first, yet, though Beethoven scrupled to call it such, that third movement is a scherzo.

The few attempts which Chopin made to express himself in the larger forms all appear to be more or less desultory. They are offshoots from the general tendency of his genius. It is plain that he did not move without constraint in the sonata form, and that he could not always find in it characteristic and unembarrassed expression. For this reason there has been considerable discussion over the merits and demerits of the sonatas in B minor and B-flat minor; the one in C minor being universally admitted to be inferior. Schumann and Liszt, both admirers of Chopin, felt constrained to pronounce against the works. But whatever may be said in criticism of them on the score of their deficiencies in form and lack of unity, the opulence and beauty of their musical ideas have argued irresistibly in their behalf, and they are played as much to-day as ever they were, if not more.

This must suffice for Chopin here; some remarks on his national dances, mazurka and polonaise, may be reserved for the next chapter. Between him and the last of the really great composers there do not stand many to detain us. On one only would I like to dwell if space permitted. This is Stephen Heller (1815–1888), a musician of rare elegance and distinction, as truly a *Tondichter* as contradistinguished from a *Tonsetzer* as was Chopin. He, too, though not a Frenchman, made his home in Paris, much to the regret of Schumann, who had hailed his coming as he had hailed Chopin's, and who feared the influence of French art and life on the young Bohemian. But Heller, though he lived fifty years among the French, was not of the French. Devoted to the smaller lyric forms, he never became a salon composer in the popular sense. He wished to extend his literary and historical studies, and to that end found Paris propitious. He had started out as a virtuoso, but nervousness prevented him from pursuing the career. He taught, wrote essays for the "Gazette musicale," and composed. He wrote studies, eclogues, fantasies, caprices, ballades, and dances, besides a set of delightful effusions which are called "Flower, Fruit, and Thorn

Pieces" (after Jean Paul's book) in Germany, but for which no better title could be found in French than "Restless Nights" (*Nuits blanches*). Fickle taste has dallied with many an idol since Heller's first pieces came to charm, but he has remained the admiration of musicians. Chopin's waltzes seem to be for that society of which Heller said that the higher you went in it the denser was the ignorance which you found. Heller's waltzes are reflective, introspective, "physiognomical," as Louis Köhler wrote in 1879. They may not be waltzes to be danced, but they are at least dances to be felt and brooded over. His studies are less for the fingers than for the heart and mind. They inculcate music in its ethereal essence rather than its mechanical manifestations. Like the "Blumen, Frucht, und Dornenstücke," they are proclamations of moods— moods dreamy, fantastic, aerial, *riant*, defiant, inert, leaden, perverse, like those which possessed the creatures of Jean Paul Friedrich Richter's fecund fancy.

Adolf Henselt (1814–1885) wrote in a brilliant style and with a nobility suggestive of Chopin. He was poetical even in his Études, one of which ("If I were a Bird") won a place in the concert-room which it still holds, as does his dashing and grandiose concerto in F minor. Henselt was a pupil of Hummel for eight months as a lad, and spent the last fifty years of his life in St. Petersburg.

William Sterndale Bennett (1816–1875) was an ingratiating echo of Mendelssohn in his native England. He wrote among other things for the pianoforte four concertos, a fantasia with orchestra, a trio, and a sonata in F minor. Schumann dedicated his "Études symphoniques" to him. Bennett was in Leipsic when the work was composed, and Schumann, in a letter to his sister, wrote of him that he was "a glorious artist and a lovely poet soul." To make the tribute which he wished to pay as beautiful and fragrant as possible, and at the same time a compliment to the English people, it has been said that Schumann abandoned the theme almost completely in the final variation (the march) and built up a new melody on the basis of a phrase from the romance which *Ivanhoe* sings in praise of Richard Cœur de Lion in Marschner's opera "Templar and Jewess." It is a pretty conceit that by quoting the first phrase of the romance in which England is enjoined to rejoice in the possession of so chivalric a king as Lionheart an allusion to Bennett was intended. I do not wish wholly to destroy it, but it is nevertheless true that Schumann's finale might easily have come into being had Marschner's melody never been written; and, indeed, by a device which is frequently employed in the course of the preceding variations—viz., that of inversion. It is no strain to fancy that Schumann conceived the beginning of his march melody only as an inversion and transposition into the major mode of the beginning of the theme of the entire composition.

Woldemar Bargiel (1828–1897) wrote one fantasia which he thought worthy of a dedication to his stepsister, Clara Schumann (he was the son of the divorced wife of Friedrich Wieck), and another which he inscribed to Johannes Brahms. Joachim Raff (1822–1882) is much better known as a symphonist than as a writer for the pianoforte, yet he wrote a concerto and a suite which were very popular in their day. The programmatic tendency illustrated in his orchestral compositions is also characteristic of some of his smaller pianoforte pieces.

Schumann's successors in all departments cultivated by him called themselves "new romanticists," and the movement which they represented received a tribute in the shape of an "Hommage au Néoromantisme" composed by Raff. Among them, though not admitted by the radicals, is Johannes Brahms (1833–1897), who provided the generation which is now passing away with the best music which came into its life in all fields except the operatic. Schumann greeted him at the beginning of his career in an essay ("Neue Bahnen") which might well have turned the head of any composer, even an older; but it left Brahms unspoiled. To Schumann the sonatas which the new-comer played for him sounded like "veiled symphonies," and the suggestion of an orchestral idiom marks his pianoforte pieces, as it does those of Beethoven and Schumann himself. Yet, like those giants, Brahms was profoundly interested in the technique of the instrument. Like them, too, he disclosed the dignity and profundity of his art in his variations. He gave his first public concert when a boy of fourteen, and though the affair had been arranged by his teacher to exploit his skill as a pianist the programme contained an original set of variations on a German folksong. Ever after, in all departments to which Brahms contributed, the old love for the form asserted itself. Prominent among his works are the variations on themes by Handel, Haydn, Paganini, and Schumann.

Brahms's genius was essentially Teutonic; he was, indeed, what Wagner imagined his Tannhäuser, "German from top to toe." His devotion to German ideals was exemplified in his rugged honesty, his sturdy yet tender affection, his contempt for affectation, his simplicity, and his candor, which frequently overstepped the line of demarcation between courtesy and rudeness. Like his revered models, he represented the element of both classicism and romanticism in their best estates; and like them, too, he raised his structures polyphonically. He was a master of form, but he moulded the form to suit the contents, and he left the vessel shapely and transparent. He wrote much for the pianoforte, but never carelessly.

Carelessness, indeed, was wholly foreign to his nature. From the beginning to the end of his career he exemplified the Horatian maxim and kept many of his works away from the public, not for nine years only, but forever. He wrote two concertos, three sonatas, five sets of variations, one scherzo, one ballade, and a large number of short pieces called variously rhapsodies, intermezzos, and caprices, and published in groups. His last publications were in this form. His chamber music consists of three trios, three quartets, and one quintet for pianoforte and strings, three sonatas with violin, two sonatas with violoncello, a trio with violin and horn, a trio with clarinet and violoncello, and a set of waltzes ("Liebeslieder") for two pianofortes and four solo voices.

XI

National Schools

THOUGH in a general way I have pursued a chronological course in these studies, I have not tied myself down to dates because, as I have intimated, dates do not mark clearly the progressive steps in art, science, or learning. Neither have I tried to mention all the pianoforte composers whose names have been written brightly on the roll of fame in the course of the last century and a quarter. These studies do not make up either a historical hand-book or a guide to pianoforte literature. If this had been their design I should now be scarcely at the beginning of my task instead of near the close. Never before was so much pianoforte music written as now; but, it must be added, never before was so little of the product of the day utilized by virtuosi. If, then, the apprehension touching the critical attitude of these writings at the end which I expressed in an earlier chapter should now be verified, I shall at least be able to shield myself behind the men whose business it is to stand between the creative artist and the public. If they are unwilling to play the pianoforte music composed by their contemporaries (they are always willing to play their own), why should I be bound to discuss it? I have been frank in all things heretofore; let me continue to be frank to the end of the book, and confess that I feel very little sympathetic interest in the compositions with which pianoforte literature is being extended in this latter day. Yet this is not because of an excessive conservatism of the kind which is willing to find beauty only in that which belongs to the days of old. Music is too young an art and its progress in some departments within the last generation or two has been too obvious to give color of truth to the assertion that its capabilities have been exhausted. Nor can it be said that the public is indifferent to the creations of the present. On the contrary, every novelty from a famous pen is scrutinized with almost feverish eagerness by concert players in the hope that it may prove good enough to be included in their repertories. Yet how small is the proportion of the music given out by the writers of to-day which takes hold upon the popular heart or finds an abiding place in the popular affections! A study of the programmes of a season's concerts in New York which I made some years ago (there has been no change in conditions since, except that Brahms has died) disclosed that out of 256 miscellaneous pianoforte compositions played (concertos and sonatas being excluded) more than two-thirds were the works of masters of the past; and the remaining one-third included the productions of all living and local composers who in various ways, such as giving concerts of their own works, got their names in the list. The concertos played included practically every work of this class which has maintained itself in the concert-room, thus representing the survival of the fittest of a century's productions. Here is, however, a fact more significant still: sixteen of Beethoven's sonatas were played—a number several times greater than all the sonatas of other composers combined. Obviously, I am not alone in a want of sympathy with latter-day pianoforte compositions; it is shared by the pianists themselves.

Is there a lesson to be learned from this? I think so; but before I attempt to look for it let me draw a few other factors into the problem. Music, especially pianoforte music, was never so universally cultivated as now. Musical pedagogy never before reached the eminence which it occupies now. On its mechanical side it has profited by the patient plodding of centuries; on its intellectual it has benefited by the researches of wise men who have lifted some of the elements of interpretation almost to a science. Printed music was never so cheap as now. The pianoforte of to-day has many times the power and richness of tone of the instrument of fifty years ago. Science has lent its aid to make it an instrument capable of asserting itself against an orchestra of a hundred, and at the same time of giving voice to the tremulous and all but inaudible sigh. Why should not this be the Golden Age of pianoforte music?

First—Because it is not an artistic age in any sense. It is the age of science, politics, and commerce, the last activity determining the course and activities of the two others. It is an age shod with iron. The flowers of art do not and cannot spring up in its path. Indescribably brilliant, but hard and cruel, are the sparks which it strikes out in its thunderous progress. That is one reason. There is another, which is inherent in the development of music itself. Who it was that first made the observation I do not know, but it is an axiom that a period of highest technical achievement in art is contemporary with a period of decay in production; that is to say, the period of the mere virtuoso (and there are now virtuosi in the domain of composition) is not that of the creative artist. It is not difficult to find out some of the reasons why this should be so; a little hunting will discover them. But here is a hint as to the direction which the search may take: In old Greece when Pindar was alive and writing his odes in praise of the winners at the Pythian and Olympian games there was a flute-player, named Midas, who was one of those thus gloriously celebrated. But what feat of Midas's was it the record of which has come down to us with the tribute of Hellenic applause? At a certain concert, while playing, he lost the mouthpiece of his instrument, yet managed to finish the piece with great bravura without it. In Midas we have the prototype of the modern virtuoso, and in the Greeks who applauded him the prototype of the modern public, which in all the domains of art is more inclined to look at the manner than the matter, which comes into the concert-room to be astounded and bewildered by feats of skill rather than to enjoy music.

Interest is added to the compositions of a very considerable number of composers of the last half century by reason of the adoption by them of the idioms of the folkmusic of the peoples to which they belonged. These idioms are evidences of romanticism in two aspects—they have provided new contents as well as new forms to artistic music. They have also made possible the classification of composers and compositions into schools on lines which were unknown in the earlier history of the art. In the classical periods of operatic and church music the boundaries of so-called "schools" were composed of dates and the names of masters and the places of their principal activity. Composers and their pupils who congregated in Rome or Florence or Milan were described as representatives of the Roman, Florentine, or Milanese schools, notwithstanding that there was nothing in their music which belonged specifically to those musical capitals. For a long time, except as language and its influence upon melodic declamation modified the manifestations, there was no essential difference between Italian, French, and German opera. When national or historical subjects other than those drawn from antiquity came to be used it got to be the custom to speak of the products of the opera-houses in different political capitals as if they had patriotic significance; but as a matter of fact the musical integument was long the same whether the hero of an opera was called Alexander, Cyrus, Julius Cæsar, Charlemagne, or Gustavus Adolphus—whether the plot turned on a classic myth or a popular romance. The talk about national schools began when national subjects were chosen for operas, or titles drawn from the history, geography, literature, or folklore of a country were given to instrumental music of a descriptive or programmatic character. But the musical settings did not become "racy of the soil," as the phrase goes, until the influence of the German romantic school had made itself felt among the composers of other countries. Inasmuch, then, as composers for a while all drew their inspiration from Germany, their music had to wait until it occurred to them to go to the people's songs and dances for characteristic elements. There were sporadic cases of the use of national idioms in an earlier period, but they were not influential. Thus Beethoven used Russian melodies in two of the quartets which he composed for Count Rasoumowsky; Schubert's Op. 54 is a "Divertissement à la hongroise" for pianoforte, four hands; Haydn adapted Croatian melodies for his works, changing them to suit his purposes without giving them characteristic expression; Mozart, Beethoven, Weber, and others utilized local color borrowed from Oriental music—orchestral pieces which made large use of instruments of percussion, like cymbals, triangle, and large drum, being called "Janizary" or "Turkish" music. Mozart's "Turkish March" in the Sonata in A major, Beethoven's incidental music for "The Ruins of Athens," the tenor solo variation in the finale of the symphony in D minor, Weber's "Preciosa" and the overture to "Turandot" (built on a Chinese tune) are familiar examples.

In the sense which is to prevail in this chapter the first distinctive school in the field (all classicists belonging to the school universal) was the Scandinavian, the chief representatives of which are the Danes: J. P. E. Hartmann (1805–1900) and Niels W. Gade (1817–1890); the Norwegians: Halfdan Kjerulf (1815–1868), Johann Svendsen (1840–   ), Richard Nordraak (1842–1866), Edvard Grieg (1843–1907), and Christian Sinding (1856–   ); the Swedes: Ludwig Norman (1831–1885), J. A. Södermann (1832–1870), Andreas Hallén (1846–   ),

Emil Sjögren (1853–   ), and Wilhelm Stenhammar (1871–   ). The composers of Finland
are generally counted among the Scandinavians,
because Finland was completely under the influence of Sweden for over four hundred years,
but few of the elements of the ancient folkmusic of
the Finns (who are of Ugrian stock and more
closely connected in racial relationship with the
Hungarians than with the people of the Northland)
have got into artistic music, and in this study no
Finnish composer calls for mention, except, pos-
sibly, Jean Sibelius (1865–   ), whose most expressive instrument is the orchestra, though he has
written transcriptions of Finnish melodies for the
pianoforte.

In a general way all Scandinavian composers may
be described as romanticists, with a leaning toward
conservatism in the matter of form. Danish folk-
melodies were introduced into a Danish opera
("Elverhoe") by Kuhlau, a German, in 1828, but
little attention was paid to their idiom until after
A. P. Berggreen (1801–1880), who was one of
Gade's teachers, made his admirable collection of
folksongs. The "real founder of the national
Scandinavian school in the nineteenth century, the
creator of Danish romanticism," according to Dr.
Walter Niemann,[1] was J. P. E. Hartmann, a com-

[1] "Die Musik Scandinaviens," Leipsic, Breitkopf und Härtel,
1908.

poser of operas, dramatic overtures, and a ballet, "The Valkyria," besides a sonata, novelettes, studies, and caprices for the pianoforte. His successor in the leadership was Gade, who was also his son-in-law, the friend of Schumann and Mendelssohn, associate conductor with the latter in Leipsic and after his death long director of the Gewandhaus concerts. He wrote copiously symphonies, overtures (the "Nachklänge aus Ossian" is still a potent Bardic voice), and cantatas, but he is most specifically national in his pianoforte pieces, among which are "Norse Tone Pictures" and "Folk Dances." He dedicated a sonata in E minor to Liszt. Of recent years Ludvig Schytté (1848–) has composed some pieces with a pretty glitter. Halfdan Kjerulf, who opens the Norwegian list, was a gentle and tender lyrist in his pianoforte pieces as well as his songs. Edmund Neupert (1842–1888), to whom Grieg dedicated his pianoforte concerto, was an efficient propagandist for the music of his country, especially in America, where he spent a considerable portion of his life. Little importance attaches to the pianoforte music of Svendsen; and Nordraak, though he composed Norway's national hymn, acquires his chief significance from the influence which he exerted upon Grieg at a critical time in his life. It was a protest against Gade which put Grieg at the head of the Scandinavian school and gave it the individuality and potency which it now enjoys. In his early years Grieg had taken Gade for his model, but shortly after embarking on his artistic career he fell under the influence of Nordraak, a young musician of great talent and a Norwegian patriot of uncompromising aggressiveness. To Nordraak the nationalism of Gade seemed pallid and ineffective. It was too full of Mendelssohnian suavity. It is still possible for us to enjoy the gentle and poetic melancholy of Gade's B-flat symphony, which erstwhile awakened so much enthusiasm in Schumann; yet it must be confessed that it sounds archaic even by the side of Mendelssohn's "Scotch." But put aside modern ideals and there is a beauty in the gloom of the fjords and the shadows of the forests which pervade it and heighten the effect of the sunny delights which fell into its scherzo from the breezy mountain pastures; yet we can well understand how when Grieg, a Norwegian to the backbone (though of Scotch extraction on his father's side), acquired the needed degree of self-reliance, he resolved to be more truthful and less sophisticated than Gade had been. And so there crept out of his music some of its gentleness and mellifluous grace, and there stalked into it a strength, a grim vigor, and a sort of uncouthness which are native to the North and its people. Grieg's short mood pieces, far and away the best of his compositions, are in the key set by the North. By turns they depict the sadness and the boisterous humor natural to a people oppressed by the climatic rigors of the Scandinavian peninsula.

"Grieg is greatest in small things," says Dr. Niemenn, whose admiration is evidenced not only by the dedication to him of his book on Scandinavian music but also in the assertion that the Concerto in A minor is the most beautiful work of its kind since Schumann. "His ten books of Lyric Pieces," the same critic adds, "are the musical Testament of the Norway of the nineteenth century, the musical reflex of the land of the vikings, with its silent, light night, gilded by the midnight sun, its tempest-tossed coasts, its snow-covered highlands, lonely valleys, lakes, rivers, and innumerous cascades." The composer has suffered from the too extravagant praise of his friends, who have too persistently ignored the greater poetical tenderness of some of his Norse compatriots and the virility and broader vision of a composer like Christian Sinding. Grieg himself knew his limitations better than they and was frank in his confession of them. "Artists like Bach and Beethoven," he wrote, "erected churches and temples on the heights. I wanted, as Ibsen expresses it in one of his last dramas, to build dwellings for men in which they might feel at home and happy. In other words, I have recorded the folkmusic of my land. In style and form I have remained a German romanticist of the Schumann school; but at the same time I have dipped from the rich treasures of native folksong and sought to create a national art out of this hitherto unexploited emanation of the folksoul of Norway." Ole Olesen (1850–   ), who wrote the funeral march for Grieg, has written also a notable Suite for pianoforte and orchestra; and Agathe Backer-Gröndahl (1842–1899), even if she had not excited interest as a virtuoso and because she was a woman, would merit attention because of her "Romantische Stücke," dainty miniatures quite worthy of a place beside Grieg's instrumental lyrics.

Besides German influences, French and Italian have been at work in Sweden ever since music entered into its culture. The opera at Stockholm is still essentially an Italian institution. Nevertheless, K. Stenborg (1752–1813) introduced Swedish melodies into his operas, and the spirit of national music has been promoted by Norman, Södermann, Hallén, Sjögren, and Stenhammar. Sjögren's poetic fancy is gentle and refined and less robust than that exhibited by Stenhammar in his Concerto in B-flat.

Nine-tenths of the glory with which Polish music is surrounded shines from the name of Chopin; yet, though he has been held up persistently as a paragon among national composers, there is a point of view from which the musical expression of his patriotism might be questioned. The voice of the

Polish people is predominantly heroic, while Chopin's, though not without an infusion of healthy vigor and vivacity, is yet predominantly languid and melancholy. This trait in his music seems to me to be much more personal than national. It is not fair to the folkmusic of Poland, the expression of the people's heart, to make it responsible for the weak emotionalism which tinctures so many of Chopin's works, or for that feeling for which he could find no definition outside of the Polish word *zàl*, which, Liszt says, "means sadness, pain, sorrow, grief, trouble, repentance, etc." There is melancholy, indeed, in Polish folkmusic, and it would be impossible to avoid the effect of it while making such frequent use of the Oriental scale, with its augmented intervals, as the Polish folk-musicians did; but the spirit of Polish song speaks more truthfully in its characteristic rhythms than in its aberrations from the diatonic scale of Occidental music. Mr. Ignaz Jan Paderewski (1859–   ) is a truer musical patriot than Chopin, at least in one of the several contributions which he has made to national pianoforte music by his "Fantasie Polonaise" for pianoforte and orchestra. In Chopin's Mazurkas (of which he composed over half a hundred) we are compelled to hear a Parisian idealization of the characteristic Polish dance modulated to the key of the French salons. Mr. Paderewski is more democratic. In the second and last of the sections of his fantasia the people dance not in courtly but in peasant fashion; you hear the clatter of heavy soles and hobnails, as in the scherzo of the "Pastoral Symphony." A truer national voice is heard in Chopin's polonaises, where the form adapts itself better to proud and patriotic utterance. The polonaise was the stately dance of the Polish nobility full of gravity and courtliness, of "state and ancientry," more like a march or procession than a dance, resembling in this what the pavan must have been in its prime. The music now has an imposing and majestic rhythm in triple time, with a tendency to emphasis on the second beat of the measure and an occasional division of the first beat into two notes, with the stress of syncopation on the second, like the "Scotch snap," or the Hungarian *alla zoppa*. Mr. Paderewski has shown both learning and fine aptitude for the large and erudite forms in a sonata and his last set of variations, and his concerto is Polish to a degree.

A couple of concertos, like his symphony "Jeanne d'Arc" and his opera "Boabdil," speak of a longing for lofty flights on the part of Moritz Moszkowski (1854–   ), but his popularity among amateur pianists at least rests upon smaller things, like "Aus Allen Herren Landen," for pianoforte, four hands (in which national forms and styles are pleasingly imitated), the "Etincelles" and "Tarantelle." There is pronounced nationalism in the composi-

IGNAZ JAN PADEREWSKI.

tions of Philipp and Xaver Scharwenka (born respectively in 1847 and 1850). The latter has more closely identified himself with pianoforte music as performer and composer than his elder brother, who has devoted himself largely to teaching, and in composition has shown a predilection for the larger forms and apparatuses. Xaver Scharwenka has written four pianoforte concertos, two sonatas, and many smaller pieces, including some Polish dances.

Bohemia has a musical history which is quite as brilliant and remarkable as its literary, a love for music and aptitude in its practice seeming to be the birthright of every son of the country, be he German or Czech. For over two centuries some of the leading musicians of Europe, composers as well as performers, have come out of Bohemia. Notice must be taken of such a list as Gyrowetz (1763–1850), Vanhal (already mentioned with other compatriots), Dyonysius Weber (1766–1842), Wranitzky (1756–1808), Duschek (1736–1799), Dreyschock (to whom we shall recur when we reach the study of the virtuosi), Kalliwoda (1801–1866), the Benda family, especially Georg (1722–1795), Stamitz (1717–1761), Bendl (1838–1897), Škroup (1801–1862), Smetana (1824–1884), Dvořák (1841–1904), and Fibich (1850–1900). Not all of these men have significance in the history of pianoforte music, but Antonin Dvořák made notable contributions to the chamber music field with his quartet and quintet for pianoforte and strings, wrote a pianoforte concerto which deserves more attention than it has received from pianists, and enriched the literature of the instruments with two forms drawn from the folkmusic of his native land—the *Dumka*, of an elegiac character, and the *Furiant*, a wild scherzo.

The name of Franz Liszt (1811–1886) looms large in the annals of the pianoforte and its music. His playing established the modern cult as well as the modern technical system, bringing the latter to as high a degree of perfection as seems possible with the instrument constructed as it now is. It was Liszt's good fortune to discover capabilities in the pianoforte which up to his time had not been thought of, and the fact that he developed them more on their external side than on their spiritual is accounted for by the fact that he was a virtuoso who from childhood to his death as an old man lived in the incense of popular adulation. Quite early in his career he conceived the idea that the pianoforte was a universal instrument in the sense that it could be made to speak the language of the entire instrumental company. When he published his arrangements of Beethoven's symphonies he stated that every orchestral effect could be reproduced on the pianoforte. When Mendelssohn read this he turned to the G minor symphony of Mozart and said: "Let me hear the first eight measures with the figure in the violas played on the pianoforte so that they will sound as they do in the band, and I will believe it." It is not necessary to think that Liszt intended that his remark should be accepted in its full literalness; but the story serves to direct attention to the high merit of Liszt as a transcriber, and to the fact that with him the orchestral style came boldly into pianoforte music. It had been lurking there since Beethoven, but now it came forward as an aim not merely as a means. Since Liszt opened new paths there has been no writer for the instrument who has not been a greater composer for the orchestra than for the pianoforte. Let the names of Raff, Rubinstein, Saint-Saëns, Tschaikowsky, and Brahms be offered in evidence. Liszt's place as an original composer of pianoforte music is still undetermined, despite his two concertos, with their superb tonal effects and their firmly knit logical structure; the imposing Sonata in B minor, the "Consolations," "Harmonies poétiques et réligieuses," the "Dream Nocturnes," "Années de Pélerinage," the "Légendes," and the scintillant Études; but the transcriptions of Schubert's songs are unique and so are his "Hungarian Rhapsodies," which are much more than mere transcriptions, though they are constructed out of the folktunes of the Magyars, and frequently disclose the characteristic features of the performances which they receive at the hands of the Gypsies, from whom Liszt learned them. This fact (to which Liszt gave currency in his book, "Des Bohèmiens et de leur Musique en Hongrie") has given rise to the general belief that the folksongs of Hungary are of Gypsy origin. This belief is erroneous, as I have argued in my book, "How to Listen to Music," from which I draw what I have still to say on the subject of the Rhapsodies. The Gypsies have for centuries been the musical practitioners of Hungary, but they are not the composers of the music of the Magyars, though they have put a marked impress not only on the melodies, but also on popular taste. The Hungarian folksongs are a perfect reflex of the national character of the Magyars, and some have been traced back centuries in their literature. Though their most marked melodic peculiarity, the frequent use of a minor scale containing one or even two superfluous seconds, may be said to belong to Oriental music generally (and the Magyars are Orientalists), the songs have a rhythmical peculiarity which is a direct product of the Magyar language. This peculiarity consists of a figure in which the emphasis is shifted from the strong to the weak part by making the first take only a fraction of the time of the second. It is the "Scotch snap" already alluded to, but in Hungarian music it occurs in the middle of the measure instead of the beginning. The result is a syncopation which is peculiarly forceful. There is an indubitable Oriental relic in the profuse embellishments which the Gypsies weave around the Hungarian melodies when playing them; but the fact that they thrust the same embellishments upon Spanish and Russian music—indeed, upon all the music which they play—indicates plainly enough that the impulse to do so is native to them, and has nothing to do with the national taste of the countries for which they provide music.

Liszt's confessed purpose in writing the "Hungarian Rhapsodies" was to create what he called "Gypsy Epics." He had gathered a large number of the melodies without a definite purpose, and was pondering what to do with them when it occurred to him that

These fragmentary, scattered melodies were the wandering, floating, nebulous part of a great whole, that they fully answered the conditions for the production of a harmonious unity which would comprehend the very flower of their essential properties, their most unique beauties, . . . and might be united in one homogeneous body, a complete work, its divisions to be so arranged that each song would form at once a whole and a part, which might be severed from the rest and be examined by and for itself; but which would, nevertheless, belong to the whole through the close affinity of subject-matter, the similar character of its inner nature and unity in development.

The basis of Liszt's "Rhapsodies" being thus distinctly national, he has in a manner indicated in their character and tempo the dual character of the

Hungarian national dance, the Czardas, which consists of two movements, a *Lassu*, or slow movement, followed by a *Friss*. These alternate at the will of the dancers, who give a sign to the band when they wish to change from one to the other.

One of the formal characteristics of Liszt's concertos, though not wholly new at the time when Liszt composed the first (between 1840 and 1848), was less common then than now, and no doubt helped it to win its wide popularity. Their movements are fused into a whole by omission of the customary pauses and by community of theme. Wherein the first concerto was chiefly remarkable at the time of its composition is the consistency and ingenuity with which the principal theme of the work (the stupendously energetic phrase which the orchestra proclaims at the outset) is transformed to make it express a great variety of moods and to give unity to the work. "Thus, by means of this metamorphosis," says Edward Dannreuther, "the poetic unity of the whole musical tissue is made apparent in spite of very great diversity of details; and Coleridge's attempt at a definition of poetic beauty—unity in multiety—is carried out to the letter."

Of all the schools of composition based on folk-music the Russian is now at once the most assertive, the most vigorous, and (outside of pianoforte music, at least) the most characteristic. In orchestral works there is no mistaking the utterances of composers like Borodin (1834–1887), Balakirew

(1836–1910), and Moussorgsky (1839–1881). Their idioms are taken straight from the lips of the Russian peasantry, and compared with them Anton Rubinstein (1830–1894) and P. I. Tschaikowsky (1840–1893), who were practically the only Russians whose music was known outside of the czar's empire twenty-five years ago (Glinka can hardly be called an exception), are not striking representatives of the school to which they are supposed to belong by reason of their nationality. Rubinstein offers a troublesome proposition in several respects. That he himself realized the fact is amusingly (and yet a bit pathetically) illustrated by his remark that he was at a loss what to call himself, the Russians saying that he was a German, the Germans that he was a Russian, the Christians that he was a Jew, the Jews that he was a Christian, the classicists that he was romantic, and the romanticists that he was a classic. "Neither fish, flesh, nor fowl" might have been his comment had he been a quoter of English saws; "Issachar, a strong ass couching down between two burdens," had he had a keener sense of humor, coupled with a knowledge of the book of Genesis. With the Young Russian School (*Kuschka*) Rubinstein had only a modicum of sympathy. He says of it:

It is the outcome of the influence of Berlioz and Liszt. . . . Its creations are based on thorough control of technical resources and masterly application of color, but on total absence of outline and predominating absence of form. . . . Whether something is to be hoped for in the future from this tendency I do not know, but would not doubt it altogether, for I believe that the peculiarity of the melody and rhythm and the unusual character of Russian folkmusic may permit of a new fructification of music in general. Besides, some of the representatives of this new tendency are not without notable talent.

Balakirew was the head of this school. He, said Borodin, was the hen that laid the eggs, which were all alike at first, out of which came the chicks which were no sooner hatched than they took on plumages of their own and flew away in different directions. Balakirew and his companions, César Cui (1835), Moussorgsky and Rimsky-Korsakow, play only a small part, comparatively speaking, in pianoforte music, and of their earlier contemporaries Rubinstein and Tschaikowsky are far and away the most significant. The besetting sin of Rubinstein as a composer was his lack of a capacity for self-criticism. He felt, and correctly, that he was cut out for large things, but he was impatient of his own industry, and though inclined to Titanic thoughts, like Beethoven, whom he sometimes suggests in his slow movements, could not "learn to labor and to wait," as the supreme master did. The climax of Rubinstein's popularity as a composer was coincident with the climax of his popularity as a player. Half a generation has passed away since his death, and much has been written since of the fading of his music; but of his three concertos that in D minor still glows with beauty; pianists still perform his "Staccato Étude" and "Study on False Notes" in the concert-room; amateurs still revel in his "Mélodie" in F and the one of the numbers of his "Kammenoi Ostrow," and many players of chamber music are loath to give up his Sonata in A for pianoforte and violin (Op. 19), the three sonatas for pianoforte and violoncello, the best of the five trios, the quintet for pianoforte and strings, or the octet for pianoforte, violin, viola, violoncello, double-bass, flute, clarinet, and horn. Tschaikowsky's pianoforte solos have won little favor compared with the first of his two concertos (in B-flat minor) and the Trio in A minor. Mrs. Newmarch, reviewing his works in Grove's "Dictionary," says: "His single pianoforte sonata is heavy in material and treatment, and cannot be reckoned a fine example of its kind. A few of his fugitive pieces are agreeable, and the variations in F show that at the time of their composition he must have been interested in thematic development, but the world would not be much the poorer for the loss of all that he has written for piano solo."

Balakirew's pianoforte compositions are not many, and when his name is seen on the programme of a pianoforte recital it is in connection with his Oriental fantasy "Islamey." The majority of the pianoforte pieces of Nicholas Andrievich Rimsky-Korsakow (1844–1908) are variations, one set ending with a fugue on the familiar subject "B-a-c-h" and one set having a folksong theme. The successors of these men, the younger composers of to-day, have cultivated the field more industriously, though some of them have had to depend largely for their popularity on a single lucky hit, like Liadow's (1859) "Musical Snuff-Box" ("Tabatière à Musique") and Rachmaninow's (1873) C-sharp minor prelude. The latter musician, however, has written three concertos, and is inclined toward work of large dimensions. Other representatives of the school are Alexandre Glazounow (1865), suite on the name "S-a-s-c-h-a," étude "La Nuit," Mazurka (Op. 25, No. 3), Nocturne (Op. 37); Nicolai de Stcherbatchew (1853), "Féeries et Pantomimes," Scherzo capriccio (Op. 17), "Mosaïque" (Op. 15); Joseph Wihtol (1863), variations on a Lettish theme (Op. 6); W. Rebikow (1867), "Autumn Dreams" (Op. 8); Alexandre Scriabin (1871), sonata (Op. 6), "Allegro appassionata" (Op. 4), "Sonata-fantasie" (Op. 19), and twelve études; Felix Blumenfeld (1863), étude "La Mer," "Fantasies-études" (Op. 25), and a Polish suite (dedicated to Paderewski); S. Liapounow (1859), "Études d'execution transcendantes" (Op. 11); Antony Stemanovich Arensky (1861), "Esquisses" (Op. 24), Concerto in F, Caprices (Op. 43), and some interesting experiments in antique metres called "Lagodées" and "Péons."

Except for the works of a small coterie of men who are striving to emancipate French music from the influence of Wagner and can think of no way save to throw the diatonic system overboard, the pianoforte music of France to-day discloses no special characteristics. The whole tone scale of these men is in no sense national, and since the movement is still in an experimental stage, it follows that the taste of French music-lovers is still represented by the older composers who combine accepted systems with the individuality, elegance, and grace which distinguish French art in all its phases. Chief of these composers is Camille Saint-Saëns, born in 1835, who, though he gave his first public concert in 1846, is still, after sixty-four years, the most energetic and enterprising of French musicians. A generation ago Dr. von Bülow, describing one of his feats in *prima vista* score-reading, called him "the greatest musical mind of the day," and for sound learning it is doubtful if M. Saint-Saëns has found a rival since. Like the majority of French composers, he has written much for the lyric stage, and his operas preserve national ideals; but his propensity for travel has taken him to many parts of the earth, and in his journeys he has gathered elements of local color and utilized them in some of his pianoforte pieces, such as a "Caprice on Russian Airs" for pianoforte and three wind instruments, "Africa," a fantasia for pianoforte and orchestra, and "Caprice Arabe" for two pianofortes, four hands. Of his four concertos the second, in G minor (in the introduction to which he pays a gracious tribute to Bach), is of first-class importance, while the fourth, in C minor, still holds a place in the programmes of virtuosi. A predecessor in the serious school, but not so many-sided a musician as he, was C. H. V. M. Alkan (called Alkan *ainê*, 1813–1888), who is chiefly noteworthy now for his studies, especially those for the pedals.

César Franck (1822–1890) was an organist of great distinction, as was also Saint-Saëns in his early days; but he gave less attention than the latter to the pianoforte and devoted himself more assiduously to the ecclesiastical instrument and the forms of composition to which it directed his mind, which had a distinctly religious and mystical bent. His most notable contributions to chamber music employing the pianoforte with other instruments are four trios, a quintet, and, best of all, a sonata with violin. Of his compositions fitted to the larger concert-rooms that which has retained the greatest vitality is the "Variations symphoniques" for pianoforte and orchestra. A piece of similar dimensions and apparatus is "Les Djinns," a symphonic poem for pianoforte and orchestra, as he called it. Franck found his ideals in the music of the great Germans, and so did his pupil Vincent d'Indy, born in 1851, who, after the death of his master, became the head of the would-be revolutionists of French music. Saint-Saëns had used the pianoforte as an orchestral instrument in his symphony in C minor; d'Indy does the same, but lifts it into greater prominence in his "Symphony on a Mountain Air," in which the melody of a folksong is treated as an *idée fixe*. Chief of the younger men who in small descriptive pieces marvellous for finish of harmonic detail and intervallic novelty are Claude Achille Debussy, born in 1862, and Maurice Ravel, born in 1875.

Italy, the cradle of opera, is still its nursery to the exclusion, almost, of all other forms. Since it yielded the sceptre to Germany in the eighteenth century it has not produced an instrumental composer of first-class importance. There are, however, a few men who stand for other things than opera, and among them are three who deserve mention in these studies. They are Giovanni Sgambati, born in 1843; Giuseppe Martucci, born in 1856, and Enrico Bossi, born in 1861. The first two began their careers as brilliant pianists and later took up composition and teaching. In Sgambati's Concerto in G minor, and two pianoforte quintets, Martucci's Concerto in B-flat minor, quintet with strings and sonata with violoncello, as well as in the smaller solo works of the two men, their consummate mastery of the resources of the instrument is much in evidence. Bossi is an organist and composer for the organ in the first instance, which fact explains his leaning toward chamber music and the large sacred forms.

England's glory in the field of music for keyboard stringed instruments is in the distant past; that of the United States is yet to come. America has produced a considerable number of sterling musicians within the last fifty years, but those among them who have distinguished themselves as composers for the pianoforte are not many. Chadwick, Parker, and Converse have kept their eyes fixed on other goals. Distinctly pianistic talents of a high order were possessed by Louis Moreau Gottschalk (1829–1869), and Edward A. MacDowell (1861–1907). Their ideals were far apart, Gottschalk being a salon sentimentalist and MacDowell a musical poet of fine fibre. In one thing they strove along parallel lines, though only incidentally. In his "Bananier" and "La Savane," Gottschalk used folk-melodies of the Southern plantations as themes and in his second orchestral suite and one of his "Woodland Sketches" for pianoforte solo, Mac-Dowell called into service melodies of the red men of North America. The efforts were tentative, but I have no doubt their influence will some day be felt. Of larger significance from the view-point of universal art are MacDowell's two concertos (in

A minor and D minor), his four sonatas ("Tragica," "Eroica," "Norse," and "Keltic"), and a suite in which the influence of his master Raff is as obvious as that of Grieg is in his later compositions. The sentimental salon style was tastefully and successfully cultivated by Ethelbert Nevin (1862–1901). Henry Holden Huss, born in 1862, has published a concerto besides a number of smaller pieces, and Arthur Whiting, born in 1861, a Fantasy in B-flat minor for pianoforte and orchestra, a "Suite moderne" (Op. 15), and three waltzes which are extremely interesting and in a nice sense idiomatic of the pianoforte.

Part III

The Players

XII

Virtuosi and Their Development

THE art of pianoforté playing has been developed hand in hand with the instrument and the music composed for it. The action of the evolutionary factors has been reciprocal—mechanical elements suggesting or compelling manner and limitation of performance, technical resources inviting or prohibiting the character of musical ideas, and these, in turn, urging to improvement in mechanism and technical manipulation. The manufacturer, composer, and performer are thus fellow agents in the evolution of pianoforte music, receiving encouragement in strivings toward both good and bad ends from popular taste, which is itself a product of the co-operation of all the factors in the art-sum.

With earnest endeavor, and so far as the limitations of this book permitted, I have made a study of the evolution of the instrument and the music composed for it, and I must now address myself to the third factor, the virtuoso. Were it not for the fact that he is at once a reflex and embodiment of the popular taste, of which he is also to a large extent the creator, he would not be an interesting or profitable subject of study. Idealism, and therefore unselfishness in a fine sense, which are the necessary attributes of every great creator in art, are exceptional qualities in the professional reproducer. It is, therefore, a less deplorable circumstance than it seems to be in the minds of sentimental rhapsodists that the fame of the ordinary virtuoso is evanescent, that all that posterity holds of him and his is anecdote (which is seldom valuable), or, at the best, pedagogical material.

Of course I am speaking now of the mere virtuoso. If a virtuoso be in the true sense an artist, he will be more than reproducer; he will be a creator also, giving out so much of himself as has been released by sympathetic interest along with the intellectual and emotional product of the composer. Virtuosi inflamed with generous and noble sympathies are, therefore, of infinitely higher rank than virtuosi whose bent is toward the petty and ignoble. In this lies the morality of the art. It is the former who win a reward like that of the composer, though they may not meet with the same measure of material recompense as their worldly-wise and unworthier companions. They create traditions which are fragrant; they leave a heritage which is enduring and fruitful. They live on after death in those who, possessed of the same artistic

CARL TAUSIG.

and ethical qualities, have learned from them and follow their example.

Unfortunately virtuosi of this class are not numerous and never have been. The many are those who seek success in the favor of the multitude and to win it pander to the predilections of the crowd. The crowd, however, can no more occupy the highest plane in musical appreciation than in wisdom or morality; hence, the most successful virtuosi, as a rule, are those whose capacities, physical, intellectual, emotional, and moral, are best adjusted to popular taste, not so much, perhaps, in what may be called its ground swell as in the fleeting ripples, eddies, and curling froth on its surface, the phenomena of fad and fashion. Such virtuosi can have no abiding place in the sympathy or even the interest of the serious critic or historian except as their example be used "for doctrine, for reproof, for correction, for instruction in righteousness"; there is small room for them in these articles.

Very little is known about the methods of study pursued by the early clavier performers. The music of the English virginalists indicates that fleetness of finger was as essential in the sixteenth century as it is in the twentieth, and when one reflects on the system of fingering which seems to have prevailed up to the time of Johann Sebastian Bach it is almost inconceivable how sufficient digital dexterity to play the music of the early virginalists and harpsichordists could be acquired.[1] The rules for fingering generally in use to-day date back only to C. P. E. Bach. "The earliest marked fingering of which we have any knowledge," says Mr. D. J. Blaikley, in his admirable essay on the subject in Grove's "Dictionary of Music and Musicians," "is that given by Ammerbach in his 'Orgel oder Instrument Tabulatur' (Leipsic, 1571). This, like all the fingering in use then and for long afterward, is characterized by the almost complete avoidance of the use of the thumb and little finger, the former

[1] A letter first published in 1854 by S. Caffi in a history of church music and reprinted in Weitzmann's "Geshichte des Clavierspiels und der Clavierliteratur," would seem to indicate that fully as much time was consumed in learning to play the clavichord in the sixteenth century as is required to become proficient on the pianoforte to-day. The writer of the letter was Pietro Bembo, eminent as poet and scholar in the first quarter of the sixteenth century. His daughter, a pupil in a convent school, had asked permission to learn the clavichord, or monochord as it was then also called. The father replied:

"Concerning your request to be permitted to learn to play the monochord I reply (since you cannot know the fact because of your tender age) that to play upon the instrument is suitable only to vain and frivolous women; but I want you to be the most amiable, pure, and modest woman on earth. Moreover, it would bring you little pleasure to play ill and not a little humiliation. But to play well you will have to practise ten to twelve years to the exclusion of all else. Consider for yourself, regardless of me, whether or not this would be worth while. If, now, your friends wish that you shall learn in order to give them pleasure say to them that you do not care to make a laughing-stock of yourself to your own humiliation; and content yourself with books and embroidery."

being only occasionally marked in the left hand, and the latter never employed except in the playing of intervals of not less than a fourth in the same hand."

An Italian system to which Mr. Blaikley makes no reference would seem to show that eighty-five years after the publication of Ammerbach's book an even more primitive system of fingering prevailed in Italy. In Lorenzo Penna's "Li Primo Albori musicali," published in Bologna in 1656, it is set down that ascending scales are to be played by the middle and ring fingers alternately of the right hand, and middle and index fingers of the left; in descending the process is to be reversed—middle and index fingers alternately of the right hand, and middle and ring fingers of the left. Mr. Blaikley's explanation of these stiff and awkward kinds of fingering is this:

In the first place, the organ and clavichord not being tuned upon the system of equal temperament, music for these instruments was written only in the simplest keys, with the black keys rarely used, and in the second place the keyboards of the earlier organs were usually placed so high above the seat of the player that the elbows were of necessity considerably lower than the fingers. The consequence of the hands being held in this position and of the black keys being seldom required would be that the three long fingers stretched out horizontally would be chiefly used, while the thumb and little finger, being too short to reach the keys without difficulty, would simply hang down below the level of the keyboard.

But while the pedagogues prescribed systems there were empiricists, no doubt in large numbers, who practised whatever way seemed to them best in the application of the fingers to the keys. They had a valiant champion, too, in Prætorius, who, in his "Syntagma Musicum" (1619), wrote: "Many think it matter of great importance and despise such organists as do not use this or that particular fingering, which in my opinion is not worth the talk; for let a player run up or down with either first, middle, or third finger, aye, even with his nose, if that could help him, provided that everything is done clearly, correctly, and gracefully, it does not much matter how or in what manner it is accomplished."

A sparing use of the thumb is timidly suggested by Purcell in his "Choice Collection of Lessons for the Harpsichord" (about 1700), and Couperin in his "De la Toucher le Clevecin" (1717); but when Bach took up the matter he revolutionized it completely, as indeed he had to do to make his system of equal temperament and the free use of all the modes practicable. Bach transformed the attitude of the hand at once. The three fingers, instead of lying horizontally with the keys, were bent so that their tips rested perpendicularly on the keys. This brought the hand forward on the keyboard and raised the wrists. Thus a smart blow could, when need be, take the place of pressure—a very important thing when the harpsichord gave way to the pianoforte and quilled jacks to hammers, that is, when the strings were struck instead of plucked. Bach also fixed the place of the thumb in the scale and used it and the little finger freely in all positions. In his playing Bach cultivated evenness of touch by ending each application, not by lifting the finger from the key, but drawing it inwardly toward the palm of the hand with a caressing motion, which transferred the requisite amount of pressure to the next finger in passage playing. Forkel says that the movement of Bach's fingers was so slight as to be scarcely noticeable. The position of his hand remained unchanged, and he held the rest of his body motionless.

His contemporary, Handel, who was also highly esteemed as a harpsichordist, used the same hand position. Burney said his fingers "seemed to grow to the keys, they were so curved and compact when he played that no motion, and scarcely the fingers themselves, could be discovered." C. P. E. Bach in his "Versuch," while enforcing the need of a quiet movement of the hands, nevertheless foreshadows a change to a practice which in the course of time became an abomination. The mechanical principle of the pianoforte invited a blow upon the keys. Bach, therefore, to secure power, permitted a lifting of the hands in the delivery of the blow. This, he said, was not an error, but good and necessary so long as it could be done in a manner "not too suggestive of wood-chopping." Wood-chopping would be an inexpressive simile applied to the actions of many pianists since.

The clavichord lent itself best to an expressive singing style of playing, the harpsichord to a crisp and scintillant *staccato*. The former instrument could not be used in public performances, but its greater soulfulness made it an invaluable preparatory instrument for the pianoforte. At Vienna, Burney, on his historical tour, heard a child play on the pianoforte with such nice command of *nuance* that he inquired on what instrument she had practised. He was told the clavichord, which led him to comment as follows: "This accounts for her expression and convinces me that children should learn upon this or a pianoforte very early, and be obliged to give an expression to 'Lady Coventry's Minuet,' or whatever their first tune, otherwise after long practice on a monotonous harpsichord, however useful for strengthening the hand, the case is hopeless."

The accounts of Mozart's playing are not many, but taken in connection with his comments on some of the virtuosi whom he encountered on his travels it is plain that his style was chiefly distinguished by its musical qualities; its charm came from its expressiveness, its grace and lucidity, combined with truthfulness of emotional utterance. In 1781, when he met Clementi in rivalry at the Austrian court, the two, after producing set pieces of their own composition, varied a theme which the emperor gave them. Long afterward Clementi said: "Until then I had never heard anybody play with so much intelligence and charm. I was particularly surprised by an adagio and a number of his extemporized variations on a theme chosen by the emperor, which we were obliged to vary alternately, each accompanying the other."

Mozart was less gracious in his opinion of his rival. He called the great Roman a mere "mechanician" (*Mechanicus*), with a great knack in passages in thirds, but not a pennyworth of feeling or taste. Mozart, it is plain, was prejudiced against Italian players as a rule. He had no patience, indeed, with the display of mere digital dexterity which many of the virtuosi of his day made, to the neglect of taste in tempo and expression. Kullak reviews his qualities as follows: "Delicacy and taste, with his lifting of the entire technique to the spiritual aspiration of the idea, elevate him as a virtuoso to a height unanimously conceded by the public, by connoisseurs and by artists capable of judging. . . . Dittersdorf finds art and taste combined in his playing; Haydn asseverated with tears that Mozart's playing he could never forget, for it touched his heart; his *staccato* is said to have possessed a peculiarly brilliant charm."

At the beginning of his career the instrument for

Mozart's intimate communings was the clavichord; for his public performances the harpsichord. When the pianoforte came under his notice he gave it his enthusiastic adherence at once, and he seems to have succeeded in combining in it the best qualities of its predecessors. Writing about his visit to Mannheim in 1777, his mother said: "Wolfgang is highly appreciated everywhere, but he plays very differently than he did in Salzburg, for here pianofortes are to be found on all sides, and he handles them incomparably, as they have never been heard before. In a word, everybody who hears him says that his equal is not to be found." His predilection for the instrument may be said to have led to the establishment of the Vienna school of pianoforte playing, for which the foundations were laid by his pupil Hummel, and him who would gladly have been his pupil —Beethoven. This school cultivated warmth of expression combined with limpidity and symmetry of melodic contour, while that founded by Clementi tended to virtuosity and systematic development of technique.

It was Clementi who opened the way to the modern style of playing, with its greater sonority and capacity for effects. Under him passage playing became something almost new; deftness, lightness, and fluency were replaced, or consorted with stupendous virtuosoship which rested on a full and solid tone. Clementi is said to have been able to trill in octaves with one hand. Mozart's opinion of him in 1781 looks less jaundiced when brought into juxtaposition with a confession which he made in later years than it does when contrasted with Clementi's praise of his rival. To his pupil Ludwig Berger, Clementi said that in the early part of his career he had cultivated brilliant and dashing dexterity, particularly passages in double notes, which at that time were unusual, and that he had acquired a nobler *cantabile* style later, being led thereto by careful attention to famous singers and the gradual perfection of the English pianofortes. A reposeful attitude of the hand was also one of his characteristics, for he was perhaps the first of the players who practised the device of balancing a coin on the back of his hand while in action. Among his pupils were Cramer, Field, Moscheles, and Kalkbrenner.

Beethoven as a pianist was very much what he was as a composer, viz., an epitome of what had gone before as well as a presage of what was to come. He studied composition in Vienna, but not pianoforte playing, and as a virtuoso he must have been self-developed on the foundation of what he had been taught in Bonn. His studies began when he was not more than five years old, and he seems to have been pretty thoroughly grounded in the principles of C. P. E. Bach and to have believed in them always. His first advice when he took Ries as pupil was to get Bach's "Versuch." He was only eleven and a half years old when he began to play the organ as a substitute for his teacher Neefe in the electoral chapel at Bonn; at twelve he was cembalist and at thirteen and a half he became second organist by appointment. At eighteen he played viola in the orchestra in the theatre and also in concerts. His style, formed at the clavichord and organ (perhaps to his detriment at the latter), was smooth and quiet, and despite the fact that his tone seems to have been rude he preserved the reposeful manner to a late date.

Czerny says: "His attitude while playing was masterly in its quietness, noble and beautiful, without the least grimace, though he bent forward more and more as his deafness grew upon him. He attached great importance to correct position of the fingers in his teaching (according to the school of Emanuel Bach, which he used in teaching me)." In Thayer's note-book, in which Beethoven's biographer recorded the conversations which he had with the men who had come into personal contact with the composer, I found the following memorandum under date of May 28, 1860: "I called again on Mähler and questioned him as to the above, and find that I have reported him correctly. One thing, he says, particularly attracted his attention, and that was that he played with his hands so very still. Wonderful as was his execution, there was no tossing up and about of his hands, but they seemed to glide right and left over the keys, the fingers doing the work."

The incident which Mähler (in his youth a painter who had painted a portrait of the master) had described took place in the winter of 1803 or 1804, for Beethoven was at work on the finale of the "Eroica" symphony and played some of the variations for his listeners. After that date Beethoven gradually abandoned playing in public. Two years later Pleyel describes his playing as extremely daring and fearless of all difficulties, though they were not always cleanly overcome; he "thrashed" too much, said Pleyel. Hummel's adherents found fault with his playing because of his excessive use of the pedals, "which produced a confused noise." Czerny also refers to his pedalling, and in his "School," describing the manner in which Beethoven's music ought to be played, says: "Characteristic and passionate power alternately with all the charms of cantabile are dominant. The means of expression are often developed to the extreme, particularly in respect of the humorous mood. The piquant, brilliant manner is seldom to be applied here, but all the oftener the general effect is to be attained partly through a full-voiced *legato*, partly by the use of the forte-pedal, etc. Great dexterity without pretensions to brilliancy. In adagios rhapsodical expression and emotional song."

The rudeness of Beethoven's playing harped upon by musicians who heard him in the later years of his life, such as Spohr and Moscheles, finds ample explanation in his temperament, aggravated by his deafness. If Wegeler is to be believed, it was noticeable before he had heard any really great players, but when he was twenty years old he heard Johann Franz Xaver Sterkel (1750–1817), whose playing was light and pleasing, almost effeminate, so much more finished and refined than anything that Beethoven had ever heard that he was unspeakably amazed and much persuasion was necessary to get him to the pianoforte in turn. When finally he did play, however, he astonished his friends by doing so with a perfect reproduction of Sterkel's style. Schindler says that in his later years Beethoven confessed to him that his rude manner was due to his having played the organ so much, which is altogether likely, considering the heavy action of the organs at that period, yet it may have been due also to his emotional impulsiveness and his original bent, for Carl Ludwig Junker wrote in 1791: "His playing is so different from the usual manner of handling the instrument that it seems as if he had tried to open entirely new paths for himself."

In his early years in Vienna he gave much thought to perfecting his violin playing, and it is possible that that instrument usurped a large place in his affections to the prejudice of the pianoforte.

As he grew more and more engrossed in composition the ambition which had prompted him to make concert trips to Prague, Nuremberg, and Berlin left him. Thereafter he played in public but seldom, and what we know of his playing we learn from accounts of his performances in private. These accounts all agree as to the rhapsodic eloquence and dramatic vitality of his playing, especially when improvising, and his sinking of the virtuoso in the character of the musical poet. Yet he mastered some difficulties which were appalling to his rivals. One of these was a Bohemian abbé named Joseph Gelinek (1757–1825), whom Mozart heard in Prague in 1787 and started on a prosperous career by recommending him to Count Kinsky, who appointed him his *Hauscaplan;* later he became musical director in Prague and Vienna. He was a voluminous composer of variations of the conventional order, so voluminous and so conventional that Carl Maria von Weber hit him off in a distich:

No theme on earth escaped your genius airy,
The simplest one of all—yourself—you never vary.

Gelinek's variations are lost forever, but the story of his first meeting with Beethoven will probably live as long as the fame of the great master. Czerny tells the story: One day Gelinek, meeting Czerny's father, remarked to him that he had been invited to a soirée that evening to break a lance with a new pianist: "*Den wollen wir zusam-menhauen*" ("We'll cudgel him well!") he added. The next day Czerny asked Gelinek how the affair had turned out. "Oh," replied the abbé, "I'll never forget yesterday. The devil himself is in that young man; I never heard such playing. He improvised on a theme which I gave him as I never heard even Mozart improvise. Then he played compositions of his own which were in the highest degree grand and wonderful. And he plays diffi-culties and brings effects out of the pianoforte of which we never dreamed."

What Beethoven's innovations were like we can guess in some degree from a remark in a letter which he wrote to his childhood friend, Eleonore von Breuning, in sending her a set of variations for piano-forte and violin on the melody of "Se vuol ballare" from Mozart's "Nozze di Figaro," which he had dedicated to her. In the coda occurred a passage in which a trill was imposed on other voices. Re-ferring to this Beethoven wrote: "You will find the V. a little difficult to play, especially the trills in the coda, but don't let that alarm you. It is so contrived that you need play only the trill, leaving out the other notes, because they are also in the violin part. I never would have composed a thing of the kind had I not often observed that here and there in Vienna there was somebody who, after I had improvised of an evening, noted down many of my peculiarities and made parade of them next day as his own. Foreseeing that some of these things would soon appear in print I resolved to anticipate them. Another reason that I had was to embarrass the local pianoforte masters. Many of them are my deadly enemies and I wanted to revenge myself on them, knowing that once in a while somebody would ask them to play the variations and they would make a sorry show with them." Beethoven's shafts were levelled at Gelinek.

Beethoven's single encounter with Daniel Steibelt (1765–1823) has been described in an earlier chapter of these studies. Steibelt seems to have possessed a great measure of digital skill, though it is said that a showy *tremolando* with both hands, which caught the ears of the groundlings, had for its real purpose the hiding of a weakness of the left hand. He travelled a great deal and became something of a musical lion by reason of the success of an opera, "Romeo and Juliet," produced in 1793. Not only his own character as a charlatan but also the popular taste of the time may be read in the tale of his triumphs in Vienna, whither he went in 1800. He was accompanied by an English woman who figured as his wife and who played the tambourine in catchpenny pieces called "Bacchanales." The instrument was taken up by some of the fashionable ladies of the Austrian capital, who paid the adventuress a gold ducat an hour for lessons and bought a cartload of tambourines from her husband.

A virtuoso of a very different order was Josef Woelffl, or Woelfl, with whom, though he put him to his trumps both as player and improviser, Beethoven associated on terms of amity and mutual esteem. Woelffl was a native of Salzburg and a pupil of Mozart's father and Haydn's brother. The friendly rivalry between him and Beethoven separated the music-lovers of Vienna into two camps. Describing their meetings at which, in the presence of their aristocratic adherents, the two artists measured their powers against each other, performing their own compositions and improvising on themes which they exchanged, the Chevalier von Seyfried wrote at the time: "It would have been difficult, perhaps impossible, to award the palm of victory to either one of the gladiators in respect of technical skill. Nature had been particularly kind to Woelffl in bestowing upon him a hand which enabled him to span a tenth as easily as other hands compass an octave, and permitted him to play passages of double notes in these intervals with the rapidity of lightning." He then describes the tempestuous manner of Beethoven's playing in his exalted moments, when he "tore along like a wildly foaming cataract, and the conjurer constrained his instrument to an utterance so forceful that the stoutest structure was scarcely able to withstand it. . . . Woelffl, on the contrary, trained in the school of Mozart, was always equable; never superficial, but always clear, and thus more accessible to the many. He used art only as a means to an end, never to exhibit his acquirements. He always enlisted the attention of his hearers and inevitably it was made to follow the progression of his well-ordered ideas. Whoever has heard Hummel will know what is meant by this."

We have another description of Woelffl's playing in Tomaschek's autobiography, in an account of a concert given in 1799: "Then he played Mozart's Fantasia in F minor, published by Breitkopf for four hands, just as it is printed, without omitting a note, or, for the sake of the execution, lessening the value of a single tone, as the so-called romanticists of our time love to do, thinking to equalize matters by raising the damper pedal and producing an unexampled confusion of tones. He is unique in his way. A pianoforte player who is six feet tall, whose extraordinarily long fingers span the interval of a tenth without strain, and who, moreover, is so emaciated that everything about him rattles like a scarecrow; who executes difficulties which are impossibilities to other pianists with the greatest ease and a small but neat touch, and without once disturbing the quiet posture of his body; who often plays whole passages in moderate tempo *legato* with one and the same finger (as in the andante of the

Mozart Fantasia, the long passage in sixteenth notes in the tenor voice)—such a pianist certainly is without a fellow in his art."

In 1901—that is, only nine years ago—there still lived in London an English musician who could and did tell us how some of the great pianists of the eighteenth and nineteenth centuries played. The memory of Charles Salaman went back to J. B. Cramer, who with Clementi, Hummel, and Czerny formed the first great group of creative virtuosi whose formative influence has been felt down to to-day. Salaman wrote down his recollections of the old pianists whom he had heard and his essay was printed in "Blackwood's Edinburgh Magazine" for September, 1901, only a few weeks after the death of the author. The testimony is of the highest importance, for Salaman had lived through all the phases of musical development and made experience of them from, let us say, five years before the death of Beethoven to as many after the death of Liszt—a period of more than two entire generations. His description of Cramer, for instance, carries us back into the eighteenth century and emphasizes several things which have been pointed out in these studies:

As a musician he was of the school of Mozart, whose compositions he constantly interpreted with true enthusiasm and perfect sympathy, and it was beautiful to hear him speak of Mozart, with whom he was contemporary for the first twenty years of his life. In appearance Cramer was dignified and elegant, with something of the look and bearing of the Kembles; and well can I recall the tranquil manner in which he displayed his mastery of the instrument, so different from the exhibitions of restless exaggeration and affectation one so often sees at the modern pianoforte recitals. It was a pleasure to watch the easy grace with which John Cramer moved his hands, with bent fingers covering the keys.

The youthful reader will be tempted, perhaps, to think that a little too much importance was attached to tranquillity of manner and evenness of touch by the early school of pianoforte playing, but these qualities, combined with fleetness of finger and correct taste, sufficed to give utterance to most of the music of that period, outside of the dramatic compositions of Beethoven. Studies were then exercises for the mastery of technique and no one thought of reading deeper purposes into them. This fact finds illustration in Von Lenz's interesting story of his meeting with Cramer. It was in 1842, and the Russian pianist and writer had bidden Cramer to a dinner in Paris, and seeking the way to the venerable master's confidence through his stomach and vanity, had set before him a feast of English viands (Cramer had lived long in England) and banished all music from the room except the complete works of his guest. He told Cramer of the continued popularity of his compositions in Russia and played some of them. Then he asked the old man to play and he complied with the first three of his studies. Von Lenz was amazed and disappointed; everything, he says, was "dry, wooden, rough, without cantilena, in the third study in D major, but well rounded and magisterial." Von Lenz tried to conceal his disappointment, but confesses that he was thoroughly disillusioned. He asked if an absolute *legato* was not indicated in the third study, in which Cramer had simply put the groups in the upper voice to the sword and neglected even to tie the bass progressions.

"We were not so anxious," replied Cramer; "we did not put so much into the music. These are exercises. I haven't your accents and intentions. Clementi played his 'Gradus ad Parnassum' in the same way. We knew no better, and no one sang more beautifully than Field, who was a pupil of Clementi. My model was Mozart. Nobody composed more beautifully than he! Now I am forgotten and a poor elementary teacher in a suburb of Paris, where they play the études of Bertini, which I have got to teach. You can hear them if you want to—eight pianos at once!"

Yet in his day Beethoven valued Cramer so highly that he did not think any other artist worthy of being compared with him.

As a boy Hummel lived two years in Mozart's household and studied with him; afterward Haydn, Salieri, Clementi, and Albrechtsberger had a hand in his musical education. Comparing his playing with that of Beethoven, Czerny wrote: "If Beethoven's playing was marked by immense power, individual character, and unheard-of *bravura* and dexterity, Hummel's, on the contrary, was a model of purity, clarity, and distinctness, of insinuating elegance and delicacy." Salaman heard Hummel in 1830, after he had been absent from London forty years; yet he says of his playing:

With ease and tranquil, concentrated power, with undeviating accuracy, richness of tone and delicacy of touch, he executed passages in single and double notes and in octaves of enormous technical difficulty. Above all, his playing possessed the indefinable quality of charm.

"Don't talk to me about these passage-players," said Beethoven, angrily, when somebody mentioned the name of Moscheles. The remark, which sounds ungracious, and even unjust, in view of the position which Moscheles came to occupy later in the musical world, receives an illuminating gloss from Salaman's estimate; he heard Moscheles in 1826:

Moscheles had taken Europe by storm and initiated his great reputation by his wonderful performance of the extraordinary *bravura* variations he had written on the French popular piece, "The Fall of Paris." . . . So completely did this style captivate the popular taste that he soon had a following, and became recognized as the founder of a school which continued in fashion for some years. Later on, however,

Moscheles emancipated himself from the *bravura* style, which played itself out, and he developed into a classical pianist and composer. I heard him often in the 20's, the 30's, and 40's at the Philharmonic, his own and other concerts; and more than once I had the honor of appearing on the same programme with him. I always admired his masterly command of all the resources of his instrument and the genuine art of his playing; but I confess that he seldom quite charmed me, never deeply moved me. . . . I never remember feeling in listening to the accomplished performances of Moscheles that a temperament was speaking to mine through the medium of the pianoforte, as I felt with Mendelssohn, with Liszt, with Chopin, with Thalberg, and later with Rubinstein.

Of Field, Mendelssohn, Chopin, and Henselt it can be said that their achievements as composers so far overshadow their fame as performers that these studies would be reasonably complete so far as they are concerned with the attention which they have received in an earlier chapter; yet they were all remarkable performers; all of them, indeed, might have become famous as virtuosi had they not been swayed by their loftier creative impulse. Field was a forerunner of Chopin in the style of his playing, as he was in the creation of the nocturne. "A really great player," says Salaman of him, "his style, like his compositions, romantic and poetic, as if interpreting some beautiful dream, while in the singing quality of his touch, the infinite grace and delicacy of his execution, his emotional expression, he was unrivalled in his day."

Schumann's ambition to become a virtuoso was nipped in the bud by an accident resulting from an effort to gain dexterity, flexibility, and strength of finger by mechanical means, and we can only guess at what he might have become as an interpreter of the music of other masters from his critical writings. It is, moreover, doubtful if he would ever have become so convincing a performer of his own music as his wife, Clara Wieck (1819–1896); for I was told many years ago by an excellent musician who was a student in Leipsic in the Schumann period that when he conducted he depended on his wife to indicate the tempo for each number, which she did by protruding her foot from beneath her skirts and beating time on the floor. Mr. Franklin Taylor, an excellent authority, considers that Mme. Schumann stood "indubitably in the first rank as a pianist, perhaps higher than any of her contemporaries, if not as regards the possession of natural or acquired gifts yet in the use she made of them."

While the majority of virtuosi down to Liszt, and even he during his period of greatest brilliancy, displayed their powers almost exclusively in their own compositions, Mendelssohn as a performer was also an admirable exponent of the creations of his great predecessors. Speaking of his performance of Beethoven's G major concerto, Salaman says: "A more reverential, sympathetic, and conservative reading of the old master's text I have never heard, while at the same time the interpretation was unmistakably individual—Mendelssohn's and no possible other's! His touch was exquisitely delicate, and the fairy fancies of his 'Midsummer Night's Dream' music seemed ever to haunt him in his playing, lending it a magic charm. . . . His fugue playing was strictly classical and based on Bach; his handling of octave passages was magnificent, and, as I have said, his power of improvisation boundless." Von Lenz calls Henselt "the most unique of all keyboard phenomena." "Liszt," he says, "must be accepted cosmically, universally, because of his command of all the resources of the instrument and, therefore, of all styles. . . . Chopin was too original in production to permit his reproduction to express his whole individuality, the more because of the decay of physical command over his resources. Midway between Liszt and Chopin, and in a degree as a bond between their contrasts, stands Henselt, a primitive Teutonic phenomenon, a Germania at the pianoforte."

If Chopin had longings and predilections for a virtuoso's career, he left them behind him with his youth. After he had attained fame in Paris he played only for small gatherings of sympathetic souls. "I am not fitted for public playing," he said; "the public frightens me, its breath chokes me. I am paralyzed by its inquisitive gaze and affrighted at these strange faces." So Henselt lived thirty-two years in St. Petersburg, where he was greatly esteemed, without appearing once in public; and when he went to Germany he played only before a chosen few. Yet Lenz, whose admiration for Liszt was boundless, held Henselt to be the only peer of that pianistic macrocosm. Henselt exercised his fingers indefatigably upon a dumb keyboard and practised Bach's fugues on a muted pianoforte, reading the Bible the while. "When Bach and the Bible are finished he begins again at the beginning," says his not always veracious laudator.

To return for a moment to Chopin. As a player he might be described as a descendant of Clementi's in the second generation: Clementi begat Field, Field begat Chopin. When he went to Paris he contemplated taking lessons from Kalkbrenner, a famous *bravura* player and teacher, who after hearing him play asked him if he had been Field's pupil. An instructive characterization of Chopin's playing is found in Moscheles's diary:

His *ad libitum* playing, which with the interpreters of his music degenerates into disregard of time, is with him only the most charming originality of execution; the amateurish and harsh modulations which strike me so disagreeably when I am reading his compositions no longer shock me, because his delicate fingers glide lightly over them in a fairylike way; his *piano* is so soft that he does not need any strong *forte* to produce contrasts; it is for this reason that one does not miss the orchestral effects which the German school demands from a pianoforte player, but allows one's self to be carried away as by a singer who, little concerned about the accompaniment, entirely follows his feelings.

Chopin was a master of *cantabile*. Schumann tells of hearing him "sing" his E-flat nocturne; Von Lenz describes his playing of Beethoven's sonata in A-flat, Op. 26: "He played it beautifully, but not so beautifully as his own works, not so as to take hold of you, not *en relief*, not like a romance with a climacteric development from variation to variation. He murmured *mezza voce*, but incomparably in the *cantilena*, infinitely perfect in the connection of phrases, ideally, beautifully, but *effeminately*."

Over against three great players who were pianoforte virtuosi and nothing more, the "Philistines" of Schumann's wrath—Friedrich Kalkbrenner (1784 ?– 1849), Henri Herz, to give him his Gallicized name (1806–1888), and Alexander Dreyschock (1818–1869) —I place the triumvirate of great virtuosi who were also great musicians, Liszt, Thalberg, and Tausig. If any man shall undertake to say who of these three was the greatest pianoforte performer he shall be a rock of offence to the special admirers of the two others. Only a portion of the musical world, and that a small one, sat under the spell of the youngest of them, and only for a short space, for Tausig's scintillant career spanned only a dozen years, while that of his elders compassed each two generations. And Liszt was Tausig's master, as he was the master, in practice or in precept, or in both, of nearly all the pianists of wide note during the last half century. There were three distinct periods in Liszt's career: the first when he travelled through Europe as a prodigy, with the kiss of Beethoven on his brow, and won all hearts as much by his charming naturalness of conduct as by his phenomenal skill upon the keyboard; the second when, the ripened virtuoso, he carried everything before him, bewildering the musicians no less than the mere music-lovers, widening the boundaries of the technicians, giving a new voice to the pianoforte, breaking the seven seals of the Book of Revelation of Beethoven the Divine, stimulating the manufacturers to augment the power and the brilliancy of the instrument so that it might withstand the assaults of men with

> thews of Anakim
> And pulses of a Titan's heart;

and the last when, "far from the madding crowd," he gave himself up to the unselfish labors of a doubly creative musician, composing music and fashioning artists out of the elect who flocked to him for instruction from all the ends of the earth. All critical discourse touching him runs out into metaphorical rhapsody. "Liszt is the latent history of the keyboard instruments and himself the crown of the work!" cries Von Lenz; "Liszt is a phenomenon of universal musical virtuosity such as had never before been known, not simply a pianistic miracle," he says again, and still again and again: "The pianist Liszt is an apparition not to be compressed within the bounds of the house drawn by schools and professors"; "Liszt is the past, the present, and the future of the pianoforte. . . . He is the spirit of the matter, he absorbs the conception"; "When Liszt thunders, lightens, and murmurs the great B-flat Sonata for Hammerklavier by Beethoven, this Solomon's Song of the keyboard, there is an end of all things pianistic; Liszt is making capital for humanity out of the ideas of the greatest thinker in the realm of music." And so Von Lenz goes on and others follow him. "Liszt is the father of modern pianoforte virtuosity," says Prosniz somewhat more instructively; "he developed the capacity of the instrument to the utmost; he commanded it to sing, to whisper, to thunder. From the human voice as well as the orchestra he borrowed effects. Daringly, triumphantly his technique overcame all difficulties—a technique which proclaimed the unqualified dominion of the mind over the human hand."

Liszt's great period as a virtuoso was from 1839 to 1847, and during this period he had only one rival, though a formidable one. This was Sigismund Thalberg (1812–1871), a natural son of

Prince Dietrichstein and the Baroness Wetzlar. He studied in Paris with Pixis and Kalkbrenner, and at the outset of his career divided with Liszt the *cognoscenti* of the French capital into parties as Beethoven and Woelffl had divided the Viennese a generation before. In the pen battle which ensued Fétis championed him and Berlioz, his rival. He travelled more extensively and longer than Liszt, his journeyings, as Herz's had done, carrying him to America, where for a short time in 1857 he was engaged with Ullmann in the management of Italian opera at the Academy of Music in New York. He was a true aristocrat and cultured gentleman in his bearing in society as well as at the pianoforte. We have the estimates of two fellow pianists to help us to form an opinion of his playing.

Sir Charles Hallé:

Totally unlike in style to either Chopin or Liszt, he was admirable and unimpeachable in his own way. His performances were wonderfully finished and accurate, giving the impression that a wrong note was an impossibility. His tone was round and beautiful, the clearness of his passage-playing crystal-like, and he had brought to the utmost perfection the method identified with his name, of making a melody stand out distinctly through a maze of brilliant passages. He did not appeal to the emotions except those of wonder, for his playing was statuesque, cold, but beautiful and so masterly that it was said of him, with reason, he would play with the same care and finish if roused out of the deepest sleep in the middle of the night. He created a great sensation in Paris and became the idol of the public, principally, perhaps, because it was felt that he could be imitated, which with Chopin and Liszt was out of the question.

Charles Salaman:

Perhaps brilliancy and elegance were his chief distinguishing qualities, but, of course, he had much more than these. He had deep feeling. . . . His playing quite enchanted me; his highly cultivated touch expressed the richest vocal tone, while his powers of execution were marvellous. Nothing seemed difficult to him; like Liszt, he could play the apparently impossible, but unlike Liszt, he never indulged in any affectation or extravagance of manner in achieving his mechanical triumphs on the keyboard. His strength and flexibility of wrist and finger were amazing, but he always tempered strength with delicacy. His loudest *fortissimos* were never noisy. His own compositions, which he chiefly played in public, enabled him best to display his astonishing virtuosity, but to be assured that Thalberg was a really great player was to hear him interpret Beethoven, which he did finely, classically, and without any attempt to embellish the work of the master.

While Chopin could not play in public and Henselt would not because of too great conscientiousness, Tausig, as he himself said, was at his best only on the concert platform. Cramer said of Dreyschock that he had two right hands; Von Lenz remarked of Tausig that his left hand was a second right. Peter Cornelius told of the amazement which Tausig caused as a boy of fourteen when he played for Liszt the first time: "A very devil

of a fellow; he dashed into Chopin's A-flat Polonaise and knocked us clean over with the octaves."
Von Lenz relates how he heard Tausig play the
ostinato octave figure in the trio of the polonaise
in a frenetic tempo from a murmuring *pianissimo*
to a thunderous *forte*, so that his listener cried out in
amazement.

"It's a specialty of mine," said Tausig. "You see my hand
is small and yet I ball it together. My left hand has a natural
descent from the thumb to the little finger. I fall naturally
upon the four notes (E, D-sharp, C-sharp, B); it's a freak of
nature. (He smiled.) I can do it as long as you please; it
doesn't weary me. It is as if written for me. Now, you play
the four notes with both hands; you'll not get the power into
them that I do." I tried it. "You see, you see! Very good,
but not so loud as mine, and you are already tired after a
few measures, and so are the octaves."

It is not for want of appreciation, respect, and
admiration for many of the pianists of to-day that
I choose to end my survey of pianoforte players
with Rubinstein and Hans von Bülow (1830–1894).
Of them it is possible to take a view which shall
have a proper historical perspective. A discussion
of the living, however, would of necessity have in
it much of personal equation. Unlike the virtuosi
of the pre-Lisztian period, the pianists of the present
day present themselves pre-eminently as interpreters of the music of the master composers and not
of their own; and in this fact there lies a merit the

only qualification of which arises from the fact that so few of them are in a high sense creative artists. In it, also, lies a tribute to the taste of the public of to-day; and every player who aims to maintain a high standard of appreciation deserves well in the thoughts of the musically cultured. It cannot mar the reputation of any of the living, however, to say that Rubinstein and Dr. von Bülow loom above them all as recreative artists.

Of the players to whom the older generation of to-day has listened, Rubinstein was the most eloquent and moving. He was in the highest degree subjective and emotional, his manner leonine and compelling. His prodigious technical skill seemed to give him as little concern as it did his listeners, who were as intent on taking in the full of his outpouring as he was in giving it. The technical side of Dr. von Bülow's playing was forced into greater prominence because of his pronounced objectivity; yet there was a wonderful delight in his playing for all who found intellectual and æsthetic pleasure in clear, convincing, symmetrical, and logical presentations of the composers' thoughts. Dr. Bie has hit him off in his chief capacity capitally:

"When he gave public recitals he did not, like Rubinstein, crowd a history of the piano into a few evenings. He took by preference a single author, like Beethoven, and played only the last five sonatas, or he unfolded the whole of Beethoven in four evenings. He would have preferred to play every piece twice. Great draftsman as he was, he hated all half-lights and colorations; he pointed his pencil very finely, and his paper was very white."

INDEX

ACADÉMIE ROYALE DES SCIENCES, 30.

Æschylus, 82.

Albrechtsberger, 191, 282.

Aldrich, Richard, on Schumann, 202.

Alkan *aîné*, 254.

Alla zoppa, 242.

Allemand (almain, allemande, and alman), 83, 85.

Allen, William, introduces tubular braces, 39.

"All in a Garden Green," 76.

American music and composers, 256, 257.

Ammerbach, "Orgel oder Instrument Tabulatur," 264, 265.

"Appassionata" Sonata, 163, 165.

Apollo, Greek archer god and god of music, 7, 12.

Apollodorus, 11.

Arbeau, "Orchésographie," 88.

"A-re," 64.

Arensky, 252.

Aristides Quintilian, 15.

Aristotle, 80, 82.

Aristoxenus, 82.

Arne, 82.

Assyrian dulcimer, 12.

Babcock, Alpheus, his patent iron frame, 39, 44.

Bach, C. P. E., 126; his clavecin pieces, 127, 128; "Versuch, etc.," 129, 267, 272; "La Journalière," 130; "La Complaisante," 130; "La Capriceuse," 130, 131; his preference for the clavichord, 133; use of harpsichord, 133, 264; his fingering, 267, 271.

Bach, J. C., 137.

Bach, Johann Sebastian, 21, 28, 100 *et seq.*, 107; compared with Handel, 110 *et seq.*; ancestors, 112; posts at Mühlhausen, Weimar, Cöthen and Leipsic, 112, 113; an instrumental musician, 114; "The Well-Tempered Clavichord," 114, 119; "Chromatic Fantasia and Fugue," 117; Preludes and fugues, 120; "Goldberg" variations, 173; "Capriccio on the Departure of a Brother," 182; "Musikalisches Opfer," 132; other compositions, 120; at court of Frederick the Great, 132; preference for clavichord,

Index

133; influence of the North German School, 117; equal temperament, 119; a continuator, 122; 215, 216, 239, 254; characterized, 197, 263; his clavier playing, 266.

Bach, W. F., 128.

Backer-Gröndahl, Agathe, 240.

Bacon, "Sylva Sylvarum," 68.

Balakirew, 248, 250; "Islamey," 251.

Balancement, 178.

Ballets, allegorical, 89.

Bargiel, 226.

"Base," 64.

Bebung, 178.

Beethoven, a continuator, 122; his significance, 135; unauthorized titles, 140; his comment on Prince Louis Ferdinand, 141; his pianoforte music, 146 *et seq.*; as writer of "occasionals," 147; the complete edition of his works, 149; attitude toward form, 149, 154; influence on the sonata, 151; his democracy, 153; a poet of humanity, 154; innovations in sonata form, 155; his scherzos, 157; finales, 158; last five sonatas, 158; motival development, 160; descriptive music, 161; projected pianoforte method, 162, 173; contents of his sonatas, 162; his polyphony, 168; his improvisations, 169, 171; his varia-tions, 168–173; meeting with Steibelt, 169; his pianofortes and their mechanism, 173, 179; clavichord and harpsichord, 173; compositions for harpsichord, 176; his music "claviermässig," 176–178; a classic and a romantic, 180; his pupil Czerny, 189; and Ries, 191; characterized, 197; use of folksong idioms, 235; his pianoforte playing, 271–279; studies C. P. E. Bach, 271; style formed on clavichord and organ, 272; Czerny's account of his playing, 272, 283; Mähler's account, 272; Pleyel's account, 273; pedalling, 273; rudeness, 274; Sterkel's influence, 274; Schindler's statement, 274; Junker's account, 274; public performances, 275; encounter with Gelinek, 276; with Steibelt, 277; association with Woelffl, 278; von Seyfried's account, 278; his high opinion of Cramer, 282; interpreted by Thalberg, 292.

His compositions: Sonatas for pianoforte, Op. 2, 157; Op. 7, 171; Op. 10, 158; Op. 13, 162; Op. 14, 158; Op. 26, 171, 178, 288; Op. 27, No. 2 ("Moonlight"), 161, 162, 165, 215, 216; Op. 28, 163; Op. 31, 158,

Index

161, 162; Op. 53 ("Wald-stein"), 160, 174, 175, 177; Op. 57 ("Appassionata"), 153, 162, 165; Op. 101, 157; Op. 106, 157, 290; Op. 109, 158, 171; Op. 110, 157, 161, 177; Op. 111, 158, 159, 171. Variations: "Ich bin der Schneider Kakadu," 148; on Diabelli's waltz, 168, 172, 204; in E-flat, Op. 35, 171; on "Se vuol ballare," 276; Concerto in G, 175, 285; Symphonies: "Eroica," 171, 272; C minor, 222; "Pastoral," 162, 242; in D minor ("Choral"), 172, 235; "Andante favori," 160; Trio Op. 11, 169; Bagatelles, 201; "Missa solemnis," 147; "Geschöpfe des Prometheus," 171; "Fidelio," 189; "Ruins of Athens," 235.

Miscellaneous references: 36, 186, 195, 201, 203, 215, 227, 231, 239, 245, 270, 280, 282, 291.

Beethovenhaus Verein in Bonn, 174.
Bellini, 211.
Bembo, Pietro, 264.
Benda, family of musicians, 243.
Bendl, 243.
Benedict, Julius, 193.
Bennett, William Sterndale, 225.
Berger, Ludwig, 188, 271.

Berggreen, collection of folk-songs, 236.
Berlioz, 213, 249.
Bernard, the German, 58.
Bertini, 282.
Bie, Dr. Oscar, 75, 173; on Mendelssohn, 212; on Chopin, 216; on Weber, 193; on Schubert, 201; on von Bülow, 294.
Blaikley, D. J., 264, 265.
Blitheman, William, 71.
Blow, Dr. John, 81.
"Blue Danube," waltzes, 60.
Blumenfeld, 252.
"Boabdil," 242.
Böhm, Theobald, 44.
Bösendorfer, 42.
Bohemian musicians and composers, 185, 243, 244.
Bologna, Jacopo, 58.
"Bonny Sweet Robin," 75.
Borodin, 248, 250.
Bossi, 255.
Bouquoy, Count, 187.
Bourrée, 89, 93.
Bow, primitive musical instrument, 7 et seq.
Brade, William, 77.
Brahms, Johannes, edits Couperin's works, 92; variations, 168, 227; 226, 227; compositions for pianoforte, 228; "Liebeslieder," 228, 230.
Branle (Shakespeare's brawl), 93, 126.
Breuning, Eleonore von, 276.
British Museum, 12.

Index

Broadwood, 47, 174.

"Broken music," 64.

Brown, Dr. John, 192.

Brown, Mrs. John Crosby, 31.

Bull, Dr. John, 71, 72; his career, 79, 80; "King's Hunting Jigg," 80, 81, 102.

Bullen, Anne, her taste in music, 65, 67.

"Burdens," 64.

Burney, Dr. Charles, "Present State, etc.," 128, 133, 185; on clavichord, 268, 270.

Burton, 83.

Buus, 58.

Buxtehude, 107, 182.

Byrd, 71; his "Battle," 74, 142; "The Carman's Whistle," 75; "Sellinger's Round," 76, 81.

Byrne, Albert, 72.

Byron, on the waltz, 221.

Caffi, S., 264.

Cantata, 125.

Cantus firmus, 59.

Canzona per sonar, 60.

"Carman's Whistle," 75.

Cassiodorus, 14.

Catherine of Portugal, 103.

Censorinus, 8.

Cesti, Antonio, 96.

Chaconne, 61, 85.

Chadwick, Geo. W., 256.

Chambonnières, Jacques Champion de, 90, 91.

Charles II, King of England, 103, 104.

Charles IX, King of France, his favorite dance-tune, 84.

Chickering, Jonas, invents iron frame for grand pf., 39.

Chinese tune, used by Weber, 235.

Chopin, labels on his music, 140; and national music, 213; his romanticism, 213; Huneker on, 214, 215, 217; his taste, 215; and classicism, 215; Schumann on, 215; Mendelssohn on, 215; Runciman on, 216; his morbidness, 215, 216; Niecks on, 216; Pudor on, 216; Bie on, 216; Rubinstein on, 217; Tappert on, 217; his pianoforte compositions, 218–223; his playing, 284, 286, 287, 288, 292; his Polish music, 240–242.

Compositions: Bolero, 219; Concertos, 218, 219; Fantasia on Polish airs, 218; Krakowiak, 218; Mazurkas, 219, 223, 241; Études, 219, 220; Préludes, 219, 220; Nocturnes, 192, 211, 219, 220; Waltzes, 219, 221; Polonaises, 219, 223, 242, 293; Rondos, 219; Ballades, 219, 220; Scherzos, 219, 221, 222; Sonatas, 219, 222; Impromptus, 219; Ecossaises, 219; Variations, 219; Fantasias, 219; Tarantelle,

219; Berceuse, 219; Barcarolle, 219; "Concert Allegro," 219; "Marche funébre," 219.

References, 189, 194, 200, 202, 203.

Chrysander, 92, 116.

Cithern, 68.

Claudius Ptolemy, 15.

Classicism, defined, 122; 123, 180 et seq.

Clavicembalo, 19.

Clavichord, 17, 18; expressive capacity of, 21; instrument owned by Philip II, 39; overstrung, 43, 44; touch of, 268; as preparatory instrument, 268.

Clavicymbal, 18.

Clavicytherium, 19.

Clementi, his sonatas, 127, 136, 138; "Gradus ad Parnassum," 138; Sonata in B-flat, 139; competes with Mozart, 139; "Didone abbandonata," 140, 143, 144, 173, 174, 185, 188, 193; and Mozart, 269.

Cobb, J., 72.

"Cobbler's Jig," 77.

Coleridge, definition of beauty, 248.

"Concords," 64.

Conti, Cosimo, 31.

Continuo, 133.

Contrapuntal music, 58, 59.

Converse, Frederick, 256.

Coranto, 61, 85, 93.

Cornelius, Peter, 292.

Couperin, Charles, 91.

Couperin, Françoise ("the Great"), 90, 91; his "ordres," 92, 93; his descriptive music, 93, 108; his allegories and ballets, 94; "Les Folies Françaises," 94; 126, 130, 140, 151.

Couperin, Louis, 91.

Courante, 85, 93.

Cramer, his sonatas, 127; 136, 142; "La Parodie," 142; "L'Ultima," 142; "Les Suivantes," 142; "Le Retour à Londres," 142; "Fantasie capricieuse," 142; "Un Jour de Printemps," 142; "Le petit Rien," 142; "Les Adieus à ses Amis de Paris," 142; career in London, 143; J. B. Cramer & Co., 143; Études, 144; "Pianoforte School," 144; "School of Velocity," 144; 174, 185, 189, 271, 280; his playing, 280; 282, 292.

Cristofori, 25, 29–30; his pianoforte described, 32, 33; his stringing, 40; compass of his pianoforte, 41; compared with a Steinway, 47–49.

Crosby Brown collection of musical instruments, 9, 31, 47.

Cui, César, 250.

"Cushion Dance," 83.

Czardas, 248.

Index

Czerny, edits Scarlatti's sonatas, 98; "Outline of Musical History," 173; schools of pianoforte playing, 190; on Beethoven's playing, 273; on Beethoven and Gelinek, 275, 280; on Beethoven and Hummel, 283.

DAGINCOURT, 91.
Dampers, 23, 46, 174, 175.
Dances, at the French court, 83, 84, 87, 89.
Dancing, at Italian courts, 87; at the Council of Trent, 88; in churches, 88; Cardinal Richelieu's, 88; Louis XIV's, 88; Marguerite of Valois's, 89.
Dandrieu, 91; "Les Tendres Reproches," 92.
Danish composers, 235; folk-tunes, 236.
Dannreuther, quoted, 138, 144, 188, 220, 248.
Danses basses, 89.
Daquin, "Le Coucou," 92; "L'Hirondelle," 92.
Debussy, 255.
Dehn, 121.
"Descant," 64.
Descriptive music, 182.
Diabelli, variations on his waltz, 168, 171.
Diana, 8.
Diapason normal, 41.
"Diapasons," 65.
Diedrichstein, Prince, 291.

"Dieu quel mariage," 59.
"Discords," 64.
"Divisions," 64.
Dittersdorf, his symphonies, 182; on Mozart, 269.
Döhler, 189.
Dolcimelo, 13.
Domestic music in the Middle Ages, 100.
Donizetti, 211.
Don Juan of Austria, 88.
Dorn, 188.
Dramma per musica, its influence on clavier music, 96.
Drayton, Michael, "Poly Olbion," 68.
Drexel, Joseph W., 72.
Dreyschock, 210, 243, 288, 292.
Due corde, 175.
Dulcimer, 12, 13, 26; Hebenstreit's, 27.
Dumka, 244.
"Dumps," 64.
Durante, 99.
Duschek, 243.
Dussek, 136, 140; his pianoforte compositions, 141; Sonata in F-sharp minor, 141; "La Consolation," 141; compositions on Marie Antoinette, 141; "Bataille navale," 141; 144, 186.
Dvořák, 141, 243.

EDWARD VI, KING OF ENGLAND, 67.
Egyptian harps, 11.
Ehlert, 221.

Index

Elizabeth, Queen, music in her period, 63, 64; plays on the virginal, 67, 70; her alleged virginal book, 70.

"Elverhoe," 236.

England's Golden Age of Music, 63 *et seq.*

English virginalists, 63 *et seq.*; 69 *et seq.*

English music, modern, 256.

Epinette, 19.

Equal temperament, 119.

Erard, system of stringing, 43; action, 47; piano owned by Beethoven, 174.

Erasmus, quoted, 65.

Erbach, 102.

FACKELTANZ, 84.

"Fain would I wed," 76.

Farnaby, Giles, 71, 81.

Farnaby, Richard, 71; "Jog on," 75; "Bonny Sweet Robin," 75.

Ferrari, G. G., 174.

Fibich, 243.

Field, John, 193; characterized by Liszt, 194; his compositions, 194; 201, 221, 271, 282; his playing, 284, 287.

Fingering, 35, 264, 267.

Finnish music, 236.

Fitzwilliam Virginal Book, 70 *et seq.*

Flood, Valentine, 77.

Folksong and romanticism, 105, 117; idioms, 233, 234, 235.

Forkel, 133; on Bach's fingering, 267.

Form, defined and described, 150, 151.

"Fortune my Foe," 77.

Frames of pianofortes, 36, 37.

Franck, César, 254; "Variations symphoniques," 254; "Les Djinns," 254.

Franck, Melchior, 102.

Frederick the Great, 130, 132.

"Freischütz, Der," 193.

French clavecinists, 90 *et seq.*

French music and composers, 253–255.

Frescobaldi, 96; "Capriccio," 99; "Canzone in sesto Tono," 99; "Canzona," 99; Correnti, 99.

"Frets," 64.

Fries, Count, 169.

Frimmel, Dr. Theodor, 178.

Friss, 248.

Froberger, 102–105; his adventures, 103, 104; his allemandes, 104; 182.

Furiant, 244.

GABRIELI, ANDREA, 58.

Gade, 235; his compositions for pianoforte, 237; "Nachklänge aus Ossian," 237; B-flat symphony, 238; pupil of Berggreen, 236.

Galliard, 61, 83, 84, 89.

Galuppi, 99.

"Gamut," 64.

Gavotte, 85, 89, 93.

Index

Geigenwerk, 25.

Gelinek, 275; competes with Beethoven, 276.

German Handel Society, 116.

Gibbons, Christopher, 72, 81, 103.

Gibbons, Orlando, 71, 72, 81.

Giga (and Jig), 61, 93.

Gittern, 68.

Gladkowska, Constantina, 220.

Glazounow, 252.

"Go from my Window," 76.

"Golden Treasury of Pianoforte Music," 99.

Gourds as resonators, 9, 10.

Gottschalk, 256.

"Gradus ad Parnassum," 282.

Gravicembalo, 19.

Greek harp and lyres, 11.

"Green Sleeves," 77.

Grieg, 200, 235, 237; self-estimate, 239, 240.

Grove, "Dictionary of Music and Musicians," 131, 138, 188, 251, 264.

Guicciardi, Giulietta, 163, 164.

Guido d'Arezzo, 15.

Gumpeltzhaimer, 102.

Gypsy musicians in Hungary, 246; "Gypsy Epics," 247.

Gyrowetz, 243.

HALLÉ, SIR CHARLES, 192, 391.

Hallén, Andreas, 235, 240.

Hammer-action, 33, 44, 45.

Hammerclavier, 173.

Handel, admired by Scarlatti, 97; his career, 100 et seq.; borrowings from Kerl and Muffat, 105; candidate as Buxtehude's successor, 107; compared with Bach, 110 et seq.; "Almira," 111; "Rodrigo," 111; "Agrippina," 112; oratorios, 113; harpsichord music, 115; "The Harmonious Blacksmith," 115, 189; Brahms's variations, 116; other compositions, 116; 151, 168, 227; his playing, 267.

"Hanskin," 74.

"Harmonious Blacksmith, The," 115, 189.

Harp, 5; Egyptian, 11.

Harpsichord, 18, 19; defects of, 21; improvements of, 22; Ruckers, maker of, 22; touch of, 268.

Hartmann, J. P. E., 235, 236.

Hasler, Hans Leo, 102.

Hawkins, Isaac, improves pianoforte, 39.

Haydn, Joseph, 42; a continuator, 122; 126; his clavier pieces, 127; "Andante varié," 130; Fantasia in C, 130; 133; "Genziger" and "London" sonatas, 138; 139; method of composing, 140; letters of Mrs. Schroeter, 143; 187, 188; characterized, 197; on Mozart, 227, 269; Croatian melodies, 235.

Hebenstreit, 27, 28.

Index

Heller, 223, 224; "Flower, Fruit, and Thorn Pieces" ("Nuits blanches"), 223.

Helmholtz, 28.

Henry VIII, King of England, 64, 65; his musical education, 67.

Henselt, edits Cramer's Études, 144; 224; "If I were a Bird," 224; Concerto in F minor, 224; his playing, 284.

Herz, Henri, 209, 210, 211, 288, 291.

Hipkins, "History of the Pianoforte," 31, 34; on metal frames, 38; on earliest clavier compositions, 53.

Hoffmann, E. T. A., 203.

Hohenlohe, Princess Marie, 175.

Homer, "Iliad," 7; "Odyssey," 8, 11.

"Homme armé, L'," 59, 60.

Hughes, Rupert, "The Musical Guide," 202.

Hummel, 136; Dannreuther on, 144; his "School," 145; 188, 189, 224, 270, 273, 279, 280; his studies, 282; his pianoforte playing, 283.

Huneker, James, on Chopin, 214, 215, 217; "Chopin, the Man and his Music," 217.

Hungarian music, 242, 245.

Huss, H. H., 257.

"Iliad," 7.

Indy, Vincent d', "Symphony on a Mountain Air," 255.

Instrumentalists, once legal vagabonds, 54.

Instrumental music, tardy development of, 54, 60.

Intrada, 85.

Italian composers, for clavier, 95 et seq.; modern, 255.

Jacks, in Harpsichords, 18, 19, 64.

Jean Paul Friedrich Richter, 183, 203, 224.

Jig, 61.

"Jog on, jog on," 75.

"John, come kiss me now," 76.

Josquin des Près, 67.

Junker, 174; on Beethoven's playing, 274.

Kalischer, Dr. Alfred, 164.

Kalkbrenner, 210, 271, 287, 288, 291.

Kalliwoda, 243.

Kerl, 105.

Key-action, 33, 44.

Keyboard, 14–16; shifting, 23.

Kissing, in Queen Elizabeth's time, 65.

Kjerulf, 235, 237.

Knyvett, C., 174.

Köhler, Louis, 224.

Kotzwara, "Battle of Prague," 74, 141.

Kozeluch, 186.

Index

Krehbiel, H. E., "How to Listen to Music," 24, 181, 183, 246; "Music and Manners in the Classical Period," 143, 154; "Studies in the Wagnerian Drama," 151.

Kuhlau, 191; "Elverhoe," 236.

Kuhnau, 28, 107; "Biblische Historien" (Bible sonatas), 107, 109, 182; programme music, 108, 109, 126, 140.

"LADY COVENTRY'S MINUET," 268.

"La Mara" (Fräulein Lipsius), 164.

"Lady Neville's Virginal Book," 71, 74, 77.

Landini, 57.

Lassu, 248.

Lasso, Orlando di, 81.

Lavignac, "Music and Musicians," 213.

Leicester, Earl of, his virginal book, 71.

Lenz, von, on Cramer's playing, 281, 282; on Liszt, 286, 289; on Henselt, 286; on Chopin, 288; on Tausig, 293.

Liadow, "Tabatière à Musique," 252.

Liapounow, 252.

Lightning, in music, 73.

Lipsius, Fräulein ("La Mara"), 164.

Liszt, 174, 175, 189, 192, 202, 210, 216, 237, 241, 280; "Sonnets," 221; on Chopin's sonatas, 222; on Field, 194, 201; Schubert's Fantasia in C, 198, 244; arrangements of Beethoven's symphonies, 244; orchestral style, 245; sonata in B minor, 245; "Consolations," 245; "Harmonies poétiques," 245; "Dream Nocturnes," 245; "Années de Pélerinage," 245; "Légendes," 245; Études, 245; "Hungarian Rhapsodies," 245–248; "Des Bohèmiens, etc.," 246; Concertos, 248; influence on Russian school, 249; his playing, 288–290; compared with Thalberg, 292; hears Tausig, 292.

Locke, Matthew, 72.

Longo, Alessandro, 99.

"Lord Willoughby's Welcome Home," 77.

Louis Ferdinand, Prince of Prussia, 141.

Louis XIV, 27, 85; his dancing lessons, 88; dancing at his court, 90, 95; his clavecin players, 91.

Lute, supplanted by the clavier, 102.

Luther, 67; and church music, 106.

Lyre, origin of, 11.

MACDOWELL, EDWARD A., 256, 257.

Index

Machin, Richard, 77.

Maffei, Scipione, 39, 33.

Magyar folkmusic, 245, 246.

Maitland, J. A. Fuller, 70.

"Mall Sims," 76, 77.

"Malt's come down," 76.

Marenzio, 81.

Marguerite of Valois, 89.

Marie Antoinette, 141.

Marius, 25, 29; his "Clavecin à mallets," 30.

Marot, tunes to his psalms, 106.

Marschner, his romantic operas, 181; "Templar and Jewess," 225.

Martelli, Signora Ernesta, 31.

Martini, 99.

Martucci, 255.

Mary Stuart, Queen of Scotland, 67.

Mason, Professor, 10.

Mason, William, 80.

Mattheson, 104, 107.

"Means," 64.

Medici, Catherine de, 87; introduces Italian dances in France, 89.

Medici, Prince Ferdinando dei, 30.

Melvil, Sir James, 67.

Mendelssohn, "Variations sérieuses," 168, 212; a romantic composer, 183, 188; his works, 209–213; Rubinstein's estimate, 209; "Songs without Words," 210, 211, 212; overture to "A Mid-summer Night's Dream," 211, 286; "Capriccio in F-sharp minor," 212; "Rondo Capriccio," 212; Scherzo in E minor, 212; Fantasia in F minor, 212; Étude in F, 212; "Scherzo capriccio," 212; "Allegro brillante," 212; Concerto in G minor, 213; and Chopin, 214; on Liszt's arrangement of Mozart's G minor symphony, 244; his playing, 284, 285.

Mercury, 11.

Merulo, 58.

Metropolitan Museum of Art in New York, 10, 31, 47.

Meyerbeer, 188; "Robert le Diable," 219.

Midas, Greek virtuoso, 232.

"Midsummer Night's Dream," 286.

"Minims," 64.

Minuet, 93.

Monochord, 15, 18.

Moussorgsky, 249, 250.

"Moonlight" sonata, 163, 165.

Morley, Thomas, 71.

Moscheles, 188, 205, 213, 271; on Beethoven's playing, 274; Salaman on his playing, 283; Beethoven on his playing, 283; on Chopin, 287.

Moszkowski, "Jeanne d'Arc," 242; "Boabdil," 242; "Aus allen Herren Landen," 242; "Étincelles," 242; "Tarantelle," 242.

Index

Mozart, 42, 126, 133; his instruments, 134; praises Stein's pianofortes, 135; his composition, 135; plays duets with J. C. Bach, 137; Sonata in C minor, 138; competes with Clementi, 139; "Magic Flute," 139; 152, 174, 179, 186, 188; characterized, 197; 215; Turkish march, 235; G minor symphony, 244; his playing, 268, 270, 276; and Clementi, 268; "Nozze di Figaro," 276; 278, 279; Fantasia in F minor 279; 280, 282.

Mürer, 58.

Muffat, G. (father), 105.

Muffat, G. (son), 105.

"Mulliner's Virginal Book," 71.

Munday, 71; his meteorological fantasia, 72, 142.

NATIONAL MUSEUM (IN BUDAPEST), 174.

National Schools of Music, 229–257.

National Museum in Washington, 10.

Neefe, 272.

Neupert, 237.

Neville, Lady, her virginal book, 71.

Nevin, Ethelbert, 257.

Newmarch, Mrs., 251.

New Romanticists, 226.

New York Public Library, manuscripts in, 72.

New York, a season's pianoforte music, 230.

Niemann, Dr. Walter, "Die Musik Scandinaviens," 236; on Grieg, 239.

N-kungo, an African instrument, 9, 11.

Nordraak, 235, 237.

Norman, Ludwig, 235, 240.

North German organists, 105, 117.

Norwegian composers, 235, 237 et seq.

"Nozze di Figaro," 276.

"OBERON," 212.

"Odyssey," 8.

Olesen, Ole, 240.

"O Mistress mine," 74.

Onslow, 188.

Opera, invention of, 62.

Organ, ancient, 14, 22; music for, 55, 56; influences clavier music, 101; Beethoven's playing influenced by, 272.

Orgelschläger, 55.

Oriental, color in music, 235; music, 241, 246.

PACHELBEL, "MUSICAL DEATH THOUGHTS," 107.

"Packington's Pound," 76, 77.

Paderewski (dedication); his Polish music, 241; "Fantaisie Polonaise," 241; sonata and variations, 242, 252.

Paganini, 168, 227.

Index

Palestrina, 106; a continuator, 122.

Pantaleon, 27.

Paradies, 99, 126.

Parker, Horatio, 256.

Partita, 61.

"Parthenia," 72, 78, 84.

Pasquini, 96, 99.

Passacaille, 94.

Passepied, 89, 94.

"Pastoral" sonata, 163.

"Pastoral" symphony, 162, 242.

"Pathétique" sonata, 165.

Pauer, E., "Old English Composers," 70, 82; "Alte Claviermusik," 99.

Paul, Dr. Oscar, "Geschichte des Claviers," 83, 98.

Paulmann (or Paumann), 57.

Pavane, 83.

"Peascod Time," 76.

Pedals, 23, 37, 46, 47, 174, 175.

Penna, Lorenzo, "Li Primo Albori musicali," 265.

Pepys, 69.

Pesaro, 57.

Petrarch, 57.

Phillips, P., 72, 81.

Pianoforte, its origin, 4 *et seq.*; its name, 6; defined, 6; lack of singing quality in, 24; Schroeter's invention, 25, 27; etymology of name, 29; Cristofori's invention, 29, 30; Marius's invention, 30; Cristofori's instrument described, 32; evolution of, 34, 49; frame, 36–39; upright patented, 39; stringing, 39–44; compass, 41, 42; overstrung scale, 43; hammeraction, 44, 45; Cristofori's instrument compared with a Steinway, 47–49; its universality, 100; Beethoven's, 173, 179.

Pindar, 82, 232.

Pistoia, 53.

Pixis, 291.

"Plainsong," 64.

Playford, "Introduction to the Skill of Musick," 82, 83, 85.

Pleyel, 197.

Pohl, 131.

Pole, William, metal frames, 37.

Polish music and composers, 240–243; Chopin and Paderewski, 240–242.

Polonaise, 84, 242.

Ponsicchi, Cesare, 32, 40.

Porpora, 99.

Prätorius, Hieronymus, 102.

Prätorius, Michael, 60; "Syntagma Musicum," 60, 101, 266.

"Preciosa," 213.

Price, John, 77.

"Pricksong," 64, 67.

Programme music, 182 *et seq.*

Proposto, 57.

Prosniz, "Handbuch der Clavier Literatur," 129; on Mozart, 135; on Weber, 193.

Psalterion, 13.

Pudor, on Chopin, 216, 217.

Index

Puliti, 32.

Purcell, 81, 82; use of thumb, 266; "Choice Collection of Lessons for Harpsichord," 266.

Pythagoras, 15.

"QUODLING'S DELIGHT," 76.

RACHMANINOW, PRELUDE IN C-SHARP MINOR, 252.

Raff, 226; "Hommage au Neo-romantisme," 226; 245, 257.

Raleigh, Sir Walter, 166.

Rameau, 90, 91, 92; "Les Rappel des Oiseaux," 92; "La Poule," 92; "Les tendres Plaintes," 92; "L'Égyptienne," 92; "La Timide," 92; "Les Soupirs," 92; "La Livri," 92; "Les Cyclops," 92; 108, 126, 130, 151.

Rebikow, 252.

Rasoumowsky, 235.

Ravel, 255.

Reformation, influence of, 106.

Rellstab, Ludwig, 165.

"Rests," 64.

Richelieu, Cardinal, dances a saraband, 88.

Ries, Ferdinand, on Beethoven's Sonata Op. 31, No. 2, 161; 167, 174, 191, 271.

Rigaudon, 89.

Riggadoon, 85.

Rimbault, Dr. Edw., "Collection of Specimens," etc., 71, 72; "The Pianoforte,"

33; on metal frames, 38; on strings, 40.

Rimsky-Korsakow, 250; pf. compositions, 252.

"Robert le Diable," 219.

Rogers, Dr., 72.

"Rolandston," 77.

Roman harps and lyres, 11.

Romano, Giulio, 81.

Romanticism, 180, et seq.; a definition, 183; aided by words and instruments, 195; its elements, 196; and folk-songs, 234.

Rore, 58.

Rossini, 211.

Rowe, Walter, 77.

Rowe, Walter, son of above, 77.

"Rowland," 76, 77.

Rubinstein, on Rameau, 91; on Couperin, 91; on Pasquini, 96; on Scarlatti, 98; on Beethoven's music, 52, 171; on Beethoven's C-sharp minor sonata, 165, 166; on "Pathétique," 166; on Beethoven's Op. 106, 178, 196; on Mendelssohn, 209, 212; on Chopin, 217, 245; on himself, 249; on young Russian school, 249; Concerto in D-minor, 251; "Staccato Étude," 251; "Study on False Notes," 251; Mélodie in F, 251; "Kammenoi Ostrow," 251; Sonata for pf. and violin, 251; his playing, 293, 294.

Index

Ruckers, harpsichord maker, 22.
"Ruins of Athens," 235.
Runciman, John F., on Chopin, 216, 217.
Ruskin, definition of repose in art, 150.
Russian music and composers, 248-253.
Rust, Friedrich Wilhelm, 137.
Rust, Dr. Wilhelm, 137.
Rust, Wilhelm Karl, 137.

SAINT-SAËNS, 245; von Bülow on, 253; "Caprice on Russian Airs," 253; "Africa," 254; "Caprice Arabe," 254; Concerto in G minor, 254; Symphony in C minor, 255.
Salaman, Charles, his recollections of pianists, 280, 283, 284, 285, 292.
Salieri, 282.
Salomon, 187.
Santini, Abbate, collection of Scarlatti's works, 97.
Santir, Persian dulcimer, 13.
Saraband, 85, 89, 93.
Sayn-Wittgenstein, Princess, 175.
Scandinavian composers, 235-240.
Scarlatti, Alessandro, "Capriccio," 97.
Scarlatti, Domenico, 97; "Narcissus," 97; Santini's collection of his works, 97; "Pastorale," 97; "Capriccio,"

97; editions of his works, 98; 126, 129.
Scharwenka, Philipp, 243.
Scharwenka, Xaver, 243.
Scheidt, Samuel, 102.
Scherzo, influenced by Beethoven, 167; 221, 222.
Schindler, on Beethoven's pianoforte method, 162; 166; on Beethoven's playing, 274.
Schroeter, Christoph Gottlieb, 25, 29.
Schroeter, Johann Samuel, 143.
Schubert, characterized, 197; his compositions, 198 et seq.; Quartet in D minor, 198, 199; Fantasia in C, 198, 199; Symphony in C, 198; variations, 198, 199; "Impromptu" in B-flat, 198; Adonic metre in his music, 198, 199; Quartet in A major, 199; "Der Tod und das Mädchen," 199; "Rosamunde," 199; "Wie sich die Äuglein," 191; "Die Forelle," 199; "Der Wanderer," 199; "Trockene Blumen," 199; "Momens musicals," 199, 201; Impromptus, 199, 201; chamber music, 199; "Rondeau brillant," 200; the sonatas, 200; 202; Chopin's dislike of his music, 215; "Divertissement à la Hongroise," 235.
Schumann, Clara (Wieck), 205, 207, 226, 285.

Schumann, Robert, "Carnaval," 94, 172, 204, 215; Études symphoniques," 168, 205, 225; a romantic composer, 183, 186, 203, 202–208; programme music, 203, 204; his inspirations, 203; his pianoforte compositions, 204 *et seq.*; Sonata in F-sharp minor, 205; his titles, 206; Fantasia in C, 207; "Nachtstücke," 208; "Funeral Fantasia," 208; and Weber, 210; and Mendelssohn, 210; and Gade, 238; on Chopin, 215; on Chopin's preludes, 220; "Noveletten," 221; on Chopin's Waltz in A-flat, 221; on Chopin's Scherzos, 222; on Chopin's sonatas, 222; on Brahms, 226; his theme varied by Brahms, 227; his playing, 285.

Schytté, Ludwig, 237.

"Scotch snap," 246.

Scriabin, 252.

Selden, John, "Table Talk," 83.

"Sellinger's Round," 76.

Seume, "Die Beterin," 164.

Seyfried, Chevalier von, 278.

Sgambati, 255.

Shakespeare, the music of his time, 64 *et seq.*; songs from the plays, 74, 75; sonnet to "the dark lady," 20, 36; "The Tempest," 166.

"Sharps," 64.

Shedlock, J. S., "The Pianoforte Sonata," 138; on Dussek, 142, 137.

Sibelius, 236.

Siciliano, 85.

Silbermann, his pianofortes, 132.

Simonides, 82.

Simpson, Richard, 77.

Sinding, 235.

Sjögren, 236, 240.

Škroup, 243.

Smetana, 141, 243.

Smithsonian Institution, 9.

Södermann, 235, 240.

Sonata, 60; defined, 124; evolution of, 124, 125 *et seq.*; Beethoven's influence on, 151 *et seq.*

Sound-box, evolution of, 9.

Spina, publisher, 174.

Spohr, 188.

Spinet, 19; defects of, 21.

Squarcialupi, 57.

Squire, W. Barclay, edits virginal music, 70.

Stamitz, 243.

Stanley, John, 77.

Stark, L., 199.

Stcherbatchew, 252.

Steibelt, 169; routed by Beethoven, 277.

Stein, pianoforte maker, 135, 174.

Steinway, Henry Engelhard, 44.

Steinway pianofortes, 33, 40; how strung, 40, 41; compared with a Cristofori instrument, 47–49.

Index

Stenborg, 240.

Stenhammar, 240, 326.

Sterkel, his playing, 274.

"Stops," 64.

Strauss, Richard, 108, 142.

Striggio, Alessandro, 81.

Stringed instruments, classification of, 5.

Strings, material, 22; on the Cristofori pianoforte, 32; sizes of, 32; development of, 39–44; laws of strings, 42.

Suite, 61.

Svendsen, Johann, 235, 237.

Swedish music and composers, 235; opera, 240.

Syrinx, 14.

TABOURET, "ORCHÉSOG-RAPHIE," 88.

Tallis (or Tallys), 71, 81.

Tambourin, 89.

Tannhäuser, 227.

Taubert, 188.

Tausig, 288; his playing, 292, 293; edition of Scarlatti's sonatas, 98, 192.

Taylor, Franklin, 285.

"Tell me, Daphne," 76.

"Tempest, The," 166.

"Templar and Jewess," 225.

Thalberg, 189, 288, 290–292.

Thayer, Alexander W., 177.

Timm, Henry C., edits Cramer's studies, 144.

Tomaschek, 186; on Woelffl, 279.

Tomkins, Thomas, 72.

Tregian, Francis, 70.

Trench, Archbishop, 181.

Tschaikowsky, 250; pianoforte compositions, 251; concerto in B-flat minor, 251.

"Turandot," 235.

Tutte corde, 178.

ULLMANN, 291.

Una corda, 23, 175, 178.

"VALKYRIA," BALLET BY HARTMANN, 237.

Vanhal, his clavier pieces, 127; 186, 187, 243.

Variations, the form, 168; Beethoven's on Diabelli's waltz, 168–173; Mendelssohn's, 168, 212; Schubert's, 198, 199; Schumann's, 168, 204, 225; Brahms's, 168; Bach's "Goldberg," 173.

Venice, organists of St. Mark's, 56, 95.

Viennese, School of pianoforte playing, 270.

"Viol-de-gamboys," 68.

Virginal, 19; defects of, 21; 69, 70; collections of music for, 70, 71.

Virginalists, technique, 263.

"Virginalling," 64.

Virtuosi, not productive, 232; characterized, 261–263.

Vivaldi, 118.

Vogler, Abbé, 188.

Volta, 89.

Von Arnim, Bettina, 153.

Index

Von Bülow, edits Cramer's Etudes, 144, 177, 178; his playing, 293, 294; on Saint-Saëns, 253.

WAGNER, A CONTINUATOR, 122; 216, 227, 253.
Walther and Streicher, 174.
"Walsingham," 76.
Waltz, Diabelli's, 168, 171, 172, 173; Byron's description of, 221.
Weber, Carl Maria von, his romantic operas, 181, 188; his pianoforte compositions, 191 *et seq.;* "Concertstück," 192, 193; "Invitation to the Dance," 192, 193; Sonata in E minor, 193; "Der Freischütz," 193; "Oberon," 212; "Preciosa," 213, 235; "Turandot," 235; on Gelinek, 275; Prosniz on, 193; Bie on, 193; 209, 211.
Weber, Dyonysius, 243.

Weingartner, his transcription of Weber's "Invitation," 192.
Weitzmann, "Geschichte des Clavierspiels," 99, 264; on Beethoven's sonatas, 155, 156.
"Well Tempered Clavichord," Bach's, 114.
Wetzlar, Baroness, 291.
Whiting, Arthur, his pianoforte compositions, 257.
"Why ask you," 76.
Wieck, Clara (Schumann), 205, 207, 226, 285.
Wieck, Friedrich, 226.
Wihtol, 252.
Willaert, 58, 60.
Woelffl, 278, 279, 291.
Wood, Anthony a, 72.
Wranitzky, 243.

YAQUIMA INDIANS, USE BOW AS MUSICAL INSTRUMENT, 9.

ZIEGLER, HENRY, 49.

THE MUSIC LOVER'S LIBRARY

CHARLES SCRIBNER'S SONS
PUBLISHERS

A series of popular volumes—historical, biographical, anecdotal, and descriptive—on the important branches of the art of music, by writers of recognized authority

The Pianoforte and Its Music
By H. E. KREHBIEL
Author of "How to Listen to Music," etc.

With portraits and illustrations. $1.25 *net;* postpaid $1.35

CONTENTS

I.   Principles and Primitive Prototypes
II.   Mediæval Precursors
III.   The Pianoforte of To-day
IV.   The Earliest Clavier Music
V.   The English Virginalists
VI.   French and Italian Clavecinists
VII.   The German School—Bach and Handel
VIII. Classicism and the Sonata
IX.   Beethoven—An Intermezzo
X.   The Romantic School
XI.   National Schools
XII.   Virtuosi and Their Development

The book, with portraits and cuts which explain the mechanical principles of the pianoforte, includes all the information about the pianoforte and the men who have made it what it is to-day.

THE MUSIC LOVER'S LIBRARY

Songs and Song Writers

By HENRY T. FINCK

Author of "Wagner and His Works," "Chopin and Other Musical Essays," etc.

With 8 portraits.   12mo, $1.25 *net*

CONTENTS

I.   Folk Song and Art Song
II.   German Song Writers Before Schubert
III.   Schubert
IV.   German Song Writers After Schubert
V.   Hungarian and Slavic Song Writers
VI.   Scandinavian Song Writers
VII.   Italian and French Song Writers
VIII. English and American Song Writers

Heretofore there has been no book to guide amateurs and professionals in the choice of the best songs.   Mr. Finck's new book not only does this but gives a bird's-eye view, with many interesting biographic details and descriptive remarks, of the whole field of song in the countries of Europe as well as in America.   The volume is especially rich in anecdotes.

"No one interested in the subject should miss reading this book, the work of a man who never ventures on praise or blame without practical personal knowledge of the matter in hand."—*London Spectator*.

THE MUSIC LOVER'S LIBRARY

The Orchestra and Orchestral Music

By W. J. HENDERSON

With 8 portraits.   12mo, $1.25 *net*

CONTENTS

I.   How the Orchestra is Constituted
II.   How the Orchestra is Used
III.   How the Orchestra is Directed
IV.   How the Orchestra Grew
V.   How Orchestral Music Grew

" An eminently practical work."
—H. E. KREHBIEL, in the *New York Tribune*.

The Opera, Past and Present

By WILLIAM F. APTHORP

With 8 portraits.   12mo, $1.25 *net*

PARTIAL CONTENTS

I.   Beginnings
II.   The European Conquest
III.   Gluck
IV.   Mozart
V.   The Italians
VI.   The French School
VII.   The Germans
VIII.   Wagner

This book shows in particular the æsthetic evolution of the opera—the influence of one school and period upon another.